Female Genital Cosmetic Surgery

Camille Nurka

Female Genital Cosmetic Surgery

Deviance, Desire and the Pursuit of Perfection

Camille Nurka
Mount Waverley
VIC, Australia

ISBN 978-3-030-07201-8   ISBN 978-3-319-96490-4   (eBook)
https://doi.org/10.1007/978-3-319-96490-4

Library of Congress Control Number: 2018950505

Cover design by Fatima Jamadar
Cover artwork by Margaret Mayhew

This Palgrave Macmillan imprint is published by the registered company Springer Nature Switzerland AG
The registered company address is: Gewerbestrasse 11, 6330 Cham, Switzerland

For Alison Jones and Joan Jones

ACKNOWLEDGEMENTS

Never enough thanks go to Zora Simic—for everything—but especially her many years of friendship, deep and insightful critique, and intellectual companionship. Her History of Sexuality subject, which I had the pleasure to teach, in many ways shaped this book. Zora, I could not have conceived, researched or written this book without you.

Jane 'eugenics girl' Carey for her dear friendship and fine work on eugenics, birth control, class and race, which has been absolutely indispensable to the development of my thinking about female sexuality in this book.

Special thanks go to my friend and renegade feminist artist Margaret 'Mayhem' Mayhew for her marvellous palimpsest 'pornogami' vulva cover artwork. I am deeply honoured that you said yes. Thank you to Palgrave designer Fatima Jamadar for designing the best cover an author could ask for.

Warm thanks to Christiane Kühling for her careful translations of Stratz, for checking my French translations, and helping me clarify the confusing and tortuous logic of eugenics theory. And a big thank you to Bettina Roesler for introducing us.

Victoria Reeve for her insightful and much-needed structural edit of Chapter 5 when my deadline was fast approaching.

Dirk Baltzly, who helped me out with investigating the Ancient Greek terms discussed in Chapter 2. Dirk, I hope I got the etymologies right.

The librarians at Monash University Rare Books Collection, who did a wonderful job scanning images of vulvas for me. Thank you, Daniel, Mia and Stephen.

My editors, Kyra Saniewski and Mary Al-Sayed, who kicked my butt into gear.

My cousin Bethany Jones, for caring as passionately about this topic as I do. I couldn't have asked for a better or more exciting writing partnership in the Vulvatalk research project. Thanks also to the women who took part in the Vulvatalk project and spoke honestly to us about their genitals.

Maree Pardy for being the best boss in the world (I'm not a boss, she says!), but also, and more importantly, for her friendship, intellectual mentorship and generally saving my life when I had no direction.

Shakira Hussein for being an awesome friend and co-author, making me laugh, and helping me think through the FGM/FGCS distinction.

Jane Lydon and Penny Edmonds for their enthusiastic support of this book, sage suggestions, mentorship and willingness to accept me as a historian. I love you! xx

Natalie Kamber for her unfaltering friendship and support, for being inspirational and brilliant, for our many animated conversations, and for borrowing books on my behalf when I had no university library access. (I expect this book to be on Ezra's extensive reading list).

Jennifer Dixon for her medical expertise, reading early chapter drafts, introducing me to experts in the field, and sharing insightful thoughts about the science of sex.

Daisy Little for introducing me to lots of fabulous stories and artworks dedicated to vulva love. And also for the cupcakes!

Malice Black for being the kind of gracious interviewer who puts a nervous academic at ease in front of a TV camera, and Andy McNamara for inviting me on Bent TV to talk about labiaplasty. If only I could have used your wonderful title *FGCS: A Great Work of Cliterature*.

David J. Vaughan for your interest and enthusiastic encouragement—it has meant a lot to me. I'm so glad I found your blog.

My wonderful friends, who have tirelessly put up with me talking about vulvas at dinner parties, lunches, brunches and barbeques:

The Melbourne crew and Hivesters: Naomi Grant, you are a wonderful reader and I am thankful for your intelligent editorial advice, always. Andrew Eaton, Sharon Crabb, Kerryn Herman, Rhys 'Potato' Tate, Maree & Phoebes, Leanne Morton, Polly, Minna & Quill Sorenson,

Gemma King, Anneliese Gillard, Sarah Jansen, Ange & Sonj Meyer, Mel Kells, Nadine Tier, Emma Dallas and Catherine Alizzi. Angela White for her informed and informative thoughts about porn.

The Sydney crew: Dave & Lee, Suzanne Ballard, Georgina, Gerard, Relz & Will Rummery, Michelle Christie, Ben Skidmore, Anada Jones, Anthony D'Ettore, Taels & Quinn, Kat Gaffney, Jack, Tom & Charlie Jacobson, Julia & Dean, Rhiannon Treasure-Brand, Ed Roy, Lucy Norman, Ben Peterson, Jasmine Stanton, Nadia Cameron, Belinda Norman, Clarissa & Grant, Mariella & John, Katherine & Mark.

The academic crew: Elspeth Probyn, Linnell Secomb & Susan Goodwin for their formative feminist intellectual mentorship, the indomitable Sarah Casey for being her outrageous self and creating FEMBOS, Adam Eldridge, Meredith Jones, Anthea Taylor, Tereza Hendl, Kate Gleeson, Andrew Hickey, Lisa Slater, Meredith Nash, Kyja Noack-Lundberg, Renee Middlemost, Clare Corbould, Carolyn Stevens, Hannah Forsythe, Alexis Harley, Justine McGill, Elaine Kelly, Sharon Crozier-De Rosa, Monika Dryburgh, Erica Rose Millar, Tanya Serisier, Cath Kevin, Tim Jones, Kath Albury, Jayne Persian, Gayelene Carbis, Kathleen Fallon, and especially Zoo for hir sharp mind and alerting me to the vulva beauty contest among many other useful news stories.

The UWS crew: Maria Angel for introducing me to feminist theory, Simon Campbell, Lisa Martin, Jason Whatt, Megan Casey and Ken Vimpany (no longer with us).

My two sets of parents, Alison & Serge, Vytas & Maz, who always believed in my writing and gave me the tools (books and a brain) to do it well. Mum, I cannot ever thank you enough for your unwavering love and encouragement, and providing a beautiful, quiet space to write. My awesome brother Marty and cheeky sister-in-law Becky—I hope Indie and Noah will grow up knowing that there are many types of genitalia that come in every shape and size! I wish my grandma had lived to see this book published (though I have no idea what she would have made of it!). Shout-out to the extended family—thanks for the many lively Christmas-dinner conversations.

Malcolm Connell, without whom this book would never have been written. Your generosity, support and love are without limit. Thank you for being uniquely you and for loving all of me just the way I am.

CONTENTS

LIST OF FIGURES

CHAPTER 1

Introduction: Perfectible Sex

In 2015, I came across an online education resource for Australian youth called Somazone. Created by the Australian Drug Foundation, it was set up as a safe space for young people to ask questions about mental health, depression, sex, sexuality, relationships, bullying, abuse, drugs and alcohol. Sadly, this education resource no longer exists.[1] I had discovered this site in the course of my research on cosmetic labiaplasty. What caught my attention was an anxious question posed by a young woman about her labia minora:

> OK, so 16 is the age to experiment, hey. And it's natural to fool around with your boyfriend if you're both ready to let yourselves explore each other's bodies. Well there lies my problem.
>
> I haven't told anybody. I am a reasonably popular girl who attracts lots of guy's attention. So I don't have a problem with guys, or with my body, so everyone thinks.
>
> I am slim and petite but yet I don't want to let anyone near me for fear of humiliation that my lower region isn't attractive or appealing. I am ready to have some fun experimenting but I am very ashamed because my labia sticks out and I do not want to be hurt or teased.
>
> I hope someone out there understands what I mean. I want to get a labioplasty but I don't want my parents to find out and don't know wether I have to be over 18. I feel guilty not loving my whole body.[2]

© The Author(s) 2019
C. Nurka, *Female Genital Cosmetic Surgery*,
https://doi.org/10.1007/978-3-319-96490-4_1

There are two kinds of painful emotion being expressed here: one is shame and the other is guilt over feeling ashamed. While she worries that a potential sexual partner might find her vagina ugly, she also worries that her body shame is unwarranted or illegitimate. The post prompted a litany of comments by respondents relieved to have the opportunity to express similar feelings of embarrassment, dislike, discomfort, disgust, paranoia, abnormality and unhappiness. But it also generated many body-positive responses from both women and men who reassured her that she was normal and that labia were sexy. These responses, in a safe and moderated online environment, led one commenter to say: 'I feel so much better reading about this ... I have large ones too and didn't like them but now i'm startin to feel better about them and now i know i'm normal=].'[3]

Somazone was a public health initiative, but not all sex education sites are responsible or ethical. For instance, RealSelf is an online forum that provides information for prospective clients about cosmetic surgery, where surgeons respond to women's queries about their bodies as a way to generate business. One query-poster from Florida asks: 'Is it normal for it to lol [look] this way. I've been scared to have any sexual relationships because I'm think guys will find it unattractive and I was wondering if I should get surgery?'[4] While one surgeon responds by reassuring her that her labia are normal, he nonetheless suggests that 'there is a trend to have less prominent labia' and that for women who are troubled by their labia, 'a certain surgical procedure exists to help to correct this problem and restore their femininity'.[5]

What is salient here is the prevalence of a shared sense of sexual shame and fears of abnormality in the anxious and unhappy stories posted by contemporary women about their genitals. The anxiety of inhabiting an abnormal femininity and the fear of heterosexual inadequacy are strikingly present in the accounts of genital shame given by women enquiring about labiaplasty in online forums such as Somazone and RealSelf. These women are likely to find their fears confirmed in the diagnosis of a spurious gynaecological condition known as 'hypertrophy of the labia minora', which simply means that the labia are large in size. I call this 'diagnosis' spurious because labia minora that bear no signs of malignant organic disorder other than that they are long are not diseased. 'Hypertrophy' is a denotative description of a structure and not a clinical pathology, even though it is often presented as a medical diagnosis.

This book charts the history of this diagnosis. It is not a sociological analysis of how women think about and respond to female genital cosmetic surgery, nor does it attempt to provide a theory of female agency that is able to show how contemporary women navigate the pleasures and pains of genital cosmetic surgery. Rather, this book came about because I felt that the development of medical knowledge of the female genitals could provide some answers to the vexing question of where the idea of genital normality comes from. Medicine is, of course, not the only source of sexual knowledge, but it has been overlooked in accounts in the popular media and in academic articles that put the blame for cosmetic labiaplasty primarily on internet pornography. This book sets out the argument that contemporary women's feelings of genital shame and abnormality need to be located within the broader history of medical gynaecology because of its important role in laying the discursive groundwork for the expression of these anxieties. Although the current phenomenon of female genital cosmetic surgery is embedded in contemporary late-capitalist Western culture, the questions that motivate this book are historical ones: To what extent is the genital shame driving female uptake of labiaplasty surgery strictly contemporary? How far back does the diagnosis of labial hypertrophy go? And where do our ideas about genital normality come from?

WHAT IS FEMALE GENITAL COSMETIC SURGERY?

Female genital cosmetic surgery (hereafter FGCS) refers to a range of surgical procedures that are performed on the vagina and vulva when there is no indication of gynaecological disease. These are essentially aesthetic and restorative procedures that aim to make the genitals look appropriately feminine, to reduce physical and mental discomfort, and to enhance sexual feeling. They include reduction of the labia minora, or labiaplasty; reduction of the clitoral hood (labiaplasty and clitoral hood reduction are often performed together); 'augmentation', or enlargement, of the labia majora; vaginal tightening, or vaginal 'rejuvenation', and perineoplasty; 'G-spot amplification'; clitoral reduction; and hymenoplasty, or hymen reconstruction.[6] I would also include in this list clitoral reconstruction for women who have had the clitoris excised in ritual cutting practices, otherwise known as FGM (or 'female genital mutilation'). The most common form of FGCS is labiaplasty, which involves cutting back large and protuberant labia minora so that they are either entirely hidden by or sit flush with the lips of the labia majora. Over the last couple of decades, media reports and anecdotal evidence from cosmetic surgeons have suggested a marked rise in popularity of cosmetic labiaplasty procedures. This has been borne out in the global statistics collected by the International Society of Aesthetic Plastic Surgery (ISAPS), which found that of all the cosmetic surgery procedures in 2016, labiaplasty showed the largest annual increase, rising by 45 per cent since 2015.[7]

In the medical literature detailing surgical labiaplasty techniques, protuberant labia minora are described as 'hypertrophied'. A precise definition of 'hypertrophy' in the literature is wanting, with labial measurement being anything from 2–5 cm from base to tip as the baseline requirement for diagnosis.[8] It may also be accompanied by asymmetry, where one labium is larger than the other. What is clear, however, is that labia minora that protrude *to any degree beyond the labia majora* can be classed as hypertrophic. German plastic surgeon Stefan Gress has suggested that a height of 2 cm from the interlabial fold could serve as a useful baseline, as this is the point at which 'the inner vaginal lips generally start to be visible outside the shelter of the labia majora'.[9] Surgeons usually also stress that a diagnosis of labial hypertrophy is more dependent upon how a woman feels about her protruding labia than about any specific method of measurement. As Solanki et al. put it: 'When deciding on the need for surgical intervention the symptoms described by the patient are more important than measurements alone. These issues can be functional, aesthetic and psychological'.[10] Gress justifies the need for surgery on the grounds that 'asymmetrical or greatly enlarged labia minora can distort the body image so permanently that the woman's sex life can be seriously affected. Doctors who empathise with their patients will surely understand their desire for correction'.[11]

According to accounts given by cosmetic surgeons in the clinical literature, the main reasons women give for wanting the procedure done involve concerns about aesthetic appearance, fears of abnormality, and problems with physical comfort, hygiene and sexual function.[12] Goodman found that in at least two studies the majority of patients cited aesthetic reasons for undergoing labiaplasty, followed by discomfort in clothing, entry dyspareunia (or painful penetrative sex) and discomfort with exercise. He concluded that 'the goal of these procedures is to obtain a more subjectively aesthetically pleasing appearance of the genitalia without adverse sequelae or anatomical distortion'.[13] In a 2007 qualitative study by Ros Bramwell, Claire Morland and Anne S. Garden, interviewees who had undergone labiaplasty expressed anxiety about their genital normality and dissatisfaction with their sex lives. They felt defective and abnormal, which, for some, was precipitated or confirmed by the comments of relatives. The women also expressed deeply felt sexual shame in feeling self-conscious about 'quite an ugly area that's kept as private as possible' and spoke of sexual difficulty because of labial length and swelling during arousal.[14] According to Australian cosmetic surgery chain Esteem Cosmetic Studio, the best candidates for labiaplasty 'are women who are either experiencing sexual dysfunction or embarrassment because their labia (labia minora) are over-sized or asymmetrical'.[15] Cosmetic surgery advertising also often states that localised health problems such as urinary tract and yeast infections, as well as 'hygiene' difficulties, can be caused by 'labial hypertrophy',[16] even though there is no medical evidence to support the claim that protuberant labia minora causes vaginal thrush, recurrent urinary tract infections or trouble maintaining hygiene.[17] In Australia, where I am based, labiaplasty costs roughly between AUD$3,500 and AUD$9,000, depending on the clinic.[18]

Cosmetic female genital modification practices have existed since the Egyptian pharaonic period, while amputations of normal but enlarged clitorises and labia have been cited in the ancient Greco-Roman medical literature.[19] As I will elaborate in this book, the 'condition' of elongated or 'hypertrophic' labia is also well documented in Western gynaecological and anatomical textbooks from the early modern period to today. However, in the contemporary setting, demand for labiaplasty is largely being met, and also driven, by plastic surgeons, rather than gynaecologists. Labiaplasty didn't obtain its present popularity as a cosmetic procedure until around 1998, when Los Angeles plastic surgeons Gary Alter and David Matlock 'publicized procedures … for "beautifying" the vulva and "increasing sexual responsiveness"'.[20] Plastic surgeons have claimed that they are 'treating' women for labial hypertrophy because gynaecologists are generally reluctant to remove undiseased labia minora, and that by their refusals gynaecologists trivialise and ignore women's pain.[21]

Notably, the peak bodies representing gynaecologists and obstetricians in the United States, Britain, Australia and New Zealand have all raised strong ethical objections to FGCS. In 2007, the American

College of Obstetricians and Gynecologists (ACOG) released a Committee Opinion stating that 'it is deceptive to give the impression that vaginal rejuvenation, designer vaginoplasty, revirgination, G-spot amplification, or any such procedures are accepted and routine surgical practices. Absence of data supporting the safety and efficacy of these procedures makes their recommendation untenable'.[22] This was reaffirmed in 2017. In 2008, the Royal Australian and New Zealand College of Obstetricians and Gynaecologists (RANZCOG) followed suit with its position statement that cosmetic genital surgeries were exploitative and unsupported by reliable evidence that such procedures were 'effective, enhance sexual function or improve self-image'. Interestingly, RANZCOG did not extend these reservations to reconstructive surgery following FGM.[23]

In 2013, the United Kingdom's Royal College of Obstetricians and Gynaecologists (RCOG) published an ethical opinion paper, where it stated that 'the presentation of female genital cosmetic surgery (FGCS) as an unproblematic lifestyle choice is undesirable because it misleads women as to the need for and the efficacy of such surgical procedures'. It also criticised the absence of controlled trials or prospective studies investigating the clinical effectiveness or risks of labiaplasty procedures, as well as the lack of independent evaluation.[24] All three bodies unequivocally agree that gynaecologists should be supported and encouraged to reassure women seeking labiaplasty that they are normal, to stress that there is a wide variety of vulval shapes and sizes, and to advise nonsurgical interventions. This year, RCOG and the British Society for Paediatric and Adolescent Gynaecology produced a new resource for doctors in the form of a booklet aimed at educating young people about normal vulval anatomy.[25]

From this point of view, it is important to distinguish cosmetic labiaplasty to 'correct' the aesthetic appearance of normal, healthy organs from surgeries that are a response to malignant afflictions. Cosmetic labiaplasty does not therefore include reconstructive surgery for conditions such as lichen sclerosus (or LS), which is a skin disorder in which the labia minora and clitoris can atrophy and be absorbed into the body, completely changing the structure of the vulva. The vagina can also shrink, and in some cases the vulval and vaginal adhesions necessitate surgery.[26] These changes are abnormal and deeply distressing for the women who experience them.

Feminist Criticism

Probably the first influential feminist critique of female genital cosmetic surgery was New Zealand scholar Virginia Braun's impressively comprehensive critical review published in the *Journal of Women's Health* in 2010.[27] In this article, Braun questioned surgeon claims in the clinical literature that FGCS benefits and promotes women's psychological, emotional and sexual health. Braun argued that there was no reliable evidence to support such claims and that the biomedical framework of knowledge was unable to address the broader problem of unequal gender relations underpinning the practice of FGCS. In short, Braun argued that FGCS needed to be situated as a harmful cultural product and purveyor of sexism and not a benign medical technology supporting women's health—a position I take in this book. In this article, Braun called to attention to methodological shortcomings in the clinical literature, the lack of evidence of clinical effectiveness, the problematic medicalisation of the female body, and the extent to which FGCS presents a constrained choice shaped by broader cultural pressures on women to sexually self-objectify.[28]

Along with Braun, health professionals have mounted important feminist critiques that have scrutinised the assumption by cosmetic surgeons that FGCS is an appropriate, safe and effective response to female body anxiety and that it improves female sexual function. Several prominent critics who have questioned the clinical value of FGCS are gynaecologists Sarah M. Creighton, Lina Michala, Naomi S. Crouch, Rebecca Deans and Jillian Lloyd, clinical psychologist Lih-Mei Liao, and urologist Justine Schober.[29] These authors have criticised the idiosyncratic and unreliable nature of published studies assessing health risk and outcomes, low survey response rates with self-selected samples, lack of long-term follow-up and conflict of interest where surveys and interviews have been conducted by the surgeons themselves, rather than independent researchers. This is problematic because surgeons have a financial interest in proving good health outcomes, low complication rates and patient satisfaction. Critics argue that the clinical literature minimises the potential health risks and incidence of poor aesthetic outcomes and emphasises patient satisfaction.[30] They also claim there is no clear evidence that labiaplasty and vaginal tightening procedures facilitate orgasm or solve problems with sexual arousal and penetrative pain. On the contrary, critics assert, surgery on the genitals is more likely to cause *loss* of sexual sensation.[31]

Critics express scepticism as to the clinical effectiveness of FGCS in part because it is being promoted and performed largely by surgeons in private practice whose income depends on getting patients in the door and on the operating table. Cosmetic labiaplasty costs thousands of dollars and it is not uncommon for plastic surgeons' clinics to be located in high-income suburbs.[32] Braun and others argue that women are making choices in ethically compromised and poorly regulated circumstances governed by coercive marketing and capitalist profiteering.[33] As demonstrated by Li-Meh Liao, Neda Taghinejadi and Sara M. Creighton, surgeon websites advertising FGCS are under no obligation to provide responsible information and are likely to make unsubstantiated and erroneous medical claims.[34]

Feminist critics of FGCS understand medicine to be an important site of political contestation. At the heart of this political arena of the body is the problem of normality. Both in the clinical literature and in advertising on the internet, cosmetic surgeons use the term 'hypertrophy' to give the impression of illness and abnormality. For instance, Melbourne clinic Cosmetic Surgery for Women & Men applies the term 'hypertrophy' to labia that are 'abnormally large or misshapen'.[35] As I indicated earlier, 'hypertrophy of the labia minora' is term that transforms normal female embodiment into an illness, given that, as Gress has stated, *any protrusion* beyond the labia majora can be considered hypertrophic, or abnormally large. The reason why this clinical designation is problematic is simply because labia minora are a structural part of what we designate as 'female' sexual anatomy and may be smaller or larger, just like any other part of the anatomy, such as a foot or an ear or a nipple. In short, there is nothing especially noteworthy or medically worrisome about labia minora that hang beyond the lips of the majora. Jillian Lloyd, Naomi Crouch, Catherine Minto, Lih-Mei Liao and Sarah Creighton demonstrated this point in their influential gynaecological study titled 'Female Genital Appearance: "Normality" Unfolds'. In this study, Lloyd et al. measured the labia minora of fifty asymptomatic premenopausal women aged between 18 and 50, and found great variation in size, with the upper limit being 50 mm in width.[36] The study was conducted because the researchers realised that there was no concept of 'normal' in the clinical literature. The anatomical boundaries of normality needed to be investigated, they argued, because 'implicit in a woman's desire to alter her genital appearance may be the belief that her genitals are not normal, that there is such a thing as normal female genital appearance, that the operating surgeon will know what this is, that he or she will be able to achieve this for her and that this would somehow improve her wellbeing or relationships with others'.[37] What is considered 'normal' by plastic surgeons is what they perceive to be aesthetically pleasing, rather than what actually exists. In this way, the plastic surgery literature constructs a biological norm on the basis of subjective aesthetic values evident in the pejorative descriptions of protuberant labia minora as 'grossly enlarged', looking like 'spaniels' ears' and 'deformed'.[38] On his website, Michael Goodman compares large labia to 'elephant ears', while the Sydney Cosmetic Specialists website states that 'protrusion of the lips may feel uncomfortable for many women, as it is unpleasing to the eyes'.[39] As Virginia Braun has argued, language—even clinical language—is never merely descriptive or neutral: 'Language is not simply a tool for information transfer; it is bound up in the creation of reality as it represents it. It (re)produces ideas about normality and pathology. The label hypertrophy is a perfect example of what might otherwise be normal variation becoming a legitimate problem—a *pathological* condition'.[40] That is, the language of 'hypertrophy' does not simply describe a condition of ill health that pre-exists the label; rather, the label itself brings the condition into being.

A POLITICAL PROBLEM

Feminist objections to FGCS must be situated within the broader social context of gender inequality. Cosmetic labiaplasty, like any other cosmetic surgery procedure, takes place in a commercialised health context which is heavily oriented toward women, rather than men. Women make up around 90 per cent of cosmetic surgery patients in the United Kingdom and the United States, and 86 per cent globally.[41] Likewise, according to global statistics collected by the International Society of Plastic Surgery, women make up 96 per cent of cosmetic genital surgery patients when comparing penis enlargements to the combined numbers of labiaplasties and vaginal rejuvenations.[42] In Australia, in 2016, women made up 99 per cent of cosmetic genital surgery patients.[43] This statistical evidence of substantial gender disparity is what makes female genital cosmetic surgery a feminist issue. It behoves us to enquire into the structural conditions that have brought the current phenomenon into being and gives us pause to wonder whether cosmetic surgery is not in fact enabling and reproducing female body anxiety, rather than solving it.

One pressing and complex problem that feminist critics of FGCS come up against is the issue of individual choice, and the risk of erasing the agent from the scene of surgery by privileging the structural gender relations of power over individual locatedness and experience within those relations of power. If a woman experiences surgery as self-affirming and it brings her happiness, then why deny her the opportunity to explore the pleasures of a new self? Cosmetic surgeons are usually the first to declare that FGCS is a liberating procedure that brings wellbeing and happiness, and they cite high consumer satisfaction as proof that procedures like labiaplasty benefit women's mental health. In a recent study, independent Australian researchers Gemma Sharp, Marika Tiggemann and Julie Mattiske found high satisfaction rates among women who had had cosmetic labiaplasty, except for those who experienced post-surgical complications and those who were not satisfied with the aesthetic result.[44] The authors concluded: 'Women appear to be very satisfied with the results of their labiaplasty and they also seem to experience improvements in their sexual satisfaction and psychological well-being. Physical/functional motivations for undergoing labiaplasty are associated with greater satisfaction with outcomes.'[45] By this, they meant that women who were more appearance-focused were more likely to be unhappy with the cosmetic outcome. This paper was published in the *Aesthetic Surgery Journal* in 2017. Unsurprisingly, prominent American aesthetic surgeon Michael P. Goodman congratulated the team for reinforcing evidence in the existing literature 'that LP and vaginal tightening operations "*work*"'.[46] For Goodman, the fact that this evidence was coming from independent researchers was an excellent endorsement of FGCS and its practitioners. Feminist critics, he suggested, were errant in negating women's concerns about their labia minora as 'frivolous because the organ in question falls within a vaguely defined and wide range of "…normal." These are real concerns and as such are to be respected'.[47]

The argument that emphasising the harms of cosmetic surgery denies female pleasure is a persuasive one, and from a liberal standpoint, I am loath to deny any person the right to bodily autonomy and happiness. Yet we nonetheless need a theoretical framework that can take account of individual experience in relation to the structural conditions of which we catch a glimpse in the cosmetic surgery statistics and in the discursive construction of 'labial hypertrophy'. A glaring drawback of Sharp et al.'s research is the methodological assumption that women's body satisfaction after surgery can somehow be measured without reference to the social and historical conditions that produce the female body as unsatisfying. It is to quarantine the emotional experience of cosmetic surgery from the emotionalised structures of gender inequality that produce the female genitals as a source of shame. As historian Joan Scott has eloquently argued, 'experience' in and of itself is not enough to comprehend the broader political picture within which feelings about oneself and one's relationships with others make sense.[48] Women's experiences of surgery can give us insight into the various 'dimensions of human life and activity',[49] but we would be mistaken in thinking that 'the evidence of experience' provides direct access to some sort of undigested truth. As Scott argues, when it becomes an attribute of individuals, agency is decontextualised, separated from the discursive, institutional, social and historical ideological systems of representation through which experience obtains meaning and cohesion.[50] When I speak of 'women' in this book, I am referring both to individuals and a group of people who obtain this identity through the social and historical patterns of a sexually ordered world.

In grappling with this question of agency, Braun and others have argued that FGCS is framed by the neoliberal rhetoric of consumer choice and freedom, even though it is imposing a restrictive norm that makes surgery seem like the best, indeed the *only*, option.[51] Braun describes the figure of the neoliberal subject as an autonomous unit making 'individualised choices, removed from any contextual constraints, structural or otherwise, free from the influence of cultural norms and expectations'.[52] Feminist critics, including myself, have pointed out that this presumption of consumer choice produces a problematic distinction between empowered, autonomous Western women who elect to have their genitals surgically cut for health reasons and disempowered, victimised African, Asian and Middle Eastern women who have been subjected to FGM. These critiques highlight the difficulty of upholding a hypocritical separation between oppressive FGM and therapeutic FGCS.[53] I address this comparison of FGCS and FGM in Chapter 7.

Within the Western context, there are a number of hypotheses as to the factors that may be motivating the present unprecedented trend of FGCS. While I argue in this book that there are historical precedents, it is clear that the current labiaplasty phenomenon is a historical product of the twentieth-century development of aesthetic plastic surgery and its increasing availability in late-capitalist consumer society. The popular, academic, and clinical literature suggests that there are a number of other interlocking sociocultural influences motivating women to seek labiaplasty surgery apart from the normalisation of cosmetic surgery. These include the influence of specific types of media, including pornography, women's magazines, surgeon advertising and reality television; frequency of pubic hair removal; the proliferation of the image in the digital age; and the intensification of sexualisation.[54]

Pornography is conspicuous in these discussions as the purported culprit behind the 'clean slit' ideal,[55] with online news outlets displaying headlines such as 'Rise in Girls Asking GPs about Genital Cosmetic Surgery Is Blamed on Online Porn' and 'Labiaplasty Surgery Increase Blamed on Pornography'.[56] Feminist researchers cite anecdotal evidence from surgeons that women are bringing images of vulvas from soft porn magazines into their consultations[57] to demonstrate that 'heterosexual pornography informs the model or ideal that [labiaplasty surgery] clients have for their post-operative genitalia'.[58] Braun attributes the youthful, pre-pubescent aesthetic in which the labia minora are hidden from view to 'the "unreal" vulvas displayed in heterosexual male-oriented pornography'.[59] Similarly, Vanessa R. Schick, Brandi N. Rima, and Sarah K. Calabrese suggest that exposure to pornographic images influences women's genital satisfaction.[60] In their study, women rated pre-labiaplasty images of vulvas as less attractive than post-labiaplasty vulvas and those found in *Playboy* centrefolds. From their review of trends in genital detail displayed in *Playboy* centrefolds, the researchers concluded that 'a "tucked-in look" is one aspect of the prototypical genital appearance that is promoted by pornographic imagery and, consequently, sought and desired by women'.[61] In their study of images of vulvas in online porn, medical textbooks and feminist publications, Helena Howarth, Volker Sommer and Fiona M. Jordan found less variation in vulval size in porn sources than feminist ones.[62] Theorists have also pointed to the growing trend in pubic hair removal, which brings greater visual attention to the genitals and accentuates exposed labia minora.[63] Bethany Jones and I have criticised what we call the 'porn thesis' firstly because women are not the main target audience for pornography and are therefore unlikely to consume it to the extent that they become dissatisfied with their genitals, and secondly because there is no singular or monolithic 'porn ideal' governing labia minora size.[64] While soft-core porn magazines are known to airbrush out the labia minora, we must be guarded about applying this rule to pornography in general.

As porn performer Angela White told me, not only is labiaplasty 'not popular in porn', but 'big labia can equal big dollars'.[65] After all, one of the most successful porn stars of the last decade, Alexis Texas, is well known for her ample buttocks (she won Favourite Ass Awards from F.A.M.E. and Night Moves in 2008) and visibly protuberant labia minora. All one has to do to see big labia in porn is type 'big labia, porn star' into Google. In a Reddit thread, for instance, a user asks about porn stars with big labia and is given a list of names to follow up: Christy Mack, Dominika C, Andie Valentino (who crops up twice), Kacey Jordan, Sabrina Maree and Luna Lane.[66] Every single one of these porn stars has markedly protuberant labia that would without doubt be classified as 'hypertrophic' by plastic surgeons. This suggests to me that any conception that women—and even male plastic surgeons—may have of *the* porn star look is not based on the empirically observable range of vulvas that are easily accessible on the internet to anyone who wishes to look for them for the purpose of comparison. Simone Weil Davis has made the same observation in her excellent article 'Loose Lips Sink Ships', where she points out the class difference in the airbrushed, 'flaw-free and glossy' vulval presentation in high-end magazines like *Playboy* and *Penthouse*, compared with '*Hustler*'s aggressive celebration of vulgarity', which is not shy in showing genital detail.[67]

Other sources of visual comparison can be found in women's magazines. Lindy Joan McDougall cited an issue of *Cleo* magazine, which featured nude photographs of ordinary women (rather than celebrities) aged 25–32 years, whose 'genitals were amazingly uniform, clean slits with no dangling labia in sight … and would hardly be reassuring for any women whose labia minora protrude'.[68] Leonore Tiefer notes that 'makeover' and surgical reality shows capitalise on a 'fantasy body fix' which insert the transformation of the body into a fairytale narrative of success and happiness.[69] As feminist Cultural Studies theorist Meredith Jones has argued, makeover culture 'valorises and rewards processes of working on the self'.[70] If, for women, part of this body work is about becoming desirable, both to themselves and imagined others, then cosmetic surgery on the vulva is a labour undertaken in the service of sexual fulfilment. The 'before' and 'after' photographs on surgeons' websites, and the stories surgeons tell about the restoration of sexual confidence, excite our desires with a visual fantasy of the person we can become through surgical transformation.

In wealthy, consumerist Western nations, rapidly evolving biomedical technologies offer up the promise of better and happier selves advertised across a multitude of digital media platforms that are now irrevocably integrated into every aspect of our lives. Women are likely to hear about labiaplasty from a range of sources, from news stories to reality television programs such as *Embarrassing Bodies*, to surgeon advertisements online. I first heard about it around 2012 from an online news article, and that was when I started finding 'before' and 'after' pictures on surgeon websites, where many of the 'after' shots looked disturbingly similar: pale-pink, hairless labia majora with the labia minora 'neatly' tucked inside. Meredith Jones locates labiaplasty in relation to her concept of 'media-bodies', which considers how 'contemporary bodies and media are conceptually, visually, and physically intertwined'.[71] Jones argues that we are now living in a media-saturated world between two and three dimensions, 'where people wish they could be Photoshopped in real life and where scalpels can be aligned with digital tools'.[72] In other words, the body-image—the conceptual and sensory apparatus that provides us with a visually coherent perception of our bodies—has become digital. I have made a similar argument elsewhere that the surgically altered genitals-without-labia are a posthuman phenomenon in a world in which we strive to leave the messy, hairy business of the biological body behind.[73] The clean slit with no visible labial protrusion has been termed the 'Barbie look',[74] which, I have argued, is an attempt to arrive at the feminine as pure form. The image of posthuman sexiness, with its perfectly smooth lines, erases the fleshiness of the organic body. In this vision of the technological evolution of the body, the labia become functionally useless evolutionary remnants that nobody wants.[75]

Beyond this, feminist theorists have explored historical and cultural constructions of the female genitals that inform present-day perceptions of genital deficiency and desirability. This work examines the historical lineage of pudendal disgust and the pathologisation of women's bodies in the Western sciences and in everyday discourses of sex and sexuality.[76] Historicised accounts of FGCS draw our attention to the practice of medical clitoridectomy in Victorian England,[77] and the notorious white colonial representations of the labia of Khoi women from the Cape of Good Hope, which European naturalists called the 'Hottentot Apron'.[78]

HISTORICISING FEMALE GENITAL COSMETIC SURGERY

This book contributes to the feminist project of situating FGCS in historical context. It is an attempt to move away from explanations concerned with present late-capitalist formations of identity to uncover hitherto unexplored narratives that situate FGCS within a larger medical history of the vulva. The research questions that inform this book are directed toward tracing the historical threads of a medical conception of vulval abnormality, which reveals the historically far-reaching complicity of medicine in giving us an image of what genital 'normality' looks like. In short: the question I ask of history is where did the diagnosis of labial hypertrophy come from?

In order to answer this query, the book traverses medico-scientific understandings of the vulva in the ancient Greco-Roman, Renaissance, Early Modern, Victorian and early twentieth-century eras to examine developments in the medical technologies and epistemologies that have shaped the context for current Western cosmetic surgical practices on the female genitals. In particular, I trace the historical threads linking the surgical management of the vulva to the cultural regulation of aberration and normality. I argue that the drive for genital perfection is rooted in an array of historical practices and knowledges that have served to define 'normal' and 'abnormal' sex and sexuality within gendered, sexualised, raced and classed relations of power.

One of the things I want to do in this book is to situate scientific texts as participating in the making of narrative and visual cultures of the body, following the influential and illuminating work of scholars of the sciences such as Anne Fausto-Sterling, Londa Schiebinger, Thomas Laqueur and Sander Gilman.[79] In the discipline of Cultural Studies, it is tempting to place under the banner of 'culture' narrative genres found, for example, in literature, religion, art, and the mass media. It is not quite so easy to place Western science wholly within these cultural traditions due to the distinct and special nature of its empiricist inquiry. And yet the sciences are no less visual or richly descriptive as the arts. Visual representations such as illustrations and photographs are embedded in the scientific process of elaborating genital typologies and topographies; and denotative names for the genitals have been formed through the poetic intersections of vision and language, where a part of the human anatomy gains its name from some other part of nature like a myrtle-berry, a lily or a moth's wing.

I argue in this book that this history of medicine, with its naming conventions, inventive descriptions and pictorial examples, is saturated with cultural prejudices that inform our fantasies about what 'normal' and 'abnormal' genitals look like. Medical science plays a central role in determining the limits of anatomical normality because that is its *raison d'être*: in order to build its understanding of the body, medicine is constantly creating, refining and revising its categories of health and sickness, order and disorder. In this book, I use the binary coupling of normality/abnormality as an analytical tool to make sense of the development of the concept of labial 'hypertrophy'. This is not without its perils. In their recent book on the history of normality, Peter Cryle and Elizabeth Stephens warn that in reducing normality to one end of a binary, scholars have tended to efface the historicity of the normal. They suggest that like Foucault's excavation of sexuality as a modern phenomenon, the concept of normality, too, is an idea with a specific genealogy.[80] Yet at the risk of courting anachronism (that is, of being a bad historian), I do want to keep open the possibility of a generalisable idea of 'normal' to mean a thing that is variously taken to be natural, expected, frequently encountered, desirable and most of all, familiar. The history of the hypertrophied labia is one of deviance, which only makes sense if there is a concomitant concept of a normal or ideal vulva. I suggest that in the medical sphere, some idea of normality as regularity is always at work in the body submitted to medical assessments of good or bad health, which may also determine whether or not a body is seen to need surgical, or some other, intervention. If the historical sources in this volume can be relied upon, then there is a strong and present discourse in medical texts, from the ancient Greeks onwards, of the natural and normal human body and the laws of equilibrium that are thought to govern it. The human vulva is a part of a scientific history of naming and classifying, which sorts bodies and body parts into normal and abnormal. This book aims to trace the discursive continuities and shifts in these ideas across different historical periods to the present day.

CHAPTERS

Chapter 2 begins with Hippocratic medicine (c. 450–350 BCE) in order to establish what was known about the anatomical structure and diseases of the female external genitals in the ancient world. I trace ancient Greek naming conventions for the female genitals to argue that there was not, at this stage, a concept of labial hypertrophy firstly because the labia minora and majora were themselves confused and indeterminate genital structures, and secondly because anatomical structure of bodies was less important to the Greeks than their humoral composition. It must be noted here that intersex embodiment was known to both Greek and Roman medical writers and signals a probable origin point for the medical conception of morphological genital 'abnormality', which is still with us today (I look at the overlap between the categories of 'intersex' and 'hypertrophy' in Chapter 7). However, I restrict my focus in Chapters 2 and 3 to an examination of sexually dimorphic anatomical naming because I want to show the historical development of medical understanding of *biotypical* vulval anatomy.[81]

Chapter 3 departs from the ancient Greek physician Galen (c. 129–216 CE) to show how his analogic model of sexed bodies, where the female sex organs were portrayed as inverted male organs, laid the groundwork for the expression of anxieties among later Roman physicians (400–700 CE) about the enlarged clitoris. In Roman medical texts, the enlarged clitoris was likened to a penis and signified abnormal femininity. I locate this Roman obsession with the problem of the enlarged clitoris as the first medical diagnosis of 'hypertrophy' of a vulval structure, which precipitated arguments about whether it was a sign of hermaphroditism (an actual penis) or a female deformity (an enlarged clitoris). I hypothesise that it wasn't until the sixteenth century, with the work of anatomist Andreas Vesalius, that the labia minora would acquire a stable identity in anatomical nomenclature. From the sixteenth century, we begin to see racialised references to elongated labia minora in Egyptian women. In seventeenth-century gynaecology the 'normal' (European) labia minora gradually acquired their own identity, and by the eighteenth century, the pendulous labia of the post-partum vulva were being unfavourably compared to the ideal virginal vulva, with its firm, pink, small labia minora.

Chapter 4 explores the historically pivotal moment in which 'abnormally' elongated labia minora became fixed in the white colonial scientific imagination as an anatomical feature specific to African women. In the seventeenth to the nineteenth centuries, beginning with the establishment of the Cape Colony in the Cape of Good Hope by the Dutch, European colonial travellers, doctors and naturalists began to share stories of their encounters with the Indigenous Khoi women who lived there. In this period, white anthropologists became fascinated with the length of the labia of these women, to which they gave the name the 'Hottentot apron'. I show how the apron became embroiled in debates about race and evolution in the white sciences between 'monogenists', who believed that the races descended from the same human ancestor, and 'polygenists', who believed that the races were distinct species. The latter drew on the Hottentot apron as evidence of their theory of species difference, and as proof that only the white race could legitimately lay claim to full human citizenship.

Chapter 5 explores the work of early twentieth-century French gynaecologist Félix Jayle, who, to my knowledge, was the first medical author to attempt to catalogue the range of dimensions of the labia minora and to sort them into types. His classificatory system identi-fied four distinct types: 'short' (small and hidden), 'membraniform' (leaf-shaped), 'aliform' (wing-shaped) and 'hypertrophic' (enlarged and considered to be a racial characteristic specific to black women). Jayle's work is important for being the first systematic attempt to understand labial variation through painstaking measurement of his female patients. He proposed that the 'normal' adult nymphae meas-ured between 2 and 4 cm. This was not the only part of the female body Jayle measured, however. The purpose of his book on gynae-cology, published in 1918, was to provide a comprehensive overview of the whole anatomy of the 'normal' European female. His statisti-cal concept of anatomical normality came from the eugenic racial sciences, and his genital typologies were part of a larger eugenic pro-ject that sought to cultivate 'normal', healthy white bodies in the service of strengthening the white races of the French nation. The association of the hypertrophied labia minora with the Hottentot apron acquired renewed meaning in early twentieth-century France, as emblematic of national anxiety over French imperial decline and racial degeneration.

Chapter 6 crosses the Atlantic to examine the work of influential early twentieth-century American gynaecologist and sexologist Robert Latou Dickinson. This chapter draws on Dickinson's highly detailed anthropometric studies of 'hypertrophic' labia minora, which he took to be an unquestionable sign of masturbation. Masturbation was wor-risome because it was thought to cause gynaecological and mental disorders. In supposing labial hypertrophy to be the result of masturba-tion, Dickinson referenced a medical tradition that associated abnormal genitals with abnormal sexual desire. In this alienist framework, women who masturbated were believed to be excessively sexual and either already were or were likely to become nymphomaniacs. But Dickinson had also surmised that it was useful to know if a woman was a chronic masturbator because it may impact upon, or allude to problems in, her marital sex life. In the Freudian twentieth-century, female masturbation signalled a refusal to accept adult heterosexuality. Hence, Dickinson believed that women who masturbated were potential lesbians: such women could, however, be averted from lesbianism if men were taught how to pleasure women. Dickinson was essentially a proto-sex-therapist who believed that the gynaecologist had a crucial role to play in promoting happy and healthy marriages. If women were sexually happy with their husbands, then this would lead to stable families and normal, well-adjusted children.

Chapter 7 moves on from Dickinson's sex-education program to the consumer context of present-day elective female genital cosmetic surgery (FGCS). This is a speculative chapter which proposes that FGCS appeals to a cultural fantasy of 'normality', or what it means to be a 'normal' woman. I argue that this norm is enmeshed in heterosexuality and the two-sex/gender system, which also regulates other forms of cosmetic cutting of the genitals: specifically, surgery on ambiguous intersex infant genitals and ritual female genital cutting (or FGM). I also acknowledge that what it means to be 'normal' is culturally and racially inflected and offer a critical examination of the cosmetic procedure of 'clitoral reconstruction' surgery for women who have undergone ritual clitoral excision. This process involves unearthing the erectile clitoral tissue buried under the pubis to construct a pseudo glans clitoris. In offering reconstructive surgery to African women, white plastic surgeons divert black feminist political action away from self-definition and autonomy and toward dependence on white benevolence. I consider 'clitoral reconstruction' to be in the cosmetic-surgery category because of its dubious health benefits and empty promises of sexual restoration that it cannot possibly fulfil (for the simple reason that once the glans clitoris has been excised, it is gone and cannot be restored, even by a skilled plastic surgeon—one cannot restore that which no longer exists). I end by proposing a conception of bodily autonomy that challenges the normalising fantasies of sex and gender through an inclusive materialist concept of biodiversity.

NOTES

1. For information on the Somazone site, see Ruth Webber and Julie Wilmot, 'Young People Seeking Help for Sexual Assault: A Question-and-Answer Online Environment', *Youth Studies Australia* 32, no. 2 (2013): 30–38.
2. Anonymous poster, 'Not Loving My Whole Body', Somazone, accessed 13 February 2015, www.somazone.com.au/index.php?option=com_stories&task=view_detail&id=95 (site discontinued). In all online quotations in this chapter, the original spelling and syntax have been retained.
3. Anonymous commenter, 'Not Loving My Whole Body', Somazone, accessed 13 February 2015, www.somazone.com.au/index.php?option=com_stories&task=view_detail&id=95 (site discontinued).
4. ilovemoms, 'It looks like I have too much skin around my vagina and it looks wrinkly. Should I get surgery?', RealSelf, 2018, https://www.realself.com/question/florida-fl-skin-vagina-wrinkly%23.
5. ilovemoms, 'It looks like I have too much skin around my vagina and it looks wrinkly. Should I get surgery?', RealSelf, 2018, https://www.realself.com/question/florida-fl-skin-vagina-wrinkly%23.
6. Gary J. Alter, 'Clitoral Reduction', Gary J. Alter MD Plastic and Reconstructive Surgeon, 2018, https://www.garyalterplasticsurgeon.com/female-genital-surgery/clitoral-reduction/; Virginia Braun, 'Female Genital Cosmetic Surgery: A Critical Review of Current Knowledge and Contemporary Debates', *Journal of Women's Health* 19, no. 7 (2010): 1393; Michael P. Goodman, 'Female Genital Cosmetic and Plastic Surgery: A Review', *Journal of Sexual Medicine* 8, no. 6 (2011): 1814.
7. International Society of Aesthetic Plastic Surgery, 'Demand for Cosmetic Surgery Procedures around the World Continues to Skyrocket – USA, Brazil, Japan, Italy and Mexico Ranked in the Top Five Countries', press release 2016, accessed 12 June 2018, https://www.isaps.org/wp-content/uploads/2017/10/GlobalStatistics.PressRelease2016-1.pdf.
8. Braun, 'Female Genital Cosmetic Surgery', 1400.
9. Stefan Gress, *Aesthetic and Functional Labiaplasty* (Cham: Springer, 2017), 6.
10. N. S. Solanki, R. Tejero-Trujeque, A. Stevens-King and C. M. Malata, 'Aesthetic and Functional Reduction of the Labia Minora Using the Maas and Hage Technique', *Journal of Plastic, Reconstructive & Aesthetic Surgery* 63, no. 7 (2010): 1182.
11. Gress, *Aesthetic and Functional Labiaplasty*, vii.
12. Ros Bramwell, 'Invisible Labia: The Representation of Female External Genitals in Women's Magazines', *Sexual and Relationship Therapy* 17, no. 2 (2002): 187–90; R. Bramwell, C. Morland and A. S. Garden, 'Expectations and Experience of Labial Reduction: A Qualitative Study', *BJOG* 114, no. 12 (2007): 1493–9.

13. Goodman, 'Female Genital Cosmetic and Plastic Surgery', 1818.
14. Bramwell, Morland and Garden, 'Expectations and Experience of Labial Reduction', 1495–6.
15. Esteem Cosmetic Studio, 'Labiaplasty', 2017, http://www.esteemstudio.com.au/body/labiaplasty.
16. See for example Cosmetic Surgery for Women & Men, 'Labiaplasty and Non-Surgical Vaginal Rejuvenation: Deciding on the Best Treatment for You', 1 March 2017, https://plasticsurgeons.com.au/labiaplasty-monalisa-touch-vaginal-rejuvenationm/; Colin Moore, 'Labioplasty Surgery Sydney', The Australian Centre for Cosmetic/Genital Surgery, 2011–18, http://www.drcolinmoore.com/procedures-for-women/body/labioplasty/; Carmen Munteanu, 'Transform the Appearance of Your Labia or Improve Personal Comfort', Aesthetik Profile, 2018, http://www.drcarmen.com.au/labiaplasty-guide/; Scott Turner, 'Labiaplasty Surgery', Labiaplasty Specialist by Dr. Turner, 2017, https://labiaplastyspecialist.com.au/procedure/labiaplasty/.
17. Melbourne plastic and reconstructive surgeon Jill Tomlinson is notable for her ethical approach to labiaplasty. As she clearly states on her website: 'There is no evidence to suggest that labiaplasty surgery can reduce problems with recurrent thrush or address hygiene concerns or problems'. Jill Tomlinson, 'Labiaplasty', Dr. Jill Tomlinson Plastic and Reconstructive Surgeon, 11 December 2011, http://jilltomlinson.com/body/labiaplasty. For information on the known causes of urinary tract infections (cystitis) and vaginal thrush, see Better Health Channel, 'Cystitis', May 2018, https://www.betterhealth.vic.gov.au/health/conditionsandtreatments/cystitis; Better Health Channel, 'Vaginal Thrush', March 2018, https://www.betterhealth.vic.gov.au/health/conditionsandtreatments/vaginal-thrush.
18. See for example Skinnotion, 'Advanced Cosmetic Surgery of Vaginal [sic]', 2018, https://www.skinnotion.com.au/body/cosmetic-vaginal-surgery/ ($3,500); Esteem Studio, 'Labiaplasty', 2017, http://www.esteemstudio.com.au/body/labiaplasty ($4,400); Sydney Cosmetic Specialists, 'Labiaplasty and Vagina Surgery', 2018, http://www.sydneycosmeticspecialists.com.au/labiaplasty-and-vagina-surgery-sydney/ ($4,900); Jill Tomlinson, 'Labiaplasty', 11 December 2011, Dr. Jill Tomlinson Plastic and Reconstructive Surgeon, http://jilltomlinson.com/body/labiaplasty ($5,600); Mark Kohout, 'Genital Surgery Prices', Dr. Mark Kohout FRACS Plastic Surgeon, http://www.drmarkkohout.com.au/prices-genital-surgery ($8,100); Scott Turner, 'Labiaplasty Surgery', Labiaplasty Specialist by Dr. Turner, https://labiaplastyspecialist.com.au/procedure/labiaplasty/ ($6,000–$9,000).
19. Michael P. Goodman, 'Genital Plastics: The History of Development', in Female Genital Plastic and Cosmetic Surgery (Chichester: Wiley, 2016), 3. See also Chapter 3, this volume.

20. Leonore Tiefer, 'Female Genital Cosmetic Surgery: Freakish or Inevitable? Analysis from Medical Marketing, Bioethics, and Feminist Theory', *Feminism & Psychology* 18, no. 4 (2008): 467. Also see Braun, 'Female Genital Cosmetic Surgery', 1394.

21. For instance, in an early article on aesthetic labiaplasty published in 1984, plastic surgeons Darryl J. Hodgkinson and Glen Hait indicated that women came to them for labiaplasty surgery because they had met with refusal from gynaecologists. Darryl J. Hodgkinson and Glen Hait, 'Aesthetic Vaginal Labioplasty', *Plastic and Reconstructive Surgery* 74, no. 3 (1984): 415–16. See also Gress, *Aesthetic and Functional Labiaplasty*, vii.

22. American College of Obstetricians and Gynecologists, ACOG Committee Opinion, no. 378, September 2007 (reaffirmed 2017), https://www. acog.org/Clinical-Guidance-and-Publications/Committee-Opinions/ Committee-on-Gynecologic-Practice/Vaginal-Rejuvenation-and-Cosmetic-Vaginal-Procedures.

23. Royal Australian and New Zealand College of Obstetricians and Gynaecologists, 'Vaginal "Rejuvenation", Laser Ablation for Benign Conditions and Cosmetic Vaginal Procedures', July 2008 (reviewed March 2015), https://www.ranzcog.edu.au/RANZCOG_SITE/media/ RANZCOG-MEDIA/Women's%20Health/Statement%20and%20guide-lines/Clinical%20-%20Gynaecology/Vaginal-rejuvenation,-laser-and-cosmetic-procedures-(C-Gyn-24)-Amended-July-2016.pdf?ext=.pdf.

24. Royal College of Obstetricians and Gynaecologists, 'Ethical Opinion Paper: Ethical Considerations in relation to Female Genital Cosmetic Surgery (FGCS)', October 2013, https://www.rcog.org.uk/globalas-sets/documents/guidelines/ethics-issues-and-resources/rcog-fgcs-ethi-cal-opinion-paper.pdf.

25. BritSPAG, *So What Is a Vulva Anyway?*, accessed 12 June 2018, https:// www.brook.org.uk/data/So_what_is_a_vulva_anyway_final_booklet.pdf.

26. Amanda Oakley, 'Lichen sclerosus', DermNet NZ, last updated January 2016, https://www.dermnetnz.org/topics/lichen-sclerosus/.

27. Braun, 'Female Genital Cosmetic Surgery'.

28. Braun, 'Female Genital Cosmetic Surgery'.

29. See for example Sarah Creighton, 'AGAINST: Labiaplasty is an Unnecessary Cosmetic Procedure', *BJOG* 121, no. 6 (2014): 768; N. S. Crouch, R. Deans, L. Michala, L-M Liao and S. M. Creighton, 'Clinical Characteristics of Well Women Seeking Labial Reduction Surgery: A Prospective Study', *BJOG* 118, no. 12 (2011): 1507–1510; Rebecca Deans, Lih-Mei Liao, Naomi S. Crouch and Sarah M. Creighton, 'Why Are Women Referred for Female Genital Cosmetic Surgery?', *Medical Journal of Australia* 195, no. 2 (2011): 99; Lih-Mei Liao and Sarah M. Creighton, 'Requests for Cosmetic Genitoplasty:

How Should Healthcare Providers Respond?', *BMJ* 334, no. 7603 (2007): 1090–92; L-M Liao, L. Michala and S. M. Creighton, 'Labial Surgery for Well Women: A Review of the Literature', *BJOG* 117, no. 1 (2010): 20–5; Lih-Mei Liao, Neda Taghinejadi and Sarah M. Creighton, 'An Analysis of the Content and Clinical Implications of Online Advertisements for Female Genital Cosmetic Surgery', *BMJ Open* 2, no. 6 (2012): http://bmjopen.bmj.com/content/2/6/e001908; Jillian Lloyd, Naomi S. Crouch, Catherine L. Minto, Lih-Mei Liao and Sarah M. Creighton, 'Female Genital Appearance: "Normality" Unfolds', *BJOG* 112, no. 5: (2005): 643–6; Justine Schober, Timothy Cooney, Donald Pfaff, Lazarus Mayoglou and Nieves Martin-Alguacil, 'Innervation of the Labia Minora of Prepubertal Girls', *Journal of Pediatric and Adolescent Gynecology* 23, no. 6 (2010): 352–7.

30. Braun, 'Female Genital Cosmetic Surgery'; Liao, Michala and Creighton, 'Labial Surgery for Well Women'; Creighton, 'AGAINST'.

31. Braun, 'Female Genital Cosmetic Surgery', 1398; Creighton, 'AGAINST'; Lloyd et al., 'Female Genital Appearance', 645; Schober et al., 'Innervation of the Labia Minora', 352–7; Liao and Creighton, 'Requests for Cosmetic Genitoplasty', 1091.

32. For instance, Australian surgeons Colin Moore, Ellis Choy and Scott Turner have their clinics in the affluent Sydney regions of Bondi Junction, Northbridge and Dee Why.

33. Braun, 'Female Genital Cosmetic Surgery', 1400.

34. Liao, Taghinejadi and Creighton, 'An Analysis of the Content and Clinical Implications of Online Advertisements for Female Genital Cosmetic Surgery'.

35. Cosmetic Surgery for Women & Men, 'Labiaplasty and Non-Surgical Vaginal Rejuvenation: Deciding on the Best Treatment for You', 1 March 2017, https://plasticsurgeons.com.au/labiaplasty-monalisa-touch-vaginal-rejuvenationm/.

36. Lloyd et al., 'Female Genital Appearance'.

37. Lloyd et al., 'Female Genital Appearance', 643.

38. Liao, Michala and Creighton, 'Labial Surgery for Well Women', 22.

39. Michael Goodman, 'What Are Vulvo-Vaginal Aesthetics?', Dr. Michael Goodman MD, 2018, http://www.drmichaelgoodman.com/what-are-vulvo-vaginal-aesthetics/; Sydney Cosmetic Specialists, 'Labiaplasty and Vagina Surgery', 2018, http://www.sydneycosmeticspecialists.com.au/labiaplasty-and-vagina-surgery-sydney/.

40. Braun, 'Female Genital Cosmetic Surgery', 1402, emphasis in original.

41. See American Society of Plastic Surgeons, *Plastic Surgery Statistics Report 2016*, 2017, https://www.plasticsurgery.org/documents/News/Statistics/2016/plastic-surgery-statistics-full-report-2016.pdf; International Society of

Aesthetic Plastic Surgery, 'Demand for Cosmetic Surgery Procedures around the World Continues to Skyrocket – USA, Brazil, Japan, Italy and Mexico Ranked in the Top Five Countries', press release 2016, accessed 12 June 2018, https://www.isaps.org/wp-content/uploads/2017/10/GlobalStatistics.PressRelease2016-1.pdf; Private Clinic of Harley Street, 'How 2015 Was "the" Year for Cosmetic Surgery in the UK', 2018, https://www.theprivateclinic.co.uk/blog/2016/02/08/how-2015-was-the-year-for-cosmetic-plastic-surgery-in-the-uk.

42. Global statistics for 2016 collected by the International Society of Aesthetic Plastic Surgery show that 8434 men underwent penile enlargement compared with 55,606 women who underwent 'vaginal rejuvenation' and 138,033 women who underwent labiaplasty. International Society of Aesthetic Plastic Surgery, *The International Study on Aesthetic/Cosmetic Procedures Performed in 2016*, accessed 12 June 2018, https://www.isaps.org/wp-content/uploads/2017/10/GlobalStatistics2016-1.pdf, p. 7.

43. In 2016, there were 30 penile enlargement surgeries in comparison to 1974 labiaplasties and 920 vaginal rejuvenations. International Society of Aesthetic Plastic Surgery, *The International Study on Aesthetic/Cosmetic Procedures Performed in 2016*, accessed 12 June 2018, https://www.isaps.org/wp-content/uploads/2017/10/GlobalStatistics2016-1.pdf, p. 8.

44. Gemma Sharp, Marika Tiggemann and Julie Mattiske, 'A Retrospective Study of the Psychological Outcomes of Labiaplasty', *Aesthetic Surgery Journal* 37, no. 3 (2017): 324–31.

45. Sharp, Tiggemann and Mattiske, 'A Retrospective Study', 324.

46. Michael P. Goodman, 'Commentary on: A Retrospective Study of the Psychological Outcomes of Labiaplasty', *Aesthetic Surgery Journal* 37, no. 3 (2017): 332.

47. Goodman, 'Commentary', 332.

48. Joan Scott, 'The Evidence of Experience', in *The Lesbian and Gay Studies Reader*, ed. Henry Abelove, Michèle Aina Barale and David M. Halperin (New York and London: Routledge, 1993), 397–415.

49. Scott, 'The Evidence of Experience', 399.

50. Scott, 'The Evidence of Experience', 399.

51. Virginia Braun, '"The Women Are Doing It for Themselves": The Rhetoric of Choice and Agency around Female Genital "Cosmetic Surgery"', *Australian Feminist Studies* 24, no. 60 (2009): 233–49; Braun, 'Female Genital Cosmetic Surgery'; Camille Nurka, 'Labiaplasty and the Melancholic Breast', *Studies in Gender and Sexuality* 16, no. 3 (2015): 204–25; Claire Moran and Christina Lee, 'Selling Genital Cosmetic Surgery to Healthy Women: A Multimodal Discourse Analysis of Australian Surgical Websites', *Critical Discourse Studies* 10, no. 4 (2013): 373–91.

52. Braun, 'The Women Are Doing It for Themselves', 236.
53. See for example Braun, 'The Women Are Doing It for Themselves'; Birgitta Essén and Sara Johnsdotter, 'Female Genital Mutilation in the West: Traditional Circumcision versus Genital Cosmetic Surgery', *Acta Obstetricia et Gynecologia Scandinavica* 83, no. 7 (2004): 611–13; Fiona J. Green, 'From Clitoridectomies to Designer Vaginas: The Medical Construction of Heteronormative Female Bodies and Sexuality through Female Genital Cutting', *Sexualities, Evolution and Gender* 7, no. 2 (2005): 153–187; Shakira Hussein and Camille Nurka, 'Entitled to Be Free: Exposing the Limits of Choice', *in Freedom Fallacy: The Limits of Liberal Feminism*, ed. Miranda Kiraly and Meagan Tyler (Ballarat: Connor Court, 2015), 81–94; Sara Johnsdotter, 'Projected Cultural Histories of the Cutting of Female Genitalia: A Poor Reflection as in a Mirror', *History and Anthropology* 23, no. 1 (2012): 91–114; Nikki Sullivan, '"The Price to Pay for Our Common Good": Genital Modification and the Somatechnologies of Cultural (In)Difference', *Social Semiotics* 17, no. 3 (2007): 395–409; Simone Weil Davis, 'Loose Lips Sink Ships', *Feminist Studies* 28, no. 1 (2002): 7–35.
54. Bramwell, 'Invisible Labia'; Bramwell, Morland and Garden, 'Expectations and Experience of Labial Reduction'; Virginia Braun, 'In Search of (Better) Sexual Pleasure: Female Genital "Cosmetic" Surgery', *Sexualities* 8, no. 4 (2005): 407–24; Braun, 'Female Genital Cosmetic Surgery'; V. Braun and S. Wilkinson, 'Socio-Cultural Representations of the Vagina', *Journal of Reproductive and Infant Psychology* 19, no. 1 (2001): 17–32; Green, 'From Clitoridectomies to Designer Vaginas'; Helena Howarth, Volker Sommer and Fiona M. Jordan, 'Visual Depictions of Female Genitalia Differ Depending on Source', *Medical Humanities* 36, no. 2 (2010): 75–9; Meredith Jones, 'Expressive Surfaces: The Case of the Designer Vagina', *Theory, Culture & Society* 34, nos 7–8 (2017): 29–50; Merel Koning, Ingeborg A. Zeijlmans, Theo K. Bouman and Berend van der Lei, 'Female Attitudes Regarding Labia Minora Appearance and Reduction with Consideration of Media Influence', *Aesthetic Surgery Journal* 29, no. 1 (2009): 65–71; Lloyd et al., 'Female Genital Appearance'; Lindy Joan McDougall, 'Towards a Clean Slit: How Medicine and Notions of Normality are Shaping Female Genital Aesthetics', *Culture, Health & Sexuality* 15, no. 7 (2013): 774–87; Moran and Lee, 'Selling Genital Cosmetic Surgery to Healthy Women'; Nurka, 'Labiaplasty and the Melancholic Breast'; Sara Rodrigues, 'From Vaginal Exception to Exceptional Vagina: The Biopolitics of Female Genital Cosmetic Surgery', *Sexualities* 15, no. 7 (2012): 778–94; Vanessa R. Schick, Brandi N. Rima and Sarah K. Calabrese, 'Evulvalution: The Portrayal of Women's External Genitalia and Physique across Time and the Current Barbie Doll Ideals',

Journal of Sex Research 48, no. 1 (2011): 74–81; Tiefer, 'Female Genital Cosmetic Surgery'.

55. McDougall, 'Towards a Clean Slit'.
56. Rowenna Davis, 'Labiaplasty Surgery Increase Blamed on Pornography', *Observer*, 27 February 2011, https://www.theguardian.com/lifeandstyle/2011/feb/27/labiaplasty-surgery-labia-vagina-pornography; Telegraph Reporters, 'Rise in Girls Asking GPs about Genital Cosmetic Surgery is Blamed on Online Porn', *Telegraph*, 7 October 2016, https://www.telegraph.co.uk/health-fitness/body/rise-in-girls-asking-gps-about-genital-cosmetic-surgery-is-blame/.
57. Braun, 'In Search of (Better) Sexual Pleasure'; Green, 'From Clitoridectomies to Designer Vaginas'; Liao and Creighton, 'Requests for Cosmetic Genitoplasty'.
58. Green 2005, 'From Clitoridectomies to Designer Vaginas', 174.
59. Braun, 'In Search of (Better) Sexual Pleasure', 413.
60. Schick, Rima and Calabrese, 'E*vulva*lution'.
61. Schick, Rima and Calabrese, 'E*vulva*lution', 79.
62. Howarth, Sommer and Jordan, 'Visual Depictions of Female Genitalia Differ Depending on Source'.
63. Crouch et al., 'Clinical Characteristics of Well Women Seeking Labial Reduction Surgery'; Green, 'From Clitoridectomies to Designer Vaginas'; McDougall, 'Towards a Clean Slit'; Rodrigues, 'From Vaginal Exception to Exceptional Vagina'.
64. Bethany Jones and Camille Nurka, 'Labiaplasty and Pornography: A Preliminary Investigation', *Porn Studies* 2, no. 1 (2015): 62–75.
65. Angela White, email message to author, 24 August 2012.
66. u/kanoon2, 'Porn Star with Large Labia', Reddit, accessed 12 June 2018, https://www.reddit.com/r/ButterflyWings/comments/2iolb5/pornstar_with_large_labia/.
67. Weil Davis, 'Loose Lips Sink Ships', 11.
68. McDougall, ''Towards a Clean Slit', 779.
69. Tiefer, 'Female Genital Cosmetic Surgery', 469.
70. Meredith Jones, *Skintight: An Anatomy of Cosmetic Surgery* (Oxford and New York: Berg, 2008), 11.
71. Jones, 'Expressive Surfaces', 29.
72. Jones, 'Expressive Surfaces', 36.
73. Nurka, 'Labiaplasty and the Melancholic Breast'.
74. Gemma Sharp, Marika Tiggemann and Julie Mattiske, 'Predictors of Consideration of Labiaplasty:An Extension of the Tripartite Influence Model of Beauty Ideals', *Psychology of Women Quarterly* 39, no. 2 (2015): 183.
75. Nurka, 'Labiaplasty and the Melancholic Breast'.

76. Braun, 'In Search of (Better) Sexual Pleasure'; Virginia Braun and Celia Kitzinger, 'The Perfectible Vagina: Size Matters', *Culture, Health & Sexuality* 3, no. 3 (2001): 263–77; Braun and Wilkinson, 'Socio-Cultural Representations of the Vagina'.

77. Green, 'From Clitoridectomies to Designer Vaginas'.

78. See for example Jones, 'Expressive Surfaces'; Camille Nurka and Bethany Jones, 'Labiaplasty, Race and the Colonial Imagination', *Australian Feminist Studies* 28, no. 78 (2013): 417–42; Weil Davis, 'Loose Lips Sink Ships'.

79. See for example Anne Fausto-Sterling, 'Gender, Race, and Nation: The Comparative Anatomy of "Hottentot" Women in Europe, 1815–1817', in *Deviant Bodies: Critical Perspectives on Difference in Science and Popular Culture*, ed. Jennifer Terry and Jacqueline Urla (Bloomington and Indianapolis: Indiana University Press, 1995), 19–48; Anne Fausto-Sterling, *Sexing the Body: Gender Politics and the Construction of Sexuality* (New York: Basic Books, 2000); Londa Schiebinger, *The Mind Has No Sex? Women in the Origins of Modern Science* (Cambridge and London: Harvard University Press, 1989); Londa Schiebinger, *Nature's Body: Sexual Politics and the Making of Modern Science* (Hammersmith: Pandora, 1993); Thomas Laqueur, *Making Sex: Body and Gender from the Greeks to Freud* (Cambridge and London: Harvard University Press, 1990); Thomas Laqueur, *Solitary Sex: A Cultural History of Masturbation* (New York: Zone, 2003); Sander Gilman, 'Black Bodies, White Bodies: Toward an Iconography of Female Sexuality in Late Nineteenth-Century Art, Medicine, and Literature', *Critical Inquiry* 12, no. 1 (1985): 204–42; Sander Gilman, *Making the Body Beautiful: A Cultural History of Aesthetic Surgery* (Princeton: Princeton University Press, 1999).

80. Peter Cryle and Elizabeth Stephens, *Normality: A Critical Genealogy* (Chicago and London: University of Chicago Press, 2017).

81. For books on the scientific construction of intersex, see for example Alice Domurat Dreger, *Hermaphrodites and the Medical Invention of Sex* (Cambridge and London: Harvard University Press, 1998); Myra J. Hird, *Sex, Gender, and Science* (Houndmills: Palgrave, 2004); Katrina Karkazis, *Fixing Sex: Intersex, Medical Authority, and Lived Experience* (Durham and London: Duke University Press, 2008).

CHAPTER 2

Ancient Anatomies

This chapter examines the development of scientific nomenclature for the female external genital organs, or vulva, beginning with the fragments of medical texts of Classical antiquity, from Hippocrates (c. 450–380 BCE) to Galen (c. 129–216 CE). I trace understandings of vulval structures, disease and health and chart changes in nomenclature to explore the development of a medical language of female disease. My aim in this chapter is to show how insignificant a place the vulva occupied in ancient Greek models of female physical health and normality. I suggest that the Greeks did not have a concept for labial hypertrophy, as it could only become a clinical condition once the labia were understood as distinct organic genital structures. The Greeks were only just beginning to develop such a language within an epistemological paradigm that privileged the role of the position and movement of the womb and menstrual flows in female disorder, rather than what genital structures *looked like*. In this medical schema, of central importance was the *behaviour* of the body and its illnesses within a general metaphysical conception of balance. This physiological approach is to be distinguished from modern clinical medicine, which, as philosopher Michel Foucault has outlined, is far more concerned with identifying and classifying anatomical structures in ever greater detail to localise disease to specific body parts. Modern medicine—which, for Foucault, dates back to the late eighteenth century—is distinctive for its emphasis on understanding the truth of disease through the ascription of exhaustive description. As Foucault explains: 'In clinical medicine, to be seen and to be spoken

© The Author(s) 2019
C. Nurka, *Female Genital Cosmetic Surgery*,
https://doi.org/10.1007/978-3-319-96490-4_2

immediately communicate in the manifest truth of the disease ... There is disease only in the element of the visible and therefore statable'.[1] This chapter is organised around what was statable in the ancient Greek model of gynaecology and argues that for the ancients, the external genitals were not a primary consideration in defining what it meant to be feminine or vulnerable to female disease. This chapter, then, is an examination of the development of anatomical knowledge that preceded the modern approach to the sexed body.

SAME BUT DIFFERENT

The difficulty of reading Greek anatomical texts, from our present standpoint, is how to understand the structure of sexual difference within a cosmology that is both eerily familiar and radically alien: while many of the sexuated diagnostic and classificatory terms developed by the ancients are still in use today, what we know now is the product of transformations over millennia in scientific method, and as such, the way we understand basic reproductive biology is wildly different to how the Greeks would have understood it. It is important to remember that the genital structures for which we have names today were not always named or known, or were accorded distinctive functional roles.

In order to chart when and how labial hypertrophy became a specific disease, we need first to understand the historical context of ancient gynaecology. The ancient attitude towards female anatomy and its role in defining female health and illness must be situated within a broader examination of how the female body was envisioned within the ancient Greek sciences. In ancient Greek medicine, the female body was conceptualised in two contradictory yet linked ways: as analogous to the male body and as distinctively sexed, or 'same but different'. According to the first perspective, advanced by historians Thomas Laqueur and Londa Schiebinger, women's anatomical organs were largely undifferentiated from men's and were considered to be less-perfect expressions of the same fundamental flesh. Both Laqueur and Schiebinger argue that femininity was a cosmological principle to which processes of the female body conformed, rather than the other way around, and that there was as yet no concept of a completely distinct biological 'sex': male and female bodies, and their substances (such as sperm and menstrual blood), were governed by the same superstructural elements that, when they fell out of balance, produced disease.

In ancient Greek thought, the human body was constituted by a combination of hot, cold, dry and wet properties corresponding to the four elements foundational to all terrestrial life: fire, air, water and earth.[2] This general theory was developed by pre-Hippocratic philosophers, who sought to explain physiological phenomena through a conceptual cosmological framework, rather than working from the principle that what could be seen of the structures of the body could provide information about how the body worked. According to historian James V. Ricci, this epistemological paradigm accounts for the marked lack of interest in empiricism among the physicians to follow.[3] Empedocles (c. 500–430 BCE) was the first to theorise that the proportionality of all four elements together are at the origin of all substances and was most influential in determining the foundations of Hippocratic medicine.[4] Hippocrates translated this elemental conception into his 'humoral theory', in which the human body was constituted and regulated by four fluids or 'humors' (blood, phlegm, yellow bile, black bile), associated with varying degrees of hot and cold, wet and dry.[5] Bodily illness or irregularity was thought to ensue when the delicate balance of the four humors was disrupted by the excess of one or more of the elements, as indexed by the behaviour of the humoral fluids.[6] The humoral theory also extended to sexual temperament and grounded the belief that men and women differed with respect to temperature. Londa Schiebinger suggests that within the overall structure of heat and cold governing Greek medicine, masculinity was associated with heat and dryness while femininity was cold and moist.[7] The belief in women's constitutional 'wetness' informed the Hippocratic theory that because women absorbed more food from their diet than men, the stored surplus moisture was evacuated in menstruation.[8] However, Laqueur argues that there was nothing particularly sexuated about this 'corporeal economy', where blood could be converted to milk (which was why pregnant women didn't menstruate), or the menses could cease if diverted elsewhere, or other flows dampen when the menses began. The sexual specificity of menstruation was doubtful, he suggests, because 'what matters is losing blood in relation to the fluid balance of the body, not the sex of the subject or the orifice from which it is lost'.[9] Following on from Hippocrates, the Aristotelian view of menstruation was that it was merely the impure, or less well 'concocted', female version of male 'seed' (or semen). Influential second-century Greek physician Galen would continue on this trajectory to claim that the female organs were 'like men's', only on the inside. He believed that as heat was associated with the active principle and cold with passivity, women were deficient men (he followed Aristotle in this reasoning) who lacked the necessary heat to project their genitals outward.[10] Galen explains: 'Now just as mankind is the most perfect of all animals, so within mankind the man is more perfect than the woman, and the reason for his perfection is his excess of heat, for heat is Nature's primary instrument'.[11] Galen proposed that 'all the parts, then, that men have, women have too, the difference between them lying in only one thing, which must be kept in mind throughout the discussion, namely, that in women the parts are within [the body], whereas in men they are outside'.[12] A visual illustration of this image of the female genitals as internalised male organs is provided by sixteenth-century anatomist Vesalius in his *De humani corporis fabrica* (1543).[13] As can be seen in Fig. 2.1, the pudendum resembles the corona; the outer lips resemble the foreskin, with the inner lips as the urinary meatus; the vaginal canal resembles the shaft; and the bottom of the womb resembles the testicles, with the 'neck' forming the base of the penile shaft.

Laqueur has famously called this general inclination toward sexual analogy—and the subordination of sexed bodies to abstract principles of equivalence—the 'one-sex model', which he believes dominated anatomical science up until the eighteenth century. In this pre-Enlightenment understanding, he says, the difference between the sexes lay not within substances or anatomic structures specific to sexed bodies, but in the metaphysical categories and hierarchies that served to explain the natural world. For Laqueur, sexed bodies in ancient Greece were 'the material correlative of a higher truth', serving as physical confirmation of metaphysical principles.[14] Likewise, Schiebinger argues that unlike the biological determinism of the modern scientific understanding of gender—where sexed biological properties such as sex hormones and brain physiology are explained as the root cause of gender difference—bodies and their substances in the ancient sciences were the effect (rather than the cause) of the formalised, gendered elements that governed them. Hence, she concludes that 'gender in the ancient world was a cosmological principle' and that 'differences between the two sexes were reflections of a set of dualistic principles that penetrated the cosmos as well as the bodies of men and women'.[15]

Classical historian Helen King argues, however, that Laqueur's one-sex model is so heavily dependent upon the Galenic account of

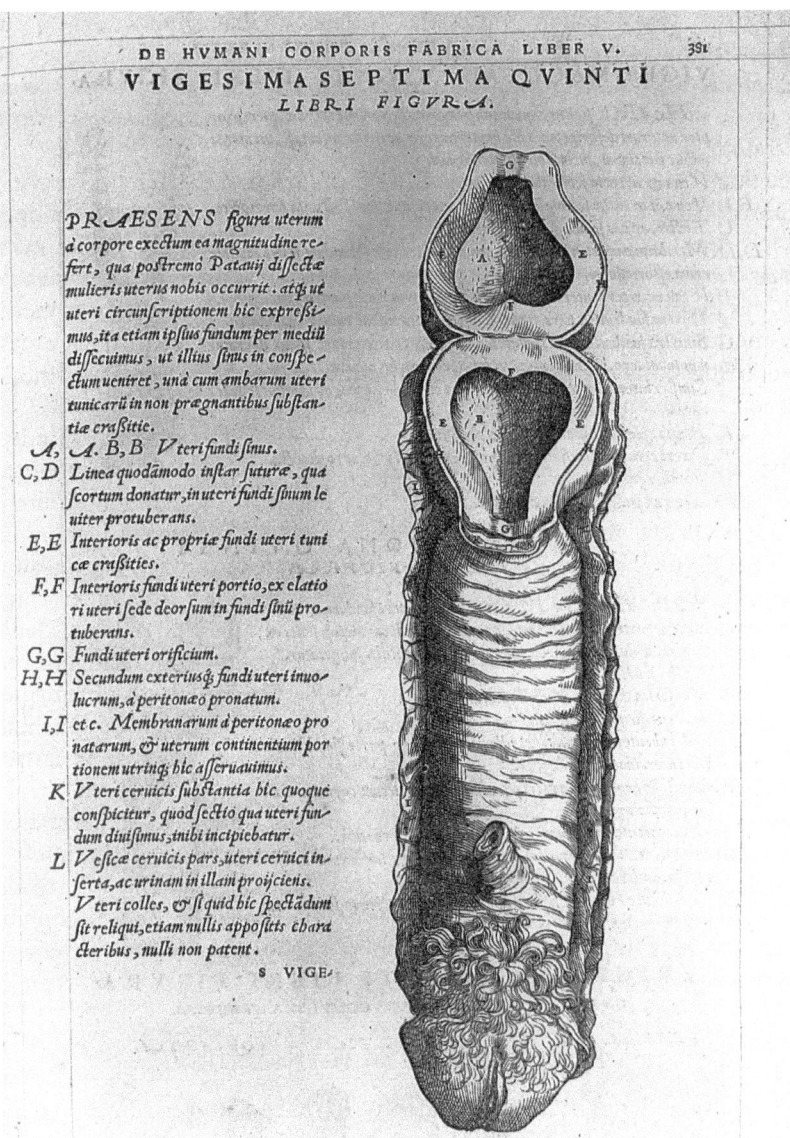

Fig. 2.1 Vesalius's interpretation of Galenic genital anatomy, with womb, vagina and vulva depicted as a penis. Andreas Vesalius, *De humani corporis fabrica* (Basileae: Joannis Oporini, 1543). Courtesy Wellcome Library, London

genital anatomy that it ignores the evidence in the Hippocratic corpus of sex difference that permeated the whole female body. Contrary to Laqueur, King asserts that the Greeks *did* have a well-developed concept of sexual difference because the very first woman in Greek myth, Pandora, was considered to be the 'origin of the "race of women"', as the poet Hesiod described her.[16] King proposes that the Hippocratic tradition of the female body in particular was one 'that could exist alongside a one-sex model, but which saw women as radically unlike men, their bodies so different that they demanded different therapies'.[17] In this perspective, women's bodies were essentially different from men's in the texture of their flesh, which was wet and spongy; in their excess fluid expelled as menstrual blood; and in their possession of a womb, a special container-organ that could 'wander' the body.[18]

I suggest, as does King, that these two perspectives existed side-by-side, and I offer the further proposition that female *vulval* anatomy was considered largely unimportant in both perspectives, but for different reasons: firstly, under the Hippocratic model of difference elaborated by King, the external genitals were merely supplementary organs supporting those organic phenomena that were pivotal in defining womanhood: menstrual blood and the uterus. Secondly, under the Galenic 'one-sex' model of sameness proposed by Schiebinger and Laqueur, no sexually specific vocabulary existed by which the labia could obtain special significance, and they were dismissed by Galen as merely ornamental. In addition, the Greeks' general lack of attention to structure in favour of elemental balance transcendent of sex rendered external genital structures largely unimportant. Hence, when disease pointed to an aberration of femininity, it had very little to do with the structures of the body—much less the shape of the genital organs—and very much more to do with the misalignment of vital elements governing the body's equilibrium (such as 'humors'), the situation of the womb and the movement or blockage of menstrual blood through the body.

FEMALE DISEASE IN HIPPOCRATES

The vulva did not figure prominently in Hippocratic writings, as the presumed causes of female disease were located elsewhere, primarily in the activities of menstrual blood and the womb, which, as King demonstrates, are detailed in the *Diseases of Women* treatises and *Places in Man*.[19] According to King, Hippocratic gynaecology defined female bodies as moist, spongy and absorbent, and consistently located the accumulation of menstrual blood (the female-specific fluid) as the source of female disease. The Hippocratics treated menstrual blood extremely seriously, as women's bodies, by their porous nature, were inclined to accumulate fluids, which could be detrimental to their health. Women were thought to possess differently textured flesh that soaked up excess blood from the stomach and then passed it out of the body as menstruation.[20] It was crucial, then, for menstrual bleeding to be regular, so that it not well up and obstruct the normal functioning of other organs: if women didn't bleed, or bled irregularly, or bled an insufficient quantity, this in itself could be considered a root cause of illness.[21]

The womb was a significant marker of difference as 'the cause of all diseases of women',[22] and also in its capacity to become dislodged or blocked. For the Hippocratics, many gynaecological problems were caused by the closure of the vulva, vagina or mouth of the womb (which may either entrap blood or dry out), or occurred when the mouth of the womb did not properly align with the vagina.[23] The womb could also shift, 'when [over]heated by hard work' or starvation, towards the liver and suffocate 'the breathing passage around the belly'.[24] Some of the common causes attributed by Hippocrates to uterine displacement were 'cold to the feet and the loins, dancing, winnowing, breaking sticks, or ... running up or down hill'.[25] Uterine displacement was also thought to be the effect of imbalance cause by excess (for example, of too much exercise, or, in the opposite direction, too much fat).[26] Certainly, Hippocrates's *Nature of Women* is filled with prolapsed, displaced, blocked, gaping, enlarged, twisted, full, inflated, inflamed, hardened and overly moist uteruses.[27]

In Greek medicine more generally, the labial lips were mentioned only when they were afflicted with warts, ulcers or tumours.[28] Classical physicians also recorded cases of atresia, in which the lips of the labia majora are sealed and require surgical cutting. Celsus (c. 53 BCE–7 CE), for example, noted that in this disease 'peculiar to women', the vagina 'does not admit of coition', and that labial adhesion may be either congenital or caused by ulceration. He recommended incising the membrane in congenital cases or cutting out the excess flesh in ulcerated cases.[29] Paulus Aegineta (c. 625–690 CE) wrote of 'imperforate' external genital parts, occurring sometimes in the alae pudendi (labia) or 'intermediate places', caused by adhesion or an obstructing substance of flesh or membrane. Cutting was necessary when the sutured skin obstructed the expulsion of menstrual blood, the entry of the penis or the birth of a baby.[30] Aetius before him spoke of a similar disorder and remedy,[31] and Soranus (second century CE) observed that atresia could be caused by the formation of a membrane between the labia.[32] A particularly extreme case of atresia encountered by anatomist Hieronymus Fabricius would be documented in graphic detail by seventeenth-century surgeon Pierre Dionis. He recounted that Fabricius treated 'a Girl, who, being wholly imperforate, could not discharge her menstruous Terms, they being detained by a Membrane which joined the *Caruncules*, and entirely locked up the Passage [occasioning] a pressing weight in the *Vagina*, accompanied with insupportable Pains'. To alleviate her suffering, Fabricius 'made an Incision lengthways in that *Membrane*, from whence issued out a great quantity of black and stinking Blood, which gave the Patient ease, and he perfectly cured her'.[33]

AMBIGUOUS ANATOMIES

Hippocratic texts were far more interested in the movements of menstrual fluid and the uterus than they were in trying to define or name female genital organs.[34] Hippocrates was not overly concerned to provide a detailed description of the external genital anatomy of either sex, usually calling the sexual organs only by αἰδοῖον (*aidoion*), or the 'shameful parts', also translated as the 'privy parts' and the 'pudenda'.[35] In the female body, the clitoris was absent from description,[36] because, as historian Lesley Dean-Jones claims, 'it played no role in health and disease',[37] while the existence of the hymen was disputed.[38] But there was some acknowledgement of the labia: in *Places in Man*, Hippocrates called the labia 'overhanging banks' (κρημνοί), and in *Nature of Women*, he used the word 'lips' (τά χείλεα) in describing adhesion of the labia (or atresia). Elsewhere in this work, the labia are implied in descriptions of and cures for aphthae (ulcers), warts, and lesions affecting the pudenda.[39] As the inner and outer lips were either subsumed under the generic label of αἰδοῖον or mentioned in general terms as a part that could be afflicted with organic problems, they were indistinguishable from one another. Hippocratic translator Paul Potter states that depending on context, the meaning of *aidoion* can be narrowed and may refer to the vagina as distinguished from the uterus, and the penis as distinguished from the testicles.[40] Hence, the vulva and vagina (external and internal) could both be collapsed together under the one term. But there was also an analogism at work in the way the different parts of the genitals of each sex were separated, as the vulva/vagina was to the penis as the uterus was to the testicles. Such analogic comparison is evident in the Hippocratic description of a prolapsed uterus, which, if it 'descends completely out of the genitalia … hangs like a scrotum'.[41]

From Hippocrates to the Latin and Medieval physicians, the female external genitals suffered from a persistent lack of definition, while the external male genitalia were better understood and became increasingly stabilised in meaning. The male genitals provided a comparatively stable reference point from which to make sense of what may have seemed to the Greeks a bewildering plurality of the female organs. According to Laqueur, Aristotle prioritised the singular *aidoion* to refer to the penis specifically and the plural to refer to genitals of both sexes,[42] which indicated that the female parts were non-specific as well as secondary to, or imitative of, the primary organ (the penis). Around the first century CE, Rufus of Ephesus stated that the penis was known as 'stem' or 'shaft', meanings contained in the Greek word καυλὸς (*kaulos*).[43] In Latin medicine, *kaulos* was translated to *caulis*, which became the standard word for 'penis' in Celsus, and it was also used by Rufus, Galen, Pollux and Diodorus.[44] *Kaulos* was used, in a narrowed gynaecological sense, by Soranus to describe the neck of the womb, and Caelius Aurelianus would extend it to the whole of the female pudenda, likening the external parts to the penis.[45] In late Latinate medical texts generally, *Veretrum* became the common word for the male organ. By contrast, there was no stable term for the external female parts (presaging the Latin term 'vulva' as we use it today) and also no standard word for labia, let alone a standard language to distinguish between minora and majora.[46] As names for the male genitals became prioritised and refined, the female genitals remained in a state of descriptive indeterminacy. By the late Medieval period, the word for the male member would become solidified as *uirga* or 'yard': the Medieval gynaecological text *Trotula*, for example, provided *uirga*, *uirga uirilis* ('male staff') and *priapus* as various names for the penis, but was vague in its names for the female external genitals, using terms such as 'pudenda', 'female members', and the 'lower parts'.[47]

Laqueur proposes that names for the female genitals were not clarified until the late seventeenth century. My research confirms this view: around the beginning of the seventeenth century gynaecological texts would use the 'nymphae' (for the labia minora) and 'alae' or 'wings' (for the labia majora) as stable descriptors.[48] For Laqueur, the ambiguity around female genital anatomical naming relative to the male is possibly 'the linguistic correlative of the corporeal telos generally: the male body is stable, the female body more open and labile'.[49] Certainly, woman's excess blood and porous flesh, as well as the openness of her vagina, which could suck in fluids or expel them (while the penis only emitted fluids), indicated a body more prone to fluctuation. But the problem of ambiguous naming among the Greeks is probably more likely to be because, firstly, the external organs were not considered to be the seat of femininity and could therefore be ignored; and secondly, because men were studying and writing on anatomy, and knew their own bodies best. If accurate naming for the ancient Greeks was unimportant, it was because the structures of the body were not where female sexual differ-ence—and the body's capacity for disease—lay; rather, the narrative of sexual difference revolved instead around the role of menstrual blood and the diseased states either caused by or showing up in the womb. Insofar as anatomical structure *did* matter, the female body, with its confounding insides and outsides, needed to be coaxed into a model of homology to be understood visually. That is, it became visible through analogy with the male parts. In this cross-gender, or, as Laqueur puts it, 'one-sex' conception of anatomy, the female body lost its distinctiveness to become a subordinate facsimile of the male body.

ARISTOTLE AND THE LOGOS OF SEX

Neither Hippocrates nor Aristotle (c. 384–322 BCE) did very much in the way of describing the external genital structures of the female, and we find the narrative of sexual difference revolving instead around the role of menstrual blood and the diseased states either caused by or showing up in the womb. In Aristotle, like Hippocrates, the external structures didn't matter because the difference lay in the active/passive principles of explicitly sexed *fluids*. For Aristotle, primary sex difference lay in 'active' semen and 'passive' menstrual blood. Menstrual blood materially exemplified the feminine principle: it was by nature inferior, cold, inert, 'prime' matter that needed the active male semen to fash-ion it into an embryo. The male body was more perfect because it was imbued with superior heat: the 'seminal ducts around the testes' were able to 'concoct' semen, which was the active ingredient in genera-tion.[50] Although he held that female menstrual blood was 'the analogous thing in females to the semen in males',[51] he also claimed that male and female bodies 'must differ in kind, and in that the *logos* of each of them is distinct'.[52] He explained that even though men and women belonged to the same species, they must be different in kind because the difference in bodily composition must be a reflection of their different logos, or essential purpose:

> Thus: there must be that which generates, and that out of which it generates; and even if these two be united in one, at any rate they must differ in kind, and in that the logos of each of them is distinct. In those animals in which these two faculties are separate, the body—that is to say the physical nature—of the active partner and of the passive must be different. Thus, if the male is the active partner, the one which originates the movement, and the female qua female is the passive one, surely what the female contributes to the semen of the male will be not semen but material. And this is in fact what we find happening; for the natural substance of the menstrual fluid is to be classed as 'prime matter'.[53]

The logos was the concept that connected the ontological, embodied, natural world with the formal, idealised principle of perfect masculinity or femininity. The active/passive pairing served as the principle that could explain why men and women look different and what happens in human reproduction.

For Aristotle, as in Hippocrates, anatomical structures were secondary to the substances: that is, *anatomy was only as important as the vital fluids it channelled*. Anatomically, the penis functioned as a 'passage' which passes a much smaller volume of highly processed, or 'matured' residue (seed), while the uterus is larger to accommodate and contain the larger volume of raw material (menses). In effect, the womb is a receptacle for female 'residue' that, by virtue of its impurity and coldness, pools in the body because it cannot be converted into semen, which is more compact and mobile.[54] Dean-Jones explains further that the function of the womb was to store 'the female seminal fluid until it was used in conception and reproduction or had reached such a volume that it *had* to be evacuated to prevent the menses from swamping the semen'.[55] Men had 'semen' that could create life, but women had 'matter' that nourished it. Female menstrual residue that welled up in the womb or expressed itself as sexual discharge during pleasurable sex was necessary to conception, but it was not the same as male seed. In particular, the function of female sexual discharge was as a signal that the womb was open to better receive the male semen, which meant that pleasure aided conception.[56]

This was an excretion specific to certain types of women—'fair-skinned women who are typically feminine, and not in dark women of a masculine appearance'—marking some women as more feminine than others.[57] It is clear here that Aristotle thought that dark-skinned women possessed masculine humoral qualities that interfered with the expression of their 'feminine' nature and procreative purpose. In ancient Greek society, a pale complexion in women, from a life indoors, was viewed as a sign of feminine beauty.[58]

Vulval anatomy was only very briefly mentioned by Aristotle to prove that there could be absolutely no equivalence between the male parts and the female parts because of the way the sexes emitted their respective fluids. He alluded to the clitoris as a region of female pleasure 'in the same place as in the male'[59] to refute arguments that its role must have been to emit female 'semen'. He rejected this claim, arguing that female 'semen' could not exist because nothing was emitted by women at the corresponding place in which men feel pleasure.[60] That is, if woman were truly like a man, then she would emit 'seed' from the same place. The clitoris did not really figure as a noteworthy organ—much less the labia—and it was only mentioned to make the point that women did not produce the same material that men did. The Hippocratic emphasis on menstrual blood as a vital substance of woman is echoed in Aristotle's theory of sex complementarity—especially in the properties of menstrual residue—and demonstrates that the ancient anatomical vocabulary did not need to be especially sophisticated, given that sex differences were located in very specific sites of physiological activity.

Thomas Laqueur and Marguerite Deslauriers have asserted, however, that as anatomical sex was thought to be the effect of abstract active and passive principles of gender, rather than the cause, men and women in Aristotle were variations of the same essential flesh.[61] Sex difference did not so much exist in the fluids themselves as in the gendered laws that gave them form. Deslauriers claims that for Aristotle, bodies were built of the same substances, but only became sexed through the presence or absence of heat as the causal principle that animates substance.[62] Aristotle ascribed active, hot 'semen' to men and passive, cold 'material' to women. Semen (the ideational, active principle) shaped the female's raw matter (the inert genetic matter), which was useless without the active principle to activate it. This led him to conclude that 'female is as it were a deformed male; and the menstrual discharge is semen, though in an impure condition; i.e., it lacks one constituent, and one only, the principle of Soul'.[63] As political scientist Giulia Sissa puts it, Aristotle's analogic paradigm 'portrays male and female bodies as quantitative variants of a single form, the *eidos* that produces itself in the *genos*'.[64] Or, as Laqueur describes the 'one-sex model', sexual difference was a matter of 'degree and not of kind'.[65]

The different way of thinking that characterises the ancient approach (at least in Hippocrates and Aristotle), as opposed to the biological sciences of today, is that there were elemental forces or qualities that animated and permeated bodies—such as masculine heat and Soul, or the feminine qualities of sponginess or inertia—which could not be empirically tested to verify their existence. This is markedly different from the modern approach, which, Laqueur says, was motivated by an epistemological desire to distinguish between 'fact and fiction'.[66] In the modern scientific paradigm, qualities like femininity and masculinity are just as mercurial, but attempts are made to prove the truth of them through examining available physiological structures, from the hormones to the brain. Thus, one of the most salient features of modern scientific rationality is, as Foucault argued, the will to truth: the desire to make the body into incontrovertible proof of a natural order of social relations.[67]

But to Hippocrates and Aristotle, femininity and masculinity, and their relationship to the elements, didn't need to be proven; rather, they were drawn upon to explain bodily disease and procreative function. As Laqueur puts it, 'Aristotle did not need the facts of sexual difference to support the claim that woman was a lesser being than man; it followed from the a priori truth that the material cause is inferior to the efficient cause'.[68] The body furnished the physician with clues as to prognosis and treatment, but it was conceived of as a whole, governed by a balance of elements; the structures and organs of the body, then, were far less important or interesting to Greek physicians than its processes.[69] By contrast, the modern sciences are characterised by a mechanistic approach, which rejects elemental principles to focus on identifying and classifying anatomical structures, which then forms the basis for the classification of identities: the more rigorous and detailed the classification, the greater the opportunity for uncovering hitherto unrecognised gender differences. In Aristotle, difference in degree was mixed up with different in kind, but the anatomical language of like—the explicit naming of female body parts after male ones—did not yet exist, or at least not comprehensively. While for Hippocrates, the external genitals of both sexes were undifferentiated, that may well have been because the *real* difference lay elsewhere, as I have already suggested. The clitoris was not yet a definable structure, nor were the ovaries yet discovered or named.

These discoveries would only come about with the anatomical investigations of the 'father of anatomy', Herophilus (c. 330–260 BCE), in the Alexandrian period. It is curious that the visible external parts of female genitals were not given sexually specific names in the Greek literature until after Herophilus, especially when we consider that one did not need to dissect a corpse in order to view these parts. As anatomical structures were discovered and named, after the anatomical interventions of Herophilus, similitude of the female to the male body would become more pronounced—the process of naming would then provide opportunity for the female genitals to become more visible as structures that could begin to define, in greater encompassing detail, what it was to be female.

MAKING SEX VISIBLE

The developing logic of empiricism would provide what psychologist James Gibson terms 'affordances' for analogic description of the female body and also for elaboration upon anomalous enlargement of hitherto ignored structures such as the clitoris and labia. The concept of affordance refers to the capacity of the physical environment and its objects or external stimuli such as vision and sound to give rise to certain performable actions, perceptions, meanings and values within the limits of that environment.[70] The interaction of the knowledge-environment of empiricism with the body-object, then, affords the evolution of a language with which to describe sex and diagnose sexed conditions of health and illness. But the practice of anatomy was also framed by the ideology of gender and relied upon the male body as the stable referent to make sense of female difference. In the anatomy texts produced in the centuries to follow, descriptions and illustrations of the male body always came first.

Herophilus and Erasistratus would play a significant role in developing empiricist method with their dissections of the corpses of executed criminals in the city of Alexandria under the reign of Ptolemy, in which the study of medicine flourished; it is unclear whether Herophilus had access to human female corpses in addition to the bodies of non-human animals in order to elaborate upon the structure of the female reproductive organs. Nevertheless, the support for scientific enquiry in the Alexandrian period meant that Herophilus could provide a more comprehensive analogy between the anatomical structures of men and women: he was the first to discover the human ovaries, and applied the appellation 'twins' (*didymi*), or the 'female testicles', thereby producing an anatomical equivalence to the male testes.[71] He also identified what we now know as the Fallopian tubes, describing them as 'spermatic ducts' (*epididymis*) and mistakenly assuming that the tubes functioned like the male ducts, passing into the bladder. It was not until Rufus and Galen that this theory would be corrected.[72] According to King, Herophilus's aim was to 'demystify the female organs', to demonstrate, as Soranus after him would do, that women did not have disease specific to them; he was also a pioneer in the propagation of the one-sex model that would so saturate Galen's anatomic philosophy.[73]

Rufus of Ephesus (80–150 CE) would be the first to correctly identify, upon the dissection of a sheep, the Fallopian tubes as terminating in the uterus (not the bladder, as Herophilus thought), equating them with the *vas deferens*.[74] He is also widely regarded as being the first to clearly catalogue the parts of the female anatomy, especially the parts of the vulva, in his treatise *On the Names of the Parts of the Human Body*. In this work, Rufus provided distinct names for the clitoris and labia, though there is no acknowledgement of inner and outer labia. McKay believes that the term 'wings' refers only to the labia majora,[75] but it is also possible that inner and outer were described as a single structure. Rufus also shifted the names of the genitals away from their religious connection to the myrtle plant, which was sacred to Aphrodite, goddess of love, beauty, pleasure and procreation[76]:

> With regard to the privates of women, the triangular extremity of the hypogastric region is called the comb (κτείς), while others call it the ἐπίσειον [pubic region]. The cleft in the genitals is called the σχίσμα [schisma]. The small fleshy body that hangs down in the mesial line is called the myrtle-berry (μύρτον). By others it is called the hypodermis, by others the clitoris (κλειτορίς); while touching the clitoris for lascivious purposes is expressed by the term κλειτοριάζειν [to clitorize]. The μυρτόχειλα [myrtle lips or *myrtokeila*] are the fleshy parts on either side of the σχίσμα. Euryphon called them also steep edges [or overhanging banks] (κρημνός). Nowadays for μυρτόχειλα we substitute wings (πτερυγώματα) and for μύρτον we substitute νύμφη [nymphe].[77]

The change in appellation wrought by Rufus away from the more poetic linguistic derivatives of 'myrtle' may have served as an attempt to encapsulate form and function, in the case of the nymphe, and to bring the body further into the scientific domain.

The social function of the clitoris, for example, was well established in the meaning of the word 'nymphe' (or νύμφη), which referred specifically to the *young* bride. As King observes, in Greek culture, what it meant to be female changed with the transition from girlhood to womanhood, from the *parthenos*, 'a girl who combines the features of being "childless, unmarried, yet of the right age for marriage"', to the *gyne*, a mature woman who both menstruates and gives birth.[78] Not only was the clitoris hidden by the labial folds—and also the hood (though this anatomical feature was not yet described, unless implied in the bridal veil)—it could also represent the virginal bride: that is, as a part of the genital body that belonged properly to the virgin girl, as mature sexuality would arrive with the menses and the admission of the penis to the vagina. This is remarkable as potentially the earliest predecessor of Sigmund Freud's modern separation of infantile clitoral and mature vaginal sexuality.

Soranus (c. 100–200 CE) would further refine Rufus's taxonomy, using the term πτερυγώματα, or wings, to refer to the labia majora and χεῖλος, or 'lip', for the labia minora,[79] and retaining nymphe for clitoris:

> The parts seen outside are called πτερυγώματα, forming, as it were, the lips of the vagina. They are thick, fleshy, and extending down beside each thigh, as it were, diverging from each other; above, they end in what we call νύμφη, which is the beginning of the two labia. In nature this fleshy prominence is muscular, and it is called 'nymphe' through its being covered as brides are veiled. Below the clitoris another fleshy prominence lies concealed, which belongs to the neck of the bladder; it is called the urethra. The rough portion forming a fold within is called χεῖλος.[80]

Soranus thus gave us the first accurate distinction in ancient Greek medicine between the clitoris (nymphe), labia majora (wings) and labia minora (lip). However, this was in spite of his belief that what could be learned from dissection was largely useless to the physician: Soranus came from the Methodist school, which identified general states of disease thought to be caused by invisible internal imbalances of the whole body, rather than being located within specific parts or organs of the body. Methodists believed that there were three main types of disease— constriction, laxity, and a mixture of both—and that the manifestation of these presupposed the cure. The school was so named because treatment was programmatically determined by the speed and severity of the presented illness. Soranus's Methodist theory of health and illness placed importance on constriction and relaxation of the pores and the movement of invisible corpuscles through channels in the body, which explains why, in his gynaecology treatise, he claimed that women did *not* have diseases specific to them.

One of the great conundrums of Greek medicine was the extent to which the diseases of women warranted their own special branch of study or were subsumed under a universal concept of bodily health applying equally to male and female bodies. Soranus had devoted a section in his gynaecology treatise to this very question, and offered the opinion that the basic causes of illness were corpuscular and common to both women and men. Soranus argued that one must distinguish between the specific functions of the female body (such as birth and lactation) and the generic diseases, or 'conditions contrary to nature', that may affect these functions:

> For in regard to generic differences, the female has her illness in common with the male, she suffers from constriction or flux, either acutely or chronically, and she is subject to the same seasonal differences, to gradations of disease, to lack of strength, and to the different foreign bodies, sores, and injuries. Only as far as particulars and specific variations are concerned does the female show conditions particularly her own, i.e. a different character of symptoms. Therefore she is subject to treatment generically the same.[81]

Soranus conceded that while women were anatomically and functionally different to men, the basic principles of balance and imbalance remained the same. As a Methodist, he was under no obligation to consider anatomy at all, as disease could be reducible to 'two or three morbid states in the body', which could then be treated programmatically.[82] He made it clear that knowledge of anatomical difference mattered little to the physician's role in treating disease—he considered dissection to be 'useless'—and that his discussion of 'the female parts' was merely cursory, included only to demonstrate he had knowledge of it.[83] In Soranus's view, men and women were essentially the same regarding their pathological afflictions, and hence, knowledge of sexual anatomy was less important than understanding the behaviour of the manifest symptoms of disease.

Soranus's dismissal of anatomy as 'useless' brings us to the question of why, when the external female genitals were on display (unlike the internal organs, which could only be seen through dissection), they were either ignored or imprecisely and confusingly labelled. I suggest that women were defined in both their sameness and their difference: a precise language for their anatomy was not needed if both male and female bodies were governed by the same elemental forces; however, there were obvious and inescapable differences in sex organs and fluids. In the Hippocratic tradition, women were, as Soranus put it, naturally different 'in their whole nature'. Even in Aristotle, says Soranus, this difference is so pronounced that he is willing to say 'that the female is imperfect, the male, however, perfect', which is taken by Soranus to support the argument that women also had diseases that reflected this nature.[84] Yet with the increased status of anatomy as a legitimate science in the Alexandrian period, the organs of the body would gradually require a standard nomenclature: this did not mean that the female genitals acquired a sex-specific character, however. On the contrary, female organs were domesticated by and reduced to the more familiar terrain of the male genitals.

Galen of Pergamum (c. 129–216 CE), the most influential physician in Western medical history, would disregard the genital taxonomies proposed by Rufus and Soranus to adopt a model of female anatomy that mirrored the male body. Galen's works became the foundation of medical science for the following 1,500 years, and thus, the rudimentary language of vulval specificity was subsequently forgotten by Galen's followers. With the anatomical contributions of Herophilus, Rufus and Soranus, Galen had access to accumulated scientific knowledge that could recuperate, in a new way, Aristotle's claim that the woman was a less 'concocted' or perfect man. Unlike Soranus, Galen reinterpreted Aristotle through the prism of anatomical sameness. It is only with the benefit of anatomical discovery that Galen could then re-read Aristotle through the genital and reproductive structures of the female body. Galen gives the following description of the female anatomy in his 'On the Usefulness of the Parts of the Body':

All the parts, then, that men have, women have too, the difference between them lying in only one thing, which must be kept in mind throughout the discussion, namely, that in women the parts are within … whereas in men they are outside, in the region called the perineum. Consider first whichever ones you please, turn outward the woman's, turn inward, so to speak, and fold double the man's, and you will find them the same in both in every respect. Then think first, please, of the man's turned in and extending inward between the rectum and the bladder. If this should happen, the scrotum would necessarily take the place of the uteri, with the testes lying outside, next to it on either side; the penis of the male would become the neck of the cavity that had been formed; and the skin at the end of the penis, now called the prepuce, would become the female pudendum ... itself. Think too, please, of the converse, the uterus turned outward and projecting. Would not the testes ... then necessarily be inside it? Would it not contain them like a scrotum? Would not the neck ... hitherto concealed inside the perineum but now pendent, be made into the male member? And would not the female pudendum, being a skinlike growth upon this neck, be changed into the part called the prepuce?[85]

As can be seen from this description, Galen had essentially reverted to a Hippocratic model that would largely regard the external parts together, though he would be more emphatic in his logic of equivalence, with the external parts considered, in explicit terms, the analogue of the male prepuce. However, unlike Hippocrates, Galen took an empiricist approach in arguing that humoral imbalances could be located in specific organs, as well as in the body as a whole. The shift towards anatomical empiricism, exemplified by Galen, brought with it a greater enthusiasm for understanding the parts of the body, though in the Galenic model, the nomenclature of sex would be based firmly in the male body: the labia would be likened to the prepuce and the clitoris would disappear from the sexual geography of woman altogether. The Galenic account of female anatomy would serve as the standard model in the centuries to come for anatomic descriptions of the female genitals, and also greatly influenced sixteenth-century anatomist Andreas Vesalius's illustration of the female reproductive tract as an inside-out penis (Fig. 2.1).

CONCLUSION

If we are assured of a break between the ancient Greek and the modern sciences and their respective categories of sexual identity, we must also not lose sight of the differences between Hippocratic, Aristotelian and Galenic models of physiology in our commitment to defining the primary historical rupture in Western medical conceptions of sex as one between ancient and modern. For to do so is to reduce the story of the female genitals in Classical antiquity to a universalising account of equivalence, when in fact, this story was subject to subtle changes, erasures, clarifications and mystifications within the historical development of scientific nomenclature.

In the ancient Greek world, how women's bodies were read shifted between sameness and difference: alternate readings positioning women as a separate 'race' or as sharing the same fundamental biology inflected how physicians represented female anatomy and disease. The Hippocratic corpus displays evidence of both. On the one hand, anatomical naming conventions rendered sex generic (*aidoion*), but on the other, women's pathologies were fundamentally different to men's because of the interactions between blood and womb. It is likely that the troublesome nomenclature ascribed to the external female organs is symptomatic of this conundrum of women's ambiguous positioning between difference and sameness: first, when considered in their difference, women were defined by their wombs and menses more so than by the external organs. Second, when women were considered to share 'the same' formal physical qualities as men, their anatomy became unimportant. When anatomical study started to gain ground, Galen's contribution was once again to relegate the external female genitals to a space of conceptual and linguistic ambiguity in a model that constructed a correlation between vulva and prepuce .

It is clear from what survives of the ancient Greek texts on medicine, from Hippocrates to Galen, that labial hypertrophy did not exist as a clinical problem in this period. The Hippocratic authors were generally unconcerned with labial length, firstly because they didn't have a precise structural vocabulary for the external genitals, and secondly, because elongation didn't constitute disease in their medical models. Female disease was only particularised when the functionality of the female organs in copulation, menstruation or childbirth was disrupted. That which indexed 'normal' or 'abnormal' femininity, for the Greeks, inhered in 'physiological processes rather than structure'.[86] This lack of attention to the structure of sex to some extent explains the reticence to classify and describe external female genital anatomy, except where the genitals were affected by pain or disease. As we have seen, the two sets of labial lips (majora and minora) were often the casualty of an impoverished vocabulary that had trouble identifying and naming them, and through which it was not uncommon for the labia minora to be ignored altogether.

Notes

1. Michel Foucault, *The Birth of the Clinic: An Archaeology of Medical Perception*, trans. A. M. Sheridan (London and New York: Routledge, [1963] 1973), 116.

2. Londa Schiebinger, *The Mind Has No Sex? Women in the Origins of Modern Science* (Cambridge: Harvard University Press, 1989), 161.
3. James V. Ricci, *The Genealogy of Gynaecology: History of the Development of Gynaecology Throughout the Ages* (Philadelphia: Blakiston Company, 1943), 46–7; 48n2.
4. Arthur J. Brock, *Greek Medicine* (New York: AMS Press, [1929] 1972), 5, 9.
5. Brock, *Greek Medicine*, 9; Helen King, *Greek and Roman Medicine* (London: Bristol Classical Press, 2001), 13–14; Schiebinger, *The Mind Has No Sex?*, 161.
6. Brock, *Greek Medicine*, 9.
7. Schiebinger, *The Mind Has No Sex?*, 161–3. A notable exception to this association of men with heat and women with cold is Parmenides, who believed instead that women were warmer, and that menstruation was caused by excess heat. Ricci, *The Genealogy of Gynaecology*, 48.
8. Helen King, *Hippocrates' Woman: Reading the Female Body in Ancient Greece* (London and New York: Routledge, 1998), 29.
9. Thomas Laqueur, *Making Sex: Body and Gender from the Greeks to Freud* (Cambridge: Harvard University Press, 1990), 37.
10. Schiebinger, *The Mind Has No Sex?*, 163.
11. Galen, *On the Usefulness of the Parts of the Body*, trans. Margaret Tallmadge May (Ithaca: Cornell University Press, 1968), 630.
12. Galen, *On the Usefulness of the Parts of the Body*, 628.
13. Andreas Vesalius, *De humani corporis fabrica* (Basileae: Joannis Oporini, 1543). Available at http://www.e-rara.ch/bau_1/content/titleinfo/6299027.
14. Laqueur, *Making Sex*, 8, 28.
15. Schiebinger, *The Mind Has No Sex?*, 161–2.
16. Helen King, *The One-Sex Body on Trial: The Classical and Early Modern Evidence* (Farnham and Burlington: Ashgate, 2013), 33.
17. Helen King, *Midwifery, Obstetrics and the Rise of Gynaecology* (Aldershot and Burlington: Ashgate, 2007), 14.
18. King, *Midwifery, Obstetrics and the Rise of Gynaecology*, 27–36.
19. King, *Hippocrates' Woman*, 35–6.
20. See King, *Hippocrates' Woman*, 28–9; Lesley Dean-Jones, *Women's Bodies in Classical Greek Science* (Oxford: Clarendon Press, 1994), 55, 59–60.
21. King, *Hippocrates' Woman*, 29–32.
22. King, *Midwifery, Obstetrics and the Rise of Gynaecology*, 11.
23. Hippocrates, 'Diseases of Women 1', trans. Ann Ellis Hanson', *Signs* 1, no. 2 (1975): 572, 573, 575; Hippocrates, *Nature of Women*, in *Hippocrates*, ed. and trans. Paul Potter, Loeb Classical Library 10 (Cambridge and London: Harvard University Press, 2012).
24. Hippocrates, 'Diseases of Women 1', 576.

25. W. J. Stewart McKay, *The History of Ancient Gynaecology* (London: Ballière, Tindall and Cox, 1901), 51.
26. McKay, *The History of Ancient Gynaecology*, 36; Ricci, *The Genealogy of Gynaecology*, 62.
27. Hippocrates, *Nature of Women*.
28. Hippocrates, *Nature of Women; New York Journal of Medicine and the Collateral Sciences*, vols 2–3 (Ithaca: Cornell University, 1843), 62–3; Ian S. C. Jones, 'Influences on the Study of Vulvar Anatomy and Disease', *Open Journal of Obstetrics and Gynecology* 2, no. 3 (2012): 224; Steven I. Hajdu, 'A Note from History: Landmarks in History of Cancer, Part 1', *Cancer* 117, no. 5 (2011): 1097–102.
29. Aulus Cornelius Celsus, *A. Cornelius Celsus of Medicine: In Eight Books*, trans. James Greive (London: Printed for D. Wilson and T. Durham, 1756), 454–5.
30. Paulus Aegineta, *The Seven Books of Paulus Aegineta*, trans. Francis Adams (London: Printed for the Sydenham Society, 1846), 383.
31. McKay, *The History of Ancient Gynaecology*, 215–16.
32. Soranus, *Gynaecology*, trans. Owsei Temkin (Baltimore: Johns Hopkins Press, 1956), 15.
33. Pierre Dionis, *A Course of Chirurgical Operations, Demonstrated in the Royal Garden at Paris*, 2nd ed. (London: J. Tonson, 1733), 152.
34. King, *Hippocrates' Woman*, 34.
35. McKay, *The History of Ancient Gynaecology*, 36; Ricci, *The Genealogy of Gynaecology*, 60, 124; Dean-Jones, *Women's Bodies in Classical Greek Science*, 77–8.
36. Ricci, *The Genealogy of Gynaecology*, 60.
37. Dean-Jones, *Women's Bodies in Classical Greek Science*, 78.
38. Giulia Sissa, 'Maidenhood Without Maidenhead: The Female Body in Ancient Greece', in *Before Sexuality: The Construction of Erotic Experience in the Ancient Greek World*, ed. David M. Halperin, John J. Winkler, and Froma I. Zeitlin (Princeton: Princeton University Press, 1990), 355. Also see Soranus, *Gynecology*, 15.
39. Hippocrates, *Nature of Women*. Also see Dean-Jones, *Women's Bodies in Classical Greek Science*, 79; McKay, *The History of Ancient Gynaecology*, 54.
40. Hippocrates, *Nature of Women*, x–xii. The Greek *orkhis* is the derivation for the Latinate *Orchidea*, so called of the orchid plant because of the tes-ticle-like appearance of its root.
41. Hippocrates, *Nature of Women*, 199.
42. Laqueur, *Making Sex*, 30.
43. Carolyn J. Gersh, 'Naming the Body: A Translation with Commentary and Interpretive Essays of Three Anatomical Works Attributed to Rufus of Ephesus' (PhD thesis, University of Michigan, 2012), available at

http://deepblue.lib.umich.edu/bitstream/handle/2027.42/95946/
cgersh_1.pdf?sequence=1.

44. For usage in Celsus, see J. N. Adams, *The Latin Sexual Vocabulary*
(London: Duckworth: 1982), 27; for usage in Galen, see *On the
Usefulness of the Parts of the Body*, 647.

45. Adams, *The Latin Sexual Vocabulary*, 26–7.

46. Adams, *The Latin Sexual Vocabulary*, 99, 227.

47. Monica H. Green, ed. and trans., *The Trotula: A Medieval Compendium of
Women's Medicine* (Philadelphia: University of Pennsylvania Press, 2001).

48. For example, see Helkiah Crooke, *Mikrokosmographia: A Description
of the Body of Man* (London: Printed by William Iaggard, 1615), 237;
Ambroise Paré, *The Workes of That Famous Chirurgion Ambrose Parey*,
trans. T. Johnson (London: T. Cotes and R. Young, 1634), 130.

49. Laqueur, *Making Sex*, 270n58.

50. Lesley Dean-Jones, 'The Cultural Construct of the Female Body in
Classical Greek Science', in *Women's History and Ancient History*, ed.
Sarah B. Pomeroy (Chapel Hill: University of North Carolina Press,
1991), 118–19.

51. Aristotle, *Generation of Animals*, trans. A. L. Peck, Loeb Classical Library
(Cambridge: Harvard University Press, 1942), 95.

52. Aristotle, *Generation of Animals*, 111.

53. Aristotle, *Generation of Animals*, 111.

54. Aristotle, *Generation of Animals*, 393–5.

55. Dean-Jones, 'The Cultural Construct of the Female Body', 121.

56. Aristotle, *Generation of Animals*, 189.

57. Aristotle, *Generation of Animals*, 101. See also Dean-Jones, *Women's
Bodies in Classical Greek Science*, 79–80.

58. Robert Garland, *Daily Life of the Ancient Greeks*, 2nd ed. (Westport:
Greenwood Press, 2009), 138.

59. Aristotle, cited in Dean-Jones, *Women's Bodies in Classical Greek Science*,
79.

60. Dean-Jones, *Women's Bodies in Classical Greek Science*, 79–80.

61. Laqueur, *Making Sex*, 28–35; Marguerite Deslauriers, 'Sex and Essence
in Aristotle's Metaphysics and Biology', in *Feminist Interpretations of
Aristotle*, ed. Cynthia A. Freeland (University Park: Pennsylvania State
University Press, 1998).

62. Deslauriers, 'Sex and Essence', 148.

63. Aristotle, *Generation of Animals*, 173–4.

64. Giulia Sissa, 'The Sexual Philosophies of Plato and Aristotle', in *A History
of Women: From Ancient Goddesses to Christian Saints*, ed. Georges Duby
and Michelle Perrot (Cambridge: Harvard University Press, 1992), 67.

65. Laqueur, *Making Sex*, 26.

66. Laqueur, *Making Sex*, 151.
67. Michel Foucault, The *History of Sexuality*, vol. 1, trans. Robert Hurley (London and New York: Penguin, 1978), 55, 79.
68. Laqueur, *Making Sex*, 151.
69. This is especially the case with physiological sexual difference. See Dean-Jones, *Women's Bodies in Classical Greek Science*, 45.
70. James Gibson, 'The Theory of Affordances', in *The Ecological Approach to Visual Perception* (Hillsdale: Lawrence Erlbaum Associates, 1986).
71. Maria Michela Sassi, *The Science of Man in Ancient Greece*, trans. Paul Tucker (Chicago: University of Chicago Press, 2001), 100; Heinrich von Staden, *Herophilus: The Art of Medicine in Early Alexandria* (Cambridge: Cambridge University Press, 1989), 167–8, 231.
72. Staden, *Herophilus*, 168.
73. King, *The One-Sex Body on Trial*, 38–40.
74. McKay, *The History of Ancient Gynaecology*, 81; Ricci, *The Genealogy of Gynaecology*, 123.
75. McKay, *The History of Ancient Gynaecology*, 248.
76. A natural affinity between the vulva and the myrtle was implied in Hippocrates's remedy of myrtle or myrtle-berry boiled in wine for aphthae and lesions of the vulva. Hippocrates, *Nature of Women*, 289, 291, 297. On the use of 'myrtle-berry' and 'myrtle' as slang words for the female genitals, see Laurence Totelin, *Hippocratic Recipes: Oral and Written Transmission of Pharmacological Knowledge in Fifth- and Fourth-Century Greece* (Leiden: Koninklijke Brill, 2009), 204; Jeffrey Henderson, ed. and trans., *3 Plays by Aristophanes: Staging Women* (London and New York: Routledge, 1996), 216n38.
77. McKay, *The History of Ancient Gynaecology*, 80.
78. King, *Hippocrates' Woman*, 23.
79. McKay, *The History of Ancient Gynaecology*, 248; A. H. Freeland Barbour, *Early Contributions of Anatomy to Obstetrics* (Edinburgh: Oliver and Boyd, 1888), 11.
80. Barbour, *Early Contributions of Anatomy to Obstetrics*, 11.
81. Soranus, *Gynaecology*, 132.
82. Simon Hornblower, Antony Spawforth, and Esther Eidinow, eds., *Oxford Classical Dictionary*, 4th ed. (Oxford: Oxford University Press, 1949), 81.
83. Soranus, *Gynaecology*, 7.
84. Soranus, *Gynaecology*, 129–30.
85. Galen, *On the Usefulness of the Parts of the Body*, 628–9.
86. Dean-Jones, *Women's Bodies in Classical Greek* Science, 45.

CHAPTER 3

Galen's Nymphs

In his *On the Usefulness of the Parts of the Body*, Galen (c. 129–216 CE) pictures the entire female genital tract as an internalised version of the penis and likens the 'skinlike growth' (undifferentiated labia) at the exterior end of the 'neck' of the womb (the vagina, imagined as the shaft of the penis) to the prepuce. Elsewhere in this same work, he says that in woman, the 'outgrowths of skin' on the pudenda 'were formed for the sake of ornament and are set in front as a covering to keep the uteri from being chilled' and that 'the part called *nympha* ... gives the same sort of protection to the uteri that the uvula gives to the pharynx; for it covers the orifice of the neck by coming down into the female pudendum and keeps it from being chilled'.[1] The relatively detailed vulval taxonomy developed by Rufus and Soranus would be changed irrevocably by Galen, if his Renaissance translators and their readers are to be believed. Seventeenth-century physician-anatomists Helkiah Crooke and Thomas Bartholin asserted that the term 'nymphae' (which they took to mean the labia minora specifically) derived from Galen, which indicates that he was responsible for shifting this descriptor from the clitoris to the labia.[2] But if Crooke and Bartholin were correct in this assumption, then Galen never managed to find a replacement word for the clitoris: perhaps the clitoris was elided because it did not fit neatly into his analogic description of the womb, vagina and vulva as the scrotum, shaft and prepuce; perhaps it was one penis too many; or perhaps it was considered so accidental a part of the female physiology that it was not worth mentioning. Galen's description of vulval anatomy is highly ambiguous: through

© The Author(s) 2019
C. Nurka, *Female Genital Cosmetic Surgery*,
https://doi.org/10.1007/978-3-319-96490-4_3

the rather vague and confusing analogy with the uvula, Galen either conflated the clitoris and labia as a singular pudendal structure or elided completely the clitoris as a unique entity from the morphology of the female anatomy: either way, it didn't exist, in marked contrast to Rufus and Soranus. As present-day physicians Vincent Di Marino and Hubert Lepidi confirm, 'no place is made for the clitoris so that the progress made by Aristotle and the physicians of Ephesus as regards the anatomy of the female sex is truly forgotten'.[3]

While Galen himself allowed no place for the clitoris, the anatomical language of similitude that he developed would ground the sensationalist reintroduction of the clitoris to the medical literature in the Latin texts of the fifth to seventh centuries. As I explore in this chapter, the clitoris would be the first vulval organ to gain notoriety for hypertrophy, as recorded in the Roman literature that reproduced ancient Greek texts now lost to us, which was then, in turn, expanded upon by Arabic doctors, and then reproduced in Renaissance Europe by physicians who were reading and translating the Roman literature for a contemporary medical audience. *Labial* hypertrophy did not become a problem until the labia minora were described and taken seriously as a distinct anatomical structure in the Renaissance. Only once the labia minora were assigned a commonly understood denotative appellation—'nymphae'—did physicians then suggest theories as to physiological function and elaborate upon their atypical characteristics, chief among them the cases thought to require surgery in which the nymphae were large enough 'to hang without *the Labia pudendi*'.[4] The labour that physicians put into describing the parts in their 'normal' situation and recording cases of 'abnormality', particularly from the seventeenth century, formed the beginnings of a new genital norm. But it must be pointed out too, that at the same time, doctors had also developed a language of genital diversity, which has now all but disappeared from the contemporary clinical literature on hypertrophy of the labia minora.

Naming is a point of capture and its history can reveal to us the fissures and flows of knowledge about the genitally defined body. What is named, or what is not—and what is forgotten—can tells us much about the shifting emphasis of cultural values that enfold and bring forth the body as a knowable object. Feminist philosopher Nancy Tuana argues that to accumulate knowledge is also to create zones of epistemological exclusion, or, as she terms it, 'epistemologies of ignorance'.[5] Ignorance is not simply a case of undiscovered knowledge waiting to be revealed, but a political condition of knowledge-making, where not knowing, or not wanting to know, or discarding what was once known can work to privilege some knowers over others. It is, then, not discoverable hidden facts but historical changes in the social organisation of knowledge-gathering processes that determine which kinds of knowledge are extrapolated and which fall into disuse: 'What was once common knowledge or even common scientific knowledge can be transferred to the realm of ignorance not because it is refuted and seen as false, but because such knowledge is no longer seen as valuable, important, or functional.'[6] Tuana argues that the history of the female sexual body and its pleasures has been powerfully shaped by patriarchal epistemologies of ignorance that hide the clitoris—the most important organ in the physiology of female sexual pleasure—from view. The concept of an epistemology of ignorance has great saliency for the questions about abnormality that have driven medical research and also for the attribution of names for the external female genitals and the kind of information that is included in their description. Following Tuana, I want to explore the medical history of genital naming as one marked by amnesia and inarticulacy, revealing masculine biases in the production of scientific knowledge about the female body. As Michel Foucault's (by now axiomatic) historical methodology demonstrates, naming is important for bringing things and identities into being, and for making them legible within available cultural repertoires of meaning.[7] The story of the vulva is told through what is named, not named, forgotten and renamed.

THE FIRST CASE OF HYPERTROPHY

Although Galen's female anatomical model omitted the clitoris, during the fifth to seventh centuries the clitoris re-emerged, gaining notoriety for its capacity to become pathologically hypertrophied. Caelius Aurelianus (c. 401–500 CE), Mustio, or Moschion (c. 400–600 CE), Aetius of Amida (c. 502–575 CE) and Paulus Aegineta (c. 625–690 CE) recuperated the clitoris in a most infamous fashion, with their descriptions of the hypertrophied clitoris and its surgical removal.[8] In the ancient Roman medical texts, the clitoris was not simply a little-known anatomical feature hitherto resurrected and appraised for its normal functional role in the production of pleasure. It was singled out specifically for its capacity to become monstrously enlarged, which rendered it a site of severe anxiety regarding the sexual status of women who possessed such a thing.

The problem of aberrant clitoral enlargement was described in Caelius's *Gynaecia*, which was a Latin translation of Soranus's treatise *Gynaikeia*. Soranus's Greek text originally contained a section entitled 'on an excessively large clitoris', but this fragment is lost to contemporary readers, and is only accessible in the writings of his Roman successor. Caelius used the vulgar appellation *landica* to describe the pathologically enlarged clitoris,[9] which unnaturally endowed upon women the lust of men: 'An uncouth size is present in certain clitorises [landicis horrida comitatur magnitude] and brings women into disorder by the deformity of the ... parts and, as most people say, those same women, affected by the lust ... of men, take on a similar desire, and they approach sexual intercourse ... only under duress'. He then gave instructions for clitoral excision, warning that it was likely to bleed copiously and advising strict post-surgical treatment.[10] And in *On Acute and Chronic Diseases*, he named women who seek to take an active role in sex with other women 'tribades' (meaning 'women that rub') and likened them to men who take the passive part in sex with other men. These were men, he said in disgust, whose unnatural excessive lust 'subjected to foul uses parts of the body that should never have been so employed'.[11] The women whom he calls *tribades* 'practise the love of either sex, are eager to have intercourse with women more than with men' and 'seek to do to other women what they are known to suffer, and winning from their double sex a pleasure from giving pleasure'.[12] In the literal reading, the tribade uses her 'doubled' sex (clitoris/penis) to penetrate other women.[13] If the anus is, for men, a part of the body that should never be penetrated by another man, then the clitoris is, by analogy, that part of the body that should never penetrate another woman. In the less literal reading, tribades are simply gender-deviant women who 'practice both kinds of sex and desire women more than men'.[14] Tribadism can indicate the exchange of pleasure between women by clitoral means, or it may refer to cunnilingus, where the mouth becomes a vagina-like receptacle for the clitoris-as-penis. What the woman with the large clitoris and the tribade have in common is their excessive desire that carries over into the wrong sexual action. The *landica* and the *tribade* are figures—one anatomical, the other psychological—that are enjoined conceptually through uncontrollable passions that are unleashed by the unnatural body (the enlarged clitoris) or that unleash unnatural acts (taking an active part in sex with other women).

The tribade as a figure of disgust appears in Martial (c. 38–103 CE) as the scorned and ridiculed Philaenis, who sodomises boys like a husband in his 'stiffened lust' and 'works eleven girls roughly every day'.[15] This reference was enough to inspire Bartholin to write that in some women, the clitoris 'grows as big as the yard of a man: so that some women abuse the same, and make use thereof in place of a man's yard, exercising carnal copulation one with another, and they are termed *confricatrices* rubsters. Which lascivious practice is said to have been invented by one Philaenis, and Sappho the Greek Poetess is reported to have practised the same.[16] Lucian (c. 120–180 CE) reportedly also makes reference to a tribade who confesses to her female lover, 'My mind, my passion and every thing else is masculine … look here, and you will see I am in no way inferior to men; *for I have something in the place of the virile member*'.[17] Evoking Sappho's birthplace, he claims that 'such women—*tribades*, they say there are in Lesbos, who will not suffer it from men, but themselves go with women, as if they were men'.[18] The women of Lesbos were not only associated with 'rubbing', however; 'to play the lesbian' colloquially meant fellatio or cunnilingus, which were treated with disgust, especially by Martial, who thought such activities defiled the mouth.[19] *Landica* was an indecent term because of its association with both lesbianism and cunnilingus, where it came to take an active, 'masculine' role in sexual relations.[20] As Classical scholar Richard W. Hooper confirms, licking the clitoris was seen to have an improper passivating effect: 'Any sexual act involving the mouth, whether cunnilingus or fellatio, was seen as extreme defilement', in part because it 'overturned the male's normal role as penetrator'.[21]

In Aetius's telling, the enlarged clitoris is a nuisance, accidentally exciting the woman to venery because it is exposed easily to the touch of garments: 'In some cases the clitoris is so large that it presents a shameful deformity, so that when irritated by the contact of the patient's garments, the woman is excited to venery.'[22] It is also believed to be a feature common to Egyptian girls: 'The Egyptian custom is to amputate it before it grows large, chiefly about the time when the girl is marriageable.'[23] As I explore later in the chapter, this reference to Egyptians would reappear in seventeenth- and eighteenth-century gynaecological texts. Physicians Mustio and Paulus also both regarded the excessive clitoris as the shameful penis-like property of the tribade and advised its surgical removal.[24] Paulus, however, distinguished clitoral enlargement from hermaphroditism. In the former, 'the nympha … is excessively large and presents a shameful deformity, insomuch that, as has been related, some women have had erections of this part like men and also venereal diseases of a like kind'.[25] In the latter, 'there is often found above the puden-dum and in the situation of the pubes the appearance of a man's privy parts, there being three bodies projecting there, one like a penis, and two like testicles'. In this instance, he advised the removal of both clitoris and labia entirely.[26]

THE REDISCOVERY OF THE CLITORIS

Yet while the clitoris was made infamous by Caelius, Mustio, Aetius and Paulus, they did little to prevent future confusion around identifying which part of the vulva was which. Historian Katharine Park explains that during the Medieval period, medical authors 'tended either to identify … [the clitoris] with the labia minora or, following the eleventh-cen-tury Persian medical authority Avicenna, to think of it as a pathologi-cal growth found in only a few women'.[27] When described in the latter terms, it was generally understood to be a sign of hermaphroditism: that is, not a clitoris which could be used *as* a penis, but, literally, a penis.[28] The clitoris was either confused with the labia (or prepuce) or it was left out of the 'normal' female anatomy altogether. With the Galenisation of Medieval Arabic medicine, Galen's perplexing description of the pro-tective prepuce as the 'nymphe' would be understood by Ali ibn Abbas Al-Majusi (Haly Abbas) as the clitoris in the context of Rufus's earlier designation, thereby creating a confusing conflation.[29] Medieval author Henri de Mondeville (1260–1316), by the same assumption, asserted that the clitoris performed the same service as the uvula did for the throat.[30] Following Galen, Mondino drew a comparison between the 'pellicula' (labia) and the prepuce,[31] and erased the clitoris. Guy de Chauliac (1363) followed Al-Majusi in his account of Galen's anatomy, in which he said that the *tentigo* (Latin for clitoris) was also the pre-puce.[32] In Bengario's *Isagogae breues et exactissimae in anatomia humani corporis* (1530), the clitoris remained undescribed, as in Mondino.[33]

This was the fraught epistemological context within which six-teenth-century anatomists Matteo Realdo Colombo and Gabriel Fallopius rivalled one another to claim discovery of the 'seat of wom-an's delight'.[34] Laqueur argues that Colombo uses the language of homology, epitomised in Galen, in describing it as 'a sort of male member'. The Renaissance writers, he suggests, accommodated the possibility of woman possessing two penises: 'the vagina only resembles the penis whereas the clitoris actually is one'.[35] Colombo used Albucasis's term *tentigo*, which was not a neutral term: for Latin writers of the Roman Empire, *tentigo* was typically used to describe the male erection and was conceptually connected to the word *landica*, which, as I have discussed, was an obscene term used to denote a hypertrophied clitoris.[36] It was obscene precisely because it was too masculine a part; and in its capacity to become erect, it violated the norms of desire dictating that men give and women receive. As French surgeon Ambroise Paré confirms by warning his readers, 'because it [the clitoris] is an obscene part, let those which desire to know more of it read the Authors which I cited [Colombo and Fallopius]'.[37]

Fallopius gave the clitoris the name we have for it today, reworking the Classical Roman notion that it could become so enlarged as to enable women to 'have sexual relations with other women as if they were men'.[38] Following Fallopius, in the seventeenth century and onward, we see mass panic among anatomists as to the threat to proper feminine embodiment, and sexual behaviour, that a hypertrophied clitoris posed.[39] In some cases it was referred to directly as a 'woman's yard',[40] and in others, the frequency of clitoral hypertrophy was vastly overstated. English physician William Sermon, for example, claimed in 1671 that '*in many women* it is well known to be as large as a man's, and doth very much trouble them in the act of generation'.[41] In 1615, Crooke spoke disapprovingly of this part 'which those wicked women do abuse called *Tribades* (often mentioned by many authors, and in some states worthily punished) to their mutual and unnatural lusts',[42] along with countless other physicians and midwives.[43] The famous herbalist Nicholas Culpeper asserted that 'the bigger the *Clitoris* is in women, the more lustful they are'.[44]

Katharine Park suggests that the revival of the tribade in sixteenth-century France represented the horror of woman attempting to overcome her natural difference.[45] Park argues, against Laqueur, that the premodern tribade complicates the theory that up until the eighteenth century the science of sex functioned by homology. As Park explains, 'French medical writers recognized analogies between the genitals of men and women, but they did not by that token deny the fundamental anatomical reality of sex difference—a difference in degree so great as to be a difference in kind'.[46] The tribade in fact represented a crisis of sex in the medical sciences as a woman who was *too much* like a man, and who therefore overstepped the boundaries of natural difference. I suggest, in sympathy with Laqueur, that it was only by anatomical analogy that the enlarged clitoris could ever have been imagined to have taken the place of the penis. The Galenic analogic model that persisted into the Renaissance functioned to domesticate the female body by making it knowable, yet at the same time, medical writers clearly had trouble imagining a female penis when women, by their sexual nature, should *not* have one. In the historical context of the influence of Galen, when it wasn't ignored, the clitoris could only be understood by reference to the penis because the latter was always the primary or first organ and much better understood. But if the clitoris became too much like a penis, it violated the natural order of sex: female desire, as reflected in the morphology of the vagina, was fundamentally different in that it was supposed to receive, not give. What the tribade represented was the sameness/difference conundrum that positioned womanhood in general: women were the same to the extent that their bodies could be scientifically understood when made to conform to a male blueprint, but different to the extent that their bodies were receptacles for penises and babies, and were naturally structured for this purpose. That is why hypertrophied clitorises necessitated cutting.

VESALIUS AND THE MISSING CLITORIS

In a rather neat metaphor for the physical genital structure itself, the story of the labia minora is intimately connected to that of the clitoris. While Colombo and Fallopius were proclaiming the discovery of the clitoris, the celebrated sixteenth-century anatomist Andreas Vesalius drew on the Galenic Medieval tradition to erase the clitoris entirely from his account: but in the process, he would assign a term to the labia minora—'nymphe'—that would establish them as a universally recognised, and distinct, body part in the medical discourse of the century to follow. Vesalius had brought Galen's anatomy to visual life in his anatomic illustrations contained in his magnum opus, *De humani corporis fabrica*, published in 1543; yet nowhere in Vesalius's depiction of the female anatomy do we encounter a description of any kind of the clitoris. The elision of the organ in Medieval anatomy was what prompted Vesalius's contemporary Fallopius to criticise the lack of attention paid to it in the medical literature, and to proclaim himself the first to provide a name for, and detailed description of, what he saw as woman's penis-like organ. Vesalius dismissed this conceit with the following remarks:

> It is unreasonable to blame others for incompetence on the basis of some sport of nature ... you have observed in some woman, and you can hardly ascribe this new and useless part, as if it were an organ, to healthy ... women. I think that such a structure appears in hermaphrodites who otherwise have well formed female genitals, as Paul of Aegina describes, but I have never once seen in any woman a penis (which Avicenna called albathara and the Greeks called an enlarged nympha and classed as an illness) or even the rudiments of a tiny phallus.[47]

As Vesalius suggests in this riposte to Fallopius, the clitoris was absent from much of the medical literature because it didn't exist in 'normal' women. It was, rather, an atypical hermaphroditic structure. He thus refused to accept Fallopius's anatomical revision, 'reading back', as it were, through Galen to support his own clitorally absent anatomy.

There is no doubt that Vesalius was highly familiar with Galen, as he was educated in medicine in an academic climate that had become heavily influenced by Nicolo Leoniceno's translations of 1514. One of Vesalius's teachers at the University of Paris, Johannes Guinther, published the first Latin translation of Galen's *On Anatomical Procedures*, which would propagate a widespread enthusiasm for Galen. Vesalius assisted Guinther with the writing of his textbook, *Anatomical Institutions According to the Opinion of Galen for Students of Medicine* (1536), and would publish a revised edition two years later.[48] In 1539, Vesalius was approached by the Guinta Press to update and edit a Latin translation of three of Galen's works, which he undertook with co-researcher John Caius. Together, they sifted through Latin and Greek manuscripts to confirm the previous translation, correct errors, or add material from newly discovered Galenic manuscripts.[49] Although Vesalius saw and remarked upon anatomical errors in Galen, against the general current of uncritical idolisation, this period of intense engagement with Galen's work would have had a significant influence on the *Fabrica*.

In his widely read and highly influential work, Vesalius distinguished the labia minora, or 'nymphae', from the labia majora, the mounds or 'wings' (consistent with Greek usage of πτερυγώματα for the labia majora), and said of the pudendum: 'There are always not only loose folds but also those cuticular caruncles or tubercles that hang down to a different extent in different women and are known to the Greeks as *nymphe*.'[50] Vesalius had preserved 'nymphe' in the original Greek script, explaining that this was the Grecian term for the 'prominent caruncles in the orifice of the neck', by which he was clearly referring to the labia minora.[51] Given Vesalius's familiarity with the Galenic corpus, it is highly probable that he took the appellation of nymphe for the labia minora from him, especially when we consider that both Rufus and Soranus before Galen had most assuredly used the term 'nympha/e' to designate the clitoris. This substitution of terms also meant that Vesalius could reinterpret the Greco-Roman accounts of clitoridectomy as labial excision. He reproduced Aetius's description of the hypertrophied clitoris in almost exactly the same detail, but applied the disease and the cure to the labia minora.

The Nymphae Discovered

In Vesalius's revised Galenic anatomy, the clitoris was consigned to invisibility to make way for the novel appearance of accurately described labia, which finally acquired a stable identity with his reintroduction of the Greek terms 'wings' (labia majora) and 'nymphe' (labia minora). Post-Vesalius, 'nymphae' would be used as standard nomenclature for the interior vulval lips in medical texts well into the nineteenth century, and eventually, it would give way to the term 'labia minora', as we know them to be called today. With the disappearance of the clitoris came the reappearance (indeed, a 'rediscovery') of two distinct labial structures, and Vesalius would be the one to provide medicine with the anatomical nomenclature for the labia minora that would go on to become conventional and long-lasting.

After Vesalius, we see a marked shift in the medical language, which gradually establishes 'nymphae' as the proper term for the labia minora. For instance, Vesalius's contemporary Paré wrote in his *Briefve collection de l'administration anatomique* of 1549, four years after the publication of the *Fabrica*, that the two excrescences of flesh are called *nymphe*.[52] In the English translation of Paré's *Works* (published in 1634), Paré distinguishes between the lips or *alae* (labia majora), the *nymphae* (labia minora), and the 'obscene part' called *Tentigo* by Colombo and

Cleitoris by Fallopius.[53] And from the turn of the seventeenth century onwards, 'nymphae' would smatter the literature to eventually become the accepted modern term for the labia minora. As the second medical dictionary published in the English language, by G. Motherby in 1775, confirmed: 'Galen, and other ancient writers, sometimes call the clitoris, and sometimes the hymen, by the name of nymphae; but what the moderns call nymphae … are two prominent folds of the inner skin of the greater or external alae.'[54]

The use of the term 'nymphae' to describe the labia minora must have come from the translations of Galen in the sixteenth century, as the word is not used in this way by notable anatomists between Galen and Vesalius.[55] For instance, after Galen, the Roman Caelius and Mustio both use *landica* for the clitoris (especially a hypertrophied one) and *pinnacula* or *fibrae* for the labia majora; *pinnacula* follows Rufus and Soranus as a Latin calque on the Greek πτερυγώματα (wings). Mustio also notes that the Greeks called the clitoris the *nymphe*.[56] Paulus, who translates Aetius, differentiates the *alae pudenda*, the Latin term for 'wings of the pudenda', from *nympha* (which is described as a member capable of becoming stiff), a division consistent with his predecessors.[57] Mondino would call attention to the '*pellicula*, which open and close to prevent the ingress of air and foreign substances in the matrix and bladder. This is called by Avicenna the *prepuce of the matrix*, since it resembles the prepuce of the penis, which protects the urethral orifice'.[58] The clitoris disappeared as the labia reasserted themselves, though which ones is not clear.

According to the early-twentieth-century sexologist Havelock Ellis, the term nymphae, in the plural, to refer to the labia minora was first introduced by Severin Pinaeu in 1599, 'mainly from the influence of these structures on the urinary stream'.[59] With Pineau, then, 'nymphe' acquired a new meaning not present in either Galen or Vesalius. Rodrigo de Castro put it in much more salacious terms: 'These fleshy growths, which stand like cock's combs by the opening of the womb in the vagina, are rightly called "nymphs". For the poets say that the satyrs pursued [the nymphs] through glades and groves, because in them were those delights of sexual congress for which [the satyrs] burned.'[60] Crooke was able to incorporate both meanings in his *Mikrokosmographia* in 1615 to state that the nymphes have their name 'because they join unto the passage of the urine, and the neck of the womb; out of which, as out of fountains (and the *Nymphes* are said to be precedents or deities of the fountains) water and humours do issue: and beside, because in them are the venereal delicacies, for the Poets say that the Nymphes lasciviously seek out the Satyrs among the woods and forests'.[61] *Bartholinus Anatomy* (1663) also offers the explanation that the 'nymphs' are so called by Galen 'either because they do first admit the bridegroom, or because they have charge of the Waters and Humors issuing forth ... Others [i.e., Vesalius] call them the Cuticular Caruncles'.[62] Not long after, Jane Sharp, in her *Midwives Book* (1671), confirmed that the labia minora 'are called '*Nymphs* because they join to the passage of the Urine and the neck of the womb, out of which as out of Fountains, whereof the *Nymphs* were called Goddesses, water and humours do flow, & besides in them is all the joy and delight of *Venus*'.[63] From de Castro to Sharp, the nymphs change their mythological expression, at first coyly hiding that which the hungry satyr (the penis) seeks out, and then becoming the guardians of female desire and pleasure. By contrast, Francois Mauriceau's *Diseases of Women with Child* (1683) is relatively brusque in its statement that they 'govern the Woman's Water, the Urine',[64] while Pierre Dionis's *Treatise of Midwifery* (1719) explains that the nymphae are so named 'because they direct the Course of the Urine; when Women make water'.[65] The 1801 edition of Hooper's medical dictionary includes a lexical note to say that the word 'nymphae' is derived from the Greek νυμφα, meaning 'a water-nymph; so called because it stands in the water-course'.[66] That 'nymphe' could easily transfer from clitoris to labia minora through its double meaning as hidden like a bride and directing the flow of urine like a water nymph was perhaps nothing more than a serendipitous accident. Nymphae would be the popular and stable term for the labia minora after Vesalius and throughout the seventeenth to the late nineteenth centuries; but it would eventually fall out of use, and its departure would bring with it the loss of the Greek mythological meanings in favour of plain, denotative terminology indicative, perhaps, of the increased secularisation of the sciences.

Defining Difference

In lending clarity to the labia minora as a structure of female anatomy, Vesalius also provided an incipient vocabulary for the capacity of this part to become abnormally hypertrophied, which obtained importance as a marker of difference *between women*. Vesalius pinched Aetius's original description of the hypertrophied clitoris to explain that the 'coriaceous caruncles [labia minora] in some women grow so large as to be ugly and embarrassing and in many cultures this is regarded as a sign of gross immorality, though the truth is rather that, being continually chafed by garments they stimulate lust and arouse the desire for venery'.[67] Continuing with his faithful reproduction of Aetius, Vesalius noted that 'it was ... the custom, particularly among the Egyptians, to cut off these caruncles so that they would not have time to grow too much; the operation was performed as soon as the girls were of marriageable age'.[68]

In the medical literature, two kinds of qualities marking differences between social classes of women are immediately apparent: one is sexual desire, and the other is race. As we shall see in the following chapters, discussions of abnormal genital anatomy would in later centuries be dominated by a preoccupation with race and sexuality. Vesalius's description of female sexual arousal conjures the image of the immoderately lustful woman that we see in Roman descriptions of the tribade, but it also recalls the maligned figure of the prostitute. In the medical literature after Vesalius, the enlarged nymphae become more conspicuously associated with frequent sex. Seventeenth-century doctor Bartholin asserted that the nymphae were particularly long in 'Whores that trade with these Parts', while his contemporary Francois Mauriceau claimed they were 'pendant in those who often copulate, or have had children'.[69] By the nineteenth century, the common assumption among medical men was that prostitutes had abnormally enlarged genitals. Nineteenth-century Italian doctor and criminologist Cesare Lombroso, for instance, conducted a sexological study of prostitute populations in prisons and concluded that they were more likely than 'normal' women to have genital abnormalities. While the occurrence of labial hypertrophy in 'normal' European was due, in his opinion, to childbirth, in prostitutes it was a sign of degeneration.[70] For Lombroso, prostitutes were a degraded of class of criminal women who needed to be understood in their relationship to 'normal women'.[71]

In Vesalius's account of the enlarged labia minora, the lascivious woman was coupled with the foreign woman. With the reappearance of the Egyptians in Vesalius's transcription of Aetius, racialised differences between women became prominent. Throughout the seventeenth and into the eighteenth century, the Egyptians, or those from the 'Eastern' nations would appear in medical texts as preternaturally disposed to enlarged clitorises and labia.[72] Crooke, purportedly drawing from Galen (or pseudo-Galen), tells us that 'sometimes they [the labia] grow to so great a length on one side, more rarely on both; and not so ordinarily in maidens as women … what through the affluence of humours, what through attrection, that for the trouble and shame (being in many Countries a notable argument of petulance and immodesty) they need the surgeon's help to cut them off … especially among the Egyptians, amongst whom this accident (as *Galen* says) is very familiar. Wherefore in Maidens before they grow too long they cut them off, and before they marry'. In a marginal note is given the helpful description, 'The Egyptian women lascivious'.[73] For Bartholin, too, '*Galen* tells us that this Disease is frequent among Egyptians; so that they are fain to cut them in Virgins that are to marry'.[74] The real Galen didn't, in fact, mention hypertrophy, much less clitoral or labial excision—at least, not in *On the Usefulness of the Parts of the Body*. Crooke and Bartholin were likely referring to a pseudo-Galenic treatise entitled *Introduction* or *Doctor*, which was probably written by a Greek doctor living in Egypt. In it, the author writes: 'the small bit of flesh that protrudes from between the lips of the crevice is called nymphe', and 'since it protrudes too much, the Egyptians think it wise to circumcise young girls'.[75]

Midwifery authority Thomas Chamberlayne notes briefly that 'sometimes these wings so far increase, that there is many times need of incision; a disease common among the Egyptians'.[76] Sharp supplements the discussion of Egyptians with an observation of what European travellers had seen in the women of Africa, remarking that in 'some Countries', the labia 'grow so long that the Chirurgion cuts them off to avoid trouble and shame, chiefly in *Egypt* … Some Sea-mem [*sic*] say that they have seen *Negro* Women go stark naked, and these wings hanging out'.[77] The author of *Treatise of the Venereal Disease* (1711) John Marten expresses concern that enlarged labia disrupt copulation and says that '*African* Maids', according to Leo Africanus, are so disposed to the problem of labial enlargement that 'Men make it their Business to walk up and down the Streets of Towns, bawling, Who wants to be Cut; which Operation is call'd *Nymphotomia*: And such indeed ought to submit to be Cut, if by that means they are unfit for Procreation'.[78] Under the entry of 'nymphotomia' (labial excision), Stephen Blancard's *Physical Dictionary* of 1715 notes briefly that the 'Egyptians cut 'em frequently'.[79] E. Chambers's medical *Cyclopaedia* of 1743 cites Galen as having observed that the Egyptians 'frequently practised the nymphotomia; but in our parts of the world, it is rarely found necessary. When it happens to be so, the casuists give their judgement that the woman is obliged to undergo it'.[80] Women's obligation to undergo labial excision was tied to their obligations both to the husband's sexual satisfaction and to their own procreative destiny, as elongated labia that impeded sexual intercourse was a great cause for medical concern and a primary deciding factor in whether or not the surgeon should cut them.

Defining Ab/Normality

The racialisation of the labia minora began with discussions of Egyptian deviance, but this also coincided with the development of more precise description of labial structure and function. Prior to Vesalius's account of labial hypertrophy, the most visible problem of abnormal genital enlargement was directed to the clitoris first and foremost[81]; but with Vesalius's rediscovery of the labia minora amid renewed interest in anatomical investigation, medical practitioners had new opportunity to define the boundaries of the normal. Renaissance physicians were pioneers in deciding what could be classed as normal or abnormal in size and structure, and where to place that line of distinction. For the Greeks, by contrast, illnesses stemming from the placement of the womb or the flow of the menses were accounted for as problems common to all women. The medical concern was about how acute these illnesses were, whether they could be resolved by intervention and by what methods. But medical writers in the Renaissance and onward built upon this knowledge to grapple with a substantially altered field of inquiry: they took a greater interest in identifying the structure of the parts (where they are situated and what they look like) and their function, and in assessing genital normality on this basis.

Many medical texts supposed that the labia had several natural functions—directing the urine, protecting the vagina, aiding childbirth and providing sexual pleasure—and also recognised that they could be asymmetrical and change their shape with age, childbirth and sexual activity (though they were quite wrong on the last point). There was thus some degree of recognition that *normal* vulval embodiment is subject to variation and change. Vesalius, for example, noted that the labia minora 'hang down to a different extent in different women' and, in the seventeenth century, Crooke stated that they 'do hang sometimes a little forth through the great cleft, without the lips of the lap ... Sometimes, they grow to so great a length on one side, more rarely on both; and not so ordinarily in maidens as women'.[82] Following Crooke, Sharp described the labia as 'longer from the middle upward, and sometimes they will hang forth a little at the great slit without the lips'.[83] English physician Thomas Gibson explained in 1688 that 'they are larger grown in Maids than in younger, and larger yet in those that have used Venery, or Born Children',[84] which John Pechey repeated in his *General Treatise on the Diseases of Maids* published eight years later.[85] Well-known French gynaecologist Pierre Dionis acknowledged that they are 'not always of the same bigness, for sometimes one is bigger than the other; some Women also have them bigger than others'.[86] In the late eighteenth century, Thomas Denman asserted 'a very great difference in the appearance of all these parts [of the vulva], especially in those who have had many children, and at various periods of life'.[87] And by the mid-nineteenth century, as terms like *nymphae* and *lips* were becoming replaced by the modern Latinate designations labia minora and majora, French anatomist Jean Cruveilhier advised that the labia minora 'vary much in size, according to age ... They also vary in different individuals: in some females being extremely small, and in others always projecting beyond the labia majora'.[88] An English translation of French surgeon Alfred Velpeau held that there are in fact 'numerous varieties ... to be observed'.[89]

Some physicians were also evidently more cautious than others in advising surgery for hypertrophied nymphae. For instance, Francois Mauriceau had evidently gained a reputation for believing that the labia minora had no use at all and could therefore be easily removed with no consequence to female sexual health. The nymphae, as he put it in 1676, were 'n'étoit utile que *pour la décoration* ['useful only for decoration'].[90] Rodrigo de Castro had counselled, in 1603, against indiscriminate cutting off of the labia, for they 'both produce great pleasure for women in intercourse, and also ... protect the womb from ... without'.[91] In a 1782 publication, gynaecologist Thomas Denman rationally explained that there is a 'very great difference' between women in vulval appearance, especially in relation to life stages, and that it is 'not unusual for one of the *labia* to be larger and more pendulous than the other'. He stressed that 'enlargement or elongation are not regarded as diseases till some inconvenience is produced by them'. He counsels doctors first and foremost to provide medicines to improve women's general health and soothing emollients, and only recommends excision if the elongation is so grievous as to 'hinder the common offices of life'.[92] In 1793, Matthew Baillie asserted that when 'very much enlarged', the labia 'pass considerably beyond the surface of the body'. He insists that 'this is a monstrous formation of no great consequence', but if necessary, the lips can be extirpated.[93] German Gynaecologist Lorenz Heister (1743) and US medical doctor John King (1858) say that the labia may be excised in instances where they prove bothersome in walking, sitting and sexual intercourse, or, as King put it, produce 'distressing symptoms'.[94]

Although, in the seventeenth century and onwards, it had been asserted that the labia can change shape with childbirth and age, the language used to describe vulval change and to identify problematic labia and its causes was by no means neutral. The state of the ageing vulva reflected the diminished value of women past their prime, in contrast to desirable young 'maids'. According to Dionis, in 'Maids', the nymphae are 'firm', but in 'used Women, they are soft and flaggy',[95] while Denman says that 'in young women they are firm and vegete, but in the old ... [they] become flaccid and withered'.[96] Charles D. Meigs espouses that the nymphae in the young are a 'lively red', thin and uncorrugated; but in post-partum women they are of a 'darker hue', 'thickened and corrugated'.[97] John King enthuses about the 'smooth, firm and red' nymphae of youthful women, in sour comparison to those that have become 'dark, flaccid, wrinkled, granulated, or elongated by frequent coitions, child-bearing, age, disease, &c.'[98] Velpeau noted that in post-partum women the nymphae 'lose their firmness and their rosy hue'.[99] The governing narrative in these anatomical descriptions is one of loss and decrepitude.

Labia minora were not only part of women's sexual desirability, but they were also important to female sexuality insofar as it was directed toward procreation and ease of access for the penis. Vesalius and Pechey after him both reasoned that the nymphae narrowed and made straight the mouth of the vagina to better accommodate the penis,[100] while Meigs suggested that the nymphae's purpose is to 'increase the surface of contact, and to bring the clitoris into contact, for the end to augment the aphrodisiac orgasm', which he thought to be 'essential as an agent in the fecundation of the germ'.[101] Any part of the woman's body that interfered with this natural order could thus be considered a problem requiring surgical intervention. Although the literature supposed that the labia minora played a crucial role in female sexual pleasure, if heterosexual sex was frustrated by their length, the most logical solution was that the woman should submit herself to be cut: it was the *woman*'s body that presented itself as a problem. As that famous gynaecological text by pseudo-Aristotle, *Aristotle's Masterpiece*, asserted, 'many times they [the nymphae] spread so far, that incision is required to make way for the Man's Instrument of Generation'.[102] This book was aimed not at medical experts, but the common reader, and brought medicine, albeit sensationalised, to a lay-audience.[103] Surgery was recommended by surgeons Marten and Heister when women's labia were so long as to 'hinder their Copulation' or 'conjugal Embraces'.[104] And famed British obstetrician William Smellie told of a case of asymmetry he encountered in a woman, in which one of the nymphae was so enlarged as to 'hang down three inches without the labia'. The mother of the unfortunate patient, he said, desired him 'to remedy this inconvenience, as the girl was to be married in a little time'.[105] American surgeon Gunning S. Bedford encouraged doctors encountering cases of labial hypertrophy to assess, first and foremost, whether it interfered with 'marital rights'.[106] Authoritative reference texts of the eighteenth century defined 'nymphotomia' in precisely these terms: Blancard's *Physical Dictionary* of 1715 defines nymphotomia as 'a cutting out of the *Nymphae,* the too great Protuberance of whereof (especially those in those Virgins that are marriageable) sometimes hinder the Enjoyment, or at least renders it difficult'.[107] Chambers's medical *Cyclopaedia* of 1743 extends the meaning of nymphotomia to include excision of the labia or clitoris 'when they are so large and tumid, as to prevent the consummation of marriage, or render it very difficult'.[108] By the late nineteenth century, such concerns were still very much a part of the medical discourse, as is evidenced by American doctor A. Reeves Jackson's chapter titled 'Sterility' in an edited collection on gynaecology, where he outlines 'hypertrophy of the labia' as a common problem 'in which congress is prevented by undue enlargement of the parts'.[109]

From the eighteenth century, elongation or hypertrophy was generally diagnosed only if the nymphae were considered to extend 'far without the labia'[110] and to interfere with sexual intercourse and activities of daily life, such as horse-riding, walking and sitting. However, there are a few accounts in the literature that suggest that in all women, labia minora that are visible beyond the outer lips can be considered hypertrophic. Dionis claimed that 'in some they [the nymphae] grow so very big, that they hang without the *Labia,* and must be cut off',[111] along with Francois Mauriceau, who said that some are so long as to necessitate excision 'so much as exceeds and grow without the Lips'.[112] Nineteenth-century American obstetrician William Potts Dewees suggests that labia minora are particularly vulnerable to illness in the form of warts and excrescences when 'they are sufficiently long to protrude beyond the labia'.[113] H T. Byford et al. claim that 'ordinarily, they project far enough for the edges to be seen'.[114] Under the heading 'Malformations of the Vulva and Hermaphroditism', a telling title indicating the ease with which large labia could be regarded as a problem of unclear assignation of sex, John David Hartley explains that hypertrophy of the nymphae is common, wherein they may 'exceed the size of the labia majora and project outside the vulva'.[115] These diagnoses confirm the common assumption that the labia minora of 'maids' and 'virgins' are typically small and concealed, while those of married women are more visible, as is noted by Velpeau, who says that 'in young virgins ... the labia almost entirely conceal the nymphae',[116] or Henry C. Coe, who affirms that 'the labia minora in the virgin ... are always covered by the external parts'.[117]

Given that labia loose and hanging in married women from 'use' was considered relatively normal, the greater concern must then have been to identify and eradicate abnormality in the youthful and desirable *virginal* vulva of the 'maid'. But the normative status of the maiden vulva was also always in some way defined through race. While there are descriptions of labiaplasty procedures dotted throughout the medical literature from Vesalius onwards, labial hypertrophy was generally regarded as anomalous among white women; it was the Egyptians who were the bearers of hypertrophic irregularity. In fact, it was these curious and exotic examples, to Western eyes, that brought the labia to visibility as two distinct sets of inner and outer lips. Like the multiple 'discoveries' of the clitoris, the dual labial structures were 'discovered' by Soranus, then forgotten or confused for several centuries, and then rediscovered with the accounts of Egyptian nymphotomies borrowed from Leo Africanus and pseudo-Galen.

CONCLUSION

The evolution of the medical condition of 'hypertrophy of the labia minora' took place alongside the development of a language with which physicians could usefully describe it. 'Hypertrophy' of the labia minora could scarcely be considered a distinct complaint if there was no standard term in use that could be unambiguously understood and applied by a community of physicians. Hence, I suggest that the establishment of the word 'nymphae' for the labia minora fulfilled an important function: it made this organ visible and legible within a *shared* medical discourse, but only after the clitoris had been recognised—as subject to scandalous enlargement—and then forgotten.

From Galen to today, medical knowledge of the normal vulva has been moulded by inarticulacy and amnesia. Rufus and Soranus were forgotten by Galen, and the language for the vulva in the Medieval period was notoriously vague, before a working vocabulary was formatively developed by Vesalius. Centuries later, as curiosity about the function of the vulval structures blossomed, physicians demonstrated that they were aware of the diversity of female genitalia. It is important to remember that this awareness competed with the idealisation of the youthful, small vulva of 'the virgin'. The virgin is a fictitious character, or figure, that incorporates the image of the healthful, desirable vulva: health and desire in medical discourse on the vulva have never been far from one another.

Our current norm, in which the labia minora are concealed by the labia majora, is partly derived from these earlier accounts of the labia in 'virgins'. Today, we can view contemporary misunderstandings of female anatomy as a legacy of the earlier gynaecological literature within which labial hypertrophy emerged as a definable condition. In the contemporary cosmetic and plastic surgery literature, the need for the surgery is often already assumed and there is very little or no consideration of labial functionality, especially in sexual pleasure—in fact, it is asserted that protruding labia greatly interfere with sexual pleasure, which, as I have shown, has a lengthy historical lineage. For us moderns, 'distressing symptoms' can be both physical and psychological, and in the volumes of current medical literature on labiaplasty, questionable judgements about appearance, rather than healthy or unhealthy function, are common. As contemporary authors Lih-Mei Liao, Lina Michala and Sarah M. Creighton found in their review of the literature, there were no attempts to define or use existing research on normal labial diversity beyond author perceptions of abnormality, by which labia were described as 'grossly enlarged', 'look[ing] like spaniels' ears' and 'deformed'.[118] What constitutes hypertrophic pathology in our modern models is largely determined by what female patients *perceive* to be excessive— and such perceptions are themselves influenced by the lack of information provided to women about *normal* vulval diversity by referring GPs and all-too-willing cosmetic surgeons. The confidence in vulval diversity espoused by physicians like Cruveilhier has today been all but forgotten, and our picture of what normal, healthy female sexuality looks like is not just lacking, but terribly skewed.

To fully appreciate the force of this historical amnesia and wilful desire *not* to understand female anatomy, we can refer to the fact that it was only in 2005 that Australia's first female urologist, Helen O'Connell, provided a comprehensive picture of the clitoral structure using MRI technology. Connell showed definitively that the clitoral nerves extend well into the vagina and are part of its tissue (as Georg Kobelt had described in 1844), and concluded that the size and reach of the clitoris had been consistently misrepresented in textbooks. Like Tuana, O'Connell has argued that this anatomical blindspot is the effect of cultural bias, concluding that 'the tale of the clitoris is a parable of culture, of how the body is forged into a shape valuable to civilization despite and not because of itself'.[119] In the same year that O'Connell's groundbreaking findings were published in the *Journal of Urology*, the outcome of the first rudimentary investigation of normal labial diversity (to my knowledge) was published by Jillian Lloyd, Naomi S. Crouch, Catherine L. Minto, Lih-Mei Liao and Sarah M. Creighton in *BJOG*.[120] Although it was less well-reported than O'Connell's findings, this journal article marks a significant turning point in the history of medical understanding of the vulva as the first study to investigate the anatomical dimensions of *normal* adult female genitalia.[121] The study was conducted in response to the emergence of cosmetic labiaplasty and the medical language of hypertrophy used to justify it. Lloyd et al. recorded 'wide variations' in the dimensions of the labia minora in their sample population, challenging claims in the literature that labia minora can be considered hypertrophic if they reach four centimetres from base to edge. Importantly, none of the women in their sample 'had expressed any personal difficulty or sought cosmetic surgical alteration'.[122] The study also amply demonstrated that medical writers in the past have made empirically unsupported claims of significant difference in labial structure according to age, sexual activity, parity and race. Lloyd et al.'s work showed that the fundamental question of what might constitute normality was conspicuously missing in the history of medical science of the vulva.

Historically, then, medical opinion on the labia minora has either focused on depicting the 'virginal' vulva as the invisible norm against which all others are measured, or, as with the Egyptian examples, focused on defining differences between women as *abnormal*, rather than satisfying any curiosity as to the extent of *normal* labial variation between women. As we shall see in the next chapter, the racial differences between women would become more pronounced as colonial forms of knowledge took hold of genital sex: descriptions of the notorious 'Hottentot apron' provided by French anatomists Henri de Blainville and Georges Cuvier (in 1816 and 1817 respectively) would come to supplement and supplant the very sparse Greek and Roman references to Egyptian women, to become the dominant model for naming and defining labial hypertrophy within the gynaecological literature up to the present day.

NOTES

1. Galen, *On the Usefulness of the Parts of the Body*, trans. Margaret Tallmadge May (Ithaca: Cornell University Press, 1968), 628–9, 660–1.
2. Helkiah Crooke, *Mikrokosmographia: A Description of the Body of Man* (London: Printed by William Iaggard, 1615), 237; Thomas Bartholin, *Bartholinus Anatomy*, trans. Nicholas Culpeper and Abdiah Cole (London: Printed by Peter Cole, 1663), 77.
3. Vincent Di Marino and Hubert Lepidi, *Anatomic Study of the Clitoris and Bulbo-Clitoral Organ* (Heidelberg, Dordrecht, London, New York: Springer, 2014), 3.
4. Lorenz Heister, *Institutions of Surgery*, vol. 2 (London: Printed for W. Innys et al., 1743), 197.
5. Nancy Tuana, 'Coming to Understand: Orgasm and the Epistemology of Ignorance', in *The Feminist Philosophy Reader*, ed. Alison Bailey and Chris Cuomo (New York: McGraw-Hill, 2008), 765–92.
6. Tuana, 'Coming to Understand', 766.
7. Michel Foucault, *The History of Sexuality*, vol. 1, trans. Robert Hurley (London and New York: Penguin, 1978).
8. Katharine Park, 'The Rediscovery of the Clitoris', in *The Body in Parts: Fantasies of Corporeality in Early Modern Europe*, ed. David Hillman and Carla Mazzio (New York: Routledge, 1997), 171–194; Bernadette J. Brooten, *Love between Women: Early Christian Responses to Female Homoeroticism* (Chicago and London: University of Chicago Press, 1996).
9. J. N. Adams, *The Latin Sexual Vocabulary* (London: Duckworth: 1982), 97–8.
10. Brooten, *Love between Women*, 164–5n59.
11. Caelius, cited in Julius Rosenbaum, *The Plague of Lust*, vol. 1, trans. An Oxford M. A. (Montmartre: Charles Carrington, 1901), 164.
12. Caelius, cited in Rosenbaum, *The Plague of Lust*, 165.
13. For this view, see Rosenbaum, *The Plague of Lust*, 161n1; Martial, *The Index Expurgatorius of Martial*, trans. anonymous (London: Printed for private circulation, 1868), 52–3n1; Adams, *The Latin Sexual Vocabulary*, 97–8; Brooten, *Love between Women*, 167.

14. See David M. Halperin, 'Is There a History of Sexuality?', *History and Theory* 28, no. 3 (1989): 267–8; Park, 'The Rediscovery of the Clitoris', 176.

15. Harriette Andreadis, *Sappho in Early Modern England: Female Same-Sex Literary Erotics 1550–1714* (Chicago and London: University of Chicago Press, 2001), 44.

16. Bartholin, *Bartholinus Anatomy*, 76.

17. Martial, *The Index Expurgatorius of Martial*, 53, emphasis in original.

18. Rosenbaum, *The Plague of Lust*, 162n1. In his sexological volume of 1824, *Antonii Panormitae Hermaphroditus*, Friedrich Karl Forberg cited Lucian as evidence for his definition of tribades, meaning '*women that rub*', as those 'who have that portion of the woman's parts which is called the clitoris grown to a size so excessive that they can use it as a penis whether for fornicating of [*sic*] for paederastia' Rosenbaum, *The Plague of Lust*, 161n1, emphasis in original.

19. John G. Younger, *Sex in the Ancient World from A to Z* (London and New York: Routledge, 2005), 69.

20. Melissa Mohr, *Holy Sh*t: A Brief History of Swearing* (Oxford and New York: Oxford University Press), 27–8.

21. Richard W, Hooper (trans.), *The Priapus Poems: Erotic Epigrams from Ancient Rome* (Urbana and Chicago: University of Illinois Press, 1999), 136n79.

22. W. J. Stewart McKay, *The History of Ancient Gynaecology* (London: Ballière, Tindall and Cox, 1901), 220.

23. McKay, *The History of Ancient Gynaecology*, 220–1.

24. On Mustio, see Brooten, *Love between Women*, 163–4n58. On Paulus Aegineta, see Paulus Aegineta, *The Seven Books of Paulus Aegineta*, trans. Francis Adams (London: Printed for the Sydenham Society, 1846), 381.

25. Paulus, *The Seven Books of Paulus Aegineta*, 381.

26. Paulus, *The Seven Books of Paulus Aegineta*, 381.

27. Park, 'The Rediscovery of the Clitoris', 173.

28. For references to a debate around whether the enlarged clitoris was a female organ or evidence of hermaphroditism, see for example Nicholas Culpeper, *A Directory for Midwives* (London: Printed by John Streater, 1671), 22–3; Thomas Gibson, *The Anatomy of Human Bodies Epitomized* (London: Printed for Awnsham Churchil, 1688), 182. Culpeper relates that he sides with those who believe that 'such kind of Creatures they call *Hermaphrodites* which they say bear the genitals both of men and women are nothing else but such women in whom the *Clitoris* hangs out externally, and so resembles the form of the Yard'. Gibson similarly says that tribades are also known as hermaphrodites, though he is sceptical that they 'are truly of both Sexes' as the clitoris is likely only 'preternaturally extended'.

29. See Plinio Prioreschi, *A History of Medicine: Byzantine and Islamic Medicine* (Omaha: Horatius Press, 2001), 408–9; James V. Ricci, *The Genealogy of Gynaecology: History of the Development of Gynaecology throughout the Ages* (Philadelphia: Blakiston Company, 1943), 227. For the original French translation of Al-Majusi, and the uncertainty of the translator around whether *nymphe* means clitoris or labia in that text, see Pieter de Koning, *Trois Traités d'Anatomie Arabes* (Leiden: E. J. Brill, 1903), 389.
30. Valeria Finucci, *The Prince's Body: Vincenzo Gonzaga and Renaissance Medicine* (Cambridge and London: Harvard University Press, 2015), 186n127.
31. Ricci, *The Genealogy of Gynaecology*, 269–70.
32. Guy de Chauliac, in *The Field Day Anthology of Irish Writing*, vol. 4, ed. Angela Burke (New York: New York University Press, 2002), 346.
33. Berengario da Carpi, *Mikrokosmographia, or, A Description of the Body of Man*, trans. H. Jackson (London : Printed for Livewell Chapman, 1664), 101–3.
34. Thomas Laqueur, *Making Sex: Body and Gender from the Greeks to Freud* (Cambridge: Harvard University Press, 1990), 64; Park, 'The Rediscovery of the Clitoris', 173.
35. Laqueur, *Making Sex*, 64–65.
36. Adams, *The Latin Sexual Vocabulary*, 103–4.
37. Ambroise Paré, *The Workes of that Famous Chirurgion Ambrose Parey*, trans. T. Johnson (London: T. Cotes and R. Young, 1634), 130.
38. Fallopius, cited in Kenneth Borris, *Same-Sex Desire in the English Renaissance: A Sourcebook of Texts*, 1470–1650 (New York and London: Routledge, 2004), 119.
39. See Park, 'The Discovery of the Clitoris'.
40. See for example William Sermon, *The Ladies Companion, or the English Midwife* (London: Printed for Edward Thomas, 1671), 195; Francois Mauriceau, *The Diseases of Women with Child, and in Child-Bed*, trans. Hugh Chamberlen (London: Printed by John Darby, 1683), 24.
41. Sermon, *The Ladies Companion*, 195, emphasis mine.
42. Crooke, *Mikrocosmographia*, 238.
43. See for example Crooke, *Mikrokosmographia*, 238; Bartholin, *Bartholinus Anatomy*, 76; Jane Sharp, *The Midwives Book* (London: Printed for Simon Miller, 1671), 45; Mauriceau, *The Diseases of Women with Child*, 24; John Pechey, *A General Treatise of the Diseases of Maids, Bigbellied Women, Child-Bed-Women, and Widows* (London: Printed for Henry Bonwick, 1696), 61.
44. Culpeper, *A Directory for Midwives*, 23.
45. Park, 'The Rediscovery of the Clitoris'.

46. Park, 'The Rediscovery of the Clitoris', 187.
47. Vesalius, cited in Park, 'The Rediscovery of the Clitoris', 177.
48. See Marie Boas Hall, *The Scientific Renaissance 1450–1630* (New York: Dover Publications, 1962), 135; Andreas Vesalius, *The Illustrations from the Works of Andreas Vesalius of Brussels*, ed. J. B. Saunders and Charles O'Malley (New York: Dover Publications, 1950), 13.
49. Stephen N. Joffe, *Andreas Vesalius: The Making, the Madman, and the Myth* (Bloomington: AuthorHouse, 2009), 95–7.
50. Andreas Vesalius, *On the Fabric of the Human Body. Book V: The Organs of Nutrition and Generation*, trans. William Frank Richardson and John Burd Carman (Novato: Jeremy Norman and Co., 2007), 173, 180.
51. For the original Latin version featuring linguistic variants of νυμφη (nymphe) in Greek script, see Andreas Vesalius, *De Humani corporis fabrica* (Basileae, 1543), 532, 536. Available at http://dx.doi.org/10.3931/e-rara-20094. For the English translation, see Vesalius, *On the Fabric of the Human Body*, 173, 184.
52. Ambroise Paré, *Briefve collection de l'administration anatomique* ['Brief Collection of the Conduct of Anatomy'] (Paris: G. Cavellat, 1549), unnumbered page following page 24.
53. Paré, *The Workes of that Famous Chirurgion Ambrose Parey*, 130.
54. G. Motherby, *A New Medical Dictionary* (London: J. Johnson, 1775). The first dictionary was compiled by a Dr. James. See *British and Foreign Medical Review: Or Quarterly Journal of Practical Medicine and Surgery*, volume 1, ed. John Forbes and John Conolly, January–April 1836 (London: Sherwood, Gilbert and Piper, 1836), 176.
55. Laqueur asserts that Berengario, who published his work *Isagogae breues et exactissimae in anatomia humani corporis* in 1530, thirteen years before Vesalius's *Fabrica*, used the word 'nymphae' to describe the labia and the prepuce. Laqueur cites an 1880 German translation. However, in the English translation of 1664, the 'skins' of the outer labia, are given as the prepuce, and the inner labia are called 'pannicular additaments'. This language is consistent with that used by Vesalius's antecedents. See Laqueur, *Making Sex*, 97–8; Berengario, *Mikrokosmographia*, 102.
56. Adams, *The Latin Sexual Vocabulary*, 97–9; Brooten, *Love between Women*, 163n58, 164n59.
57. Paulus Aegineta, *The Seven Books of Paulus Aegineta*, 381–3.
58. Ricci, *The Genealogy of Gynaecology*, 269–70, emphasis in original.
59. Havelock Ellis, *Studies in the Psychology of Sex*, vol. 2 (London: Butterworth-Heinemann, [1906] 2013), 137.
60. Rodrigo de Castro, in Borris, *Same-Sex Desire in the English Renaissance*, 142.

61. Crooke, *Mikrokosmographia*, 237–8. Henceforth, all quoted matter of archaic language taken from original seventeenth-century texts has been modernised.
62. Bartholin, *Bartholinus Anatomy*, 77.
63. Sharp, *Midwives Book*, 43.
64. Mauriceau, *The Diseases of Women*, 25; Pierre Dionis, *A General Treatise of Midwifery* (trans. London: A. Bell, J. Darby, A. Bettesworth, J. Pemberton, C. Rivington, J. Hooke, R. Cruttenden, T. Cox, F. Clay, J. Battley, and E. Symon, 1719), 38.
65. Dionis, *A General Treatise of Midwifery*, 38.
66. Robert Hooper, *A Compendious Medical Dictionary*, second edition (London: Murray and Highley; Cuthell; H. D. Symonds; Callow; Cox; and Dwyer, 1801).
67. Vesalius, *On the Fabric of the Human Body*, 184.
68. Vesalius, *On the Fabric of the Human Body*, 184.
69. Bartholin, *Bartholinus Anatomy*, 77; Mauriceau, *The Diseases of Women*, 25. Other late-seventeenth-century physicians such as John Pechey and Thomas Gibson repeated the same wisdom. See Pechey, *A General Treatise of the Diseases of Maids*, 61; Gibson, *The Anatomy of Human Bodies Epitomized*, 181.
70. Cesare Lombroso and Guglielmo Ferrero, *Criminal Woman, the Prostitute, and the Normal Woman*, trans. Nicole Hahn Rafter and Mary Gibson (Durham and London: Duke University Press, [1893] 2004), 132–4.
71. Lombroso and Ferrero, *Criminal Woman, the Prostitute, and the Normal Woman*, 36.
72. See for example Rodrigo de Castro, in Borris, 141–2; Crooke, *Mikrokosmographia*, 237; Thomas Chamberlayne, *The Compleat Midwife's Practice* (London: Printed for Nathaniel Brooke, 1656), 26; Bartholin, *Bartholinus Anatomy*, 77; Sharp, *The Midwives Book*, 45; Gibson, *The Anatomy of Human Bodies Epitomized*, 184; Pechey, *A General Treatise of the Diseases of Maids*, 62; Stephen Blancard, *The Physical Dictionary* (London: Printed by R. B. for Sam. Crouch, and John & Benj. Sprint, 1715), 245; Dionis, *A General Treatise of Midwifery*, 40; Pierre Dionis, *A Course of Chirurgical Operations, Demonstrated in the Royal Garden at Paris*, 2nd ed. (London: J. Tonson, 1733), 153–4; Lorenz Heister, *Institutions of Surgery*, vol. 2 (London: Printed for W. Innys et al., 1743), 197; E. Chambers, *Cyclopaedia: Or, an Universal Dictionary of Arts and Sciences*, 5th ed., vol. 2 (London: Printed for D. Midwinter et al., 1743), n.p.
73. Crooke, *Mikrokosmographia*, 237.
74. Bartholin, *Bartholinus Anatomy*, 77.

75. Pseudo-Galen, cited in Jacques Jouanna, *Greek Medicine from Hippocrates to Galen: Selected Papers* (Leiden: Brill, 2012), 15.
76. Chamberlayne, *The Compleat Midwife's Practice*, 26.
77. Sharp, *The Midwives Book*, 46–7.
78. John Marten, *A Treatise of the Venereal Disease* (London: Printed for the Author, 1711), 192.
79. Blancard, *The Physical Dictionary*, 245.
80. Chambers, *Cyclopaedia*, n.p.
81. There is, however, one account written by Lanfrancus (c. 1315), which, according to Sergio Musitelli and Ilaria Bossi, could possibly be the first description of labial hypertrophy and excision. In their translation, Lanfrancus writes of 'a sort of muscular panniculus forms at the orifice of the vagina and grows so much that it hangs down, troubles the woman and makes her much less loved by her partner. If you want to treat such a patient, cut away the superfluous pellicle and cauterize the wound with a golden cautery, until you have brought the part back to its natural shape'. See Sergio Musitelli and Ilaria Bossi, '"Peyronie's Disease", "Hottentot Apron" and "Kidney Stones" in the "Urologists" of the Middle Ages', Labome.org, 29 April 2014, http://www.labome. org/research/Peyronie-s-disease-Hottentot-apron-and-kidney-stones-in-the-urologists-of-the-middle-ages.html. In Monica Green's reading, Lanfrancus describes excessive or superfluous skin-like 'growths', which, in phrasing familiarly applied to the tribade, allow women 'to play the part of men with other women'. But precisely what body part Lanfrancus is referring to is unclear, a problem typical of post-Galenic medicine, in which, as I have discussed, the labia minora/majora were undifferentiated, interchangeable, ambiguously defined, missing, or confused with the clitoris. See Monica Green, *Making Women's Medicine Masculine: The Rise of Male Authority in Pre-Modern Gynaecology* (Oxford: Oxford University Press, 2008), 72.
82. Vesalius, *On the Fabric of the Human Body*, 173; Crooke, *Mikrokosmographia*, 237.
83. Sharp, *The Midwives Book*, 46.
84. Gibson, *The Anatomy of Human Bodies Epitomized*, 181.
85. Pechey, *A General Treatise of the Diseases of Maids*, 60.
86. Dionis, *A General Treatise of Midwifery*, 39.
87. Thomas Denman, *Introduction to the Practice of Midwifery* (London, no publisher, 1782), 50.
88. Jean Cruveilhier, *The Anatomy of the Human Body*, ed. Granville Sharp Pattison (New York: Harper and Brothers, 1844), 471.
89. Alfred Armand Louis Marie Velpeau, *An Elementary Treatise of Midwifery; Or, the Principles of Tokology and Embryology* (Philadelphia: Lindsay and Blakiston, 1845), 58.

90. Mauriceau, cited in Charles D. Meigs, *Woman; Her Diseases and Remedies. A Series of Letters to His Class* (Philadelphia: Lea and Blanchard, 1848), 117, my translation.

91. Rodrigo de Castro, in Borris, *Same-Sex Desire in the English Renaissance*, 142.

92. Denman, *Introduction to the Practice of Midwifery*, 50–2.

93. Matthew Baillie, *Morbid Anatomy of Some of the Most Important Parts of the Human Body* (London: Printed for J. Johnson and G. Nicol, 1793), 285.

94. Heister, *Institutions of Surgery*; John King, *Women: Their Diseases and Their Treatment* (Cincinatti: Longley Brothers, 1858), 22.

95. Dionis, *A General Treatise of Midwifery*, 39.

96. Denman, *Introduction to the Practice of Midwifery*, 50.

97. Charles D. Meigs, *Obstetrics: The Science and the Art*, second edition, revised (Philadelphia: Blanchard and Lea, 1852), 92.

98. King, *Women*, 22.

99. Velpeau, *An Elementary Treatise of Midwifery*, 89.

100. Vesalius, *On the Fabric of the Human Body*, 180; Pechey, *A General Treatise of the Diseases of Maids*, 60.

101. Charles D. Meigs, *Females and Their Diseases* (Philadelphia: Lea and Blanchard, 1848), 81.

102. Anonymous, *Aristotle's Masterpiece* (London: Printed for F. L. for J. How, 1690), 99.

103. Roy Porter, 'Sexual Advice before 1800', in *Sexual Knowledge, Sexual Science*, ed. Roy Porter and Mikuláš Teich (Cambridge: Cambridge University Press, 1994), 134–57.

104. Marten, *A Treatise of the Venereal Disease*, 192; Heister, *Institutions of Surgery*, 197.

105. William Smellie, *A Treatise on the Theory and Practice of Midwifery* (London: Printed for Alexander Cleugh and M. Watson, 1790), 173.

106. Gunning S. Bedford, *Clinical Lectures on the Diseases of Women and Children* (New York: William Wood and Co., 1866), 427.

107. Blancard, *The Physical Dictionary*, 245.

108. Chambers, *Cyclopaedia*, n.p.

109. A. Reeves Jackson, 'Sterility', in *A System of Gynecology*, ed. Matthew D. Mann (Philadelphia: Lea Brothers and Co., 1887), 447.

110. Jean-Louis Baudelocque, *A System of Midwifery*, trans. John Heath (London: Printed for the author, 1790), 105.

111. Dionis, *A General Treatise of Midwifery*, 39.

112. Mauriceau, *The Diseases of Women with Child*, 25.

113. William P. Dewees, *Treatise on the Diseases of Females* (Philadelphia: Lea and Blanchard, 1840), 23.

114. Henry T. Byford, J. M. Baldy, Edwin B. Cragin, J. H. Etheridge, William Goodell, Howard A. Kelly, Florian Krug, E. E. Montgomery, William R. Pryor and George M. Tuttle, *An American Text-Book of Gynecology, Medical and Surgical, for Practitioners and Students*, ed. J. M Baldy (Philadelphia: W. B. Saunders, 1894), 164.
115. John Davis Hartley, *A System of Gynaecology* (New York: J. B. Flint and Company, 1899), 580.
116. Velpeau, *An Elementary Treatise of Midwifery*, 89.
117. Henry C. Coe, 'The Anatomy of the Female Pelvic Organs' in *A System of Gynecology*, ed. Matthew D. Mann (Philadelphia: Lea Brothers and Co., 1887), 101.
118. Lih-Mei Liao, Lina Michala and Sarah M. Creighton, 'Labial Surgery for Well Women: A Review of the Literature', *BJOG* 117, no. 1 (2010): 22.
119. Helen O'Connell, Kalavampara V. Sanjeevan and John M. Hutson, 'Anatomy of the Clitoris', *Journal of Urology* 174, no. 4 Part 1 (2005): 1194.
120. Jillian Lloyd, Naomi S. Crouch, Catherine L. Minto, Lih-Mei Liao and Sarah M. Creighton, 'Female Genital Appearance: "Normality" Unfolds', *BJOG* 112 (2005): 643–6.
121. Lloyd et al., 'Female Genital Appearance', 643.
122. Lloyd et al., 'Female Genital Appearance', 645.

CHAPTER 4

The Colonial Race Sciences

In this chapter, I argue that white colonial encounters with African women popularised labial hypertrophy, rendering it recognisable as a condition of disorder pertaining almost exclusively to black women. By the mid-nineteenth century, medical practitioners were becoming increasingly familiar with anthropological accounts of an enlarged vulval structure supposedly found in women of southwest Africa, among the peoples the Dutch called 'Hottentots'. This anatomical curiosity was thus dubbed the 'Hottentot apron' (or *tablier*, as it was known to the French). Due to its racist heritage, the term 'Hottentot' is considered offensive, and these peoples of Southern Africa (Khoi), along with the 'Bushmen' (San), are today collectively known as the Khoisan. In this chapter, I acknowledge the periodicity of the terms 'Hottentot', 'Bushman' and 'Hottentot apron' and generally use them without quotation marks. I hope to show that the 'Hottentot apron' is a rhetorical, rather than an ontological, construct used to signify black otherness in opposition to the invisible norm that white genitals represent. I am also aware of the ethical risk of reproducing a racist gaze through the inclusion of racially offensive images taken of African women by white anthropologists. As a white researcher, I am profoundly aware of my phenomenological and temporal distance from the women presented in the images I show here. I have no desire to reinvigorate the white gaze turned upon exoticised black women; however, I argue that in order for the reader to adequately appreciate the extraordinary rhetorical power of

© The Author(s) 2019
C. Nurka, *Female Genital Cosmetic Surgery*,
https://doi.org/10.1007/978-3-319-96490-4_4

white colonial depictions of aberrant black labia, it is necessary to display those images that attest to its symbolic construction.

I locate the 'Hottentot apron' of the early colonial race sciences as influential in the historical construction of the medical model of labial hypertrophy, a diagnosis used in the present day to support and justify the need for cosmetic labiaplasty surgery in Western nations. I suggest that contemporary labiaplasty is highly invested in a colonial sexual imaginary, by which the aesthetic valuation of the labia is linked to the construction and maintenance of racial hierarchies. I speak of a 'colonial sexual imaginary' as comprising anthropological, medical and photographic accounts of female 'Hottentot' genitality that produce a normalised *invisible* white female sexuality through the spectacular depiction of aberrant black bodies. As we saw in Chapter 3, while the Galenic anatomical model made the white female body knowable through emphasising its resemblance to the male body, colonial encounters with Khoisan women fundamentally changed this mode of representation from one of similitude to radically alien difference.

Sander Gilman proposes that the intense medical interest in 'Hottentot' genitalia reflected a more general trend in the nineteenth-century sciences to look to physiological structures to explain or summarise individuals, especially in their difference: hence, 'the female genitalia' became particularly important in defining 'the female' in this period.[1] Undoubtedly, the rise of anthropometry and the measurement of the human body to organise individuals according to type predominated in the natural sciences, including medicine. In medicine, there could be no diagnosis of labial hypertrophy without a consideration of the size and shape of the female sexual parts. However, as we saw in Chapter 3, discussion among the medical community of clitoral and labial hypertrophy, which had been transcribed from Latin translations of Classical medical texts, predated the nineteenth century. What changed was not the emphasis on the genitals to define 'sex', for the form and function of the various vulval structures had already been incorporated into medical knowledge of anatomy and pathology; rather, with the introduction to medicine of anthropological ways of thinking, the *discourse* on sex changed from white likeness to black Otherness. In short, the medical concept of labial hypertrophy would be dramatically transformed with the colonial invention of race.

The white female body in the Galenic imagination functions as what Lacan would call the 'imago of the counterpart': as Dylan Evans explains, the imago of the counterpart forms the basis for the subject's identification with his/her sibling in the familial structure. Under this concept, the sibling's body is incorporated into the subject's imaginary processes of identification through its imagined likeness to the subject's own body.[2] The subject projects his/her ego onto this counterpart, by which it is assimilated into a comprehensible image. The Galenic understanding of female illness thus produced an 'other' body whose organs could be understood in their relation to those of men—'woman' did not, in fact, occupy so radically alterior a position. Attempts to explain the female body using the male body as a benchmark constituted a domestication of alterity, where otherness is brought back to the self as an 'other self'.[3] But with the appearance of the 'Hottentot', white naturalists were confronted with radical and unassimilable difference: it was now not enough simply to understand the workings of the white female body and its diseases. The *black* female body had to be made legible, not through similarity, but as a projection of essential and unbridgeable *difference*. In their encounters with black Others, white anthropologists sought to incorporate racial differences into a typological system that could explain human variation within a global ecology. Linnaean—and later Darwinian—theories of species purity and degeneration opened up new avenues for interpreting the human in Nature, and the female Hottentot body presented an excellent opportunity for white anthropologists to work through cultural anxieties regarding the natural limits of human constitution. Europeans were grappling with the problem of accounting for 'the human' as a product of the environment while attempting to uphold whites as a special, transcendental case. That is, European theories that wrestled with the problem of humanity as a product of the natural environment also situated white people as having natural dominion over all other animal-human life through the cultivation of techniques of civilisation that simultaneously overcame 'Nature' and natural dependency. Just as Europeans were coming face to face with the fact of the ecological human, the black woman's body made its appearance, conveniently so, to carry the animal abjected from the white ego. Or, as Martinican psychoanalyst Frantz Fanon described this racialised mechanism of projection:

> As ... In the degree to which I find in myself something unheard-of, something reprehensible, only one solution remains for me: to get rid of it, to ascribe its origin to someone else. In this way I eliminate a short circuit that threatens to destroy my equilibrium.[4]

This process of projection governs the colonial sexual imaginary and informs the historical development of the medicalisation of labial hypertrophy in Western science.

Understanding the significance of the Hottentot labia in early colonial constructions of sexual and racial difference is absolutely vital to the task of historicising the cultural reasons behind the growing demand for labiaplasty today. This indebtedness to a colonial sexual imaginary produces labiaplasty as 'white', where whiteness 'corresponds to one place in racism as a system of categorization and subject formation'.[5] The desire for cosmetic labiasty surgery exists, then, as part of a colonial psychic interrelation that produces white subjects, and the female body is the border object upon which the desire for whiteness is transcribed. I trace early colonial and racist discourses that emerged in the European imperial encounter with the women of the Cape of Good Hope to their 'unfolding into the present' as 'a "repertoire" of images or tropes' that inflect the cultural psychic investment in the labia as signifiers of intolerable difference and as the embodied site of a white conception of feminine perfection.[6]

ORIGINS OF THE HOTTENTOT APRON

The medical construction of anomalous elongated labia owes much to the colonial racial science narratives of the seventeenth to nineteenth centuries, when white anthropologists became obsessed with the size and shape of the labia of African women, specifically Indigenous Khoisan women from the Dutch colony of the Cape of Good Hope. Colonial travellers, naturalists and physicians propagated tales of a large flap or flaps of skin covering the genitals of Hottentot women, which was famously dubbed the 'Hottentot apron'. This figure of fascination attained a mythic status in colonial anthropology and the European popular consciousness, and became an iconic symbol of black female sexuality.

The historical development of labial hypertrophy as a racial phenomenon is embedded within anthropological accounts by figures such as Dutch doctor Ten Rhyne and his compatriot Peter Kolbe, and British explorer Captain Cook. The story of the Hottentot apron began in the seventeenth century. In one of the earliest known accounts, Dutch physician and geographer Olfert Dapper wrote in 1668 that 'the lining of the body appears to be loose, so that in certain places part of it dangles out'.[7] Vulval hypertrophy among Hottentot women was later described in greater detail by Ten Rhyne in 1686. He considered this to be an enlargement of the labia minora, which must only have served to confirm his view that these women were 'ugly' by European standards:

> The women may be distinguished from the men by their ugliness. And they have this peculiarity to distinguish them from other races, that most of them have dactyliform appendages, always two in number, hanging down from their pudenda. These are enlargements of the *Nymphae*, just as occasionally in our own countrywomen an elongation of the clitoris is observed. If one should happen to enter a hut full of women—the huts they call *kraals* in their idiom—then, with much gesticulation, and raising their leathern aprons, they offer these appendages to the view. A surgeon of my acquaintance lately dissected a Hottentot woman who had been strangled. He observed these finger-shaped prolongations of the *Nymphae* falling down from the private parts.[8]

As purported by the natural scientist and astronomer Peter Kolbe in 1719, *all* 'Hottentot' women possessed a 'strange Excrescence', which he described as a 'broad callous Part, growing just above the *Pudenda*, and flapping over and hiding them. It seems intended by Nature for the Concealment of those Parts; and is, in some, so large that it can hardly be cover'd by the *Kutt Kroffe*, as they call it, (a Piece of Sheep-Skin the Women wear for the Concealment of those Parts) but is often seen below it'.[9]

Captain Cook had sought to resolve speculation on the existence of the Hottentot apron upon his expedition to Cape Hope in 1771, making use of animal imagery in his description of the labia, a rhetorical technique by which black bodies were rendered more animal, or closer to Nature, than white ones:

> We were very desirous to determine the great question among natural historians whether the women of this country have or have not that fleshy flap or apron which has been called the Sinus pudoris, and what we learnt I shall relate. Many of the Dutch and Malays, who said they had received

favours from Hottentot women, positively denied its existence; but a physician of the place declared that he had cured many hundreds of venereal complaints, and never saw one without two fleshy, or rather skinny
appendages, proceeding from the upper part of the labia, in appearance
somewhat resembling the teats of a cow.[10]

Nearly fifty years later, the German anatomist Adolph Wilhelm Otto
included a description of the apron in his book *Seltene Beobachtungen
zur Anatomie, Physiologie und Pathologie gehörig*, which was first published in 1816 and reproduced in English in the medical journal *The
Lancet* in 1832. Synthesising the observations of travellers, he reported
that in addition to elongated labia majora and nymphae, Hottentot
women possessed a 'curious anomaly', which he described as 'an
extraordinary fleshy appendage, which descends before the vulva like a
valve, and which really in some respects deserves the suitable name of a
flesh-apron'.[11]

Other disagreements arose as to whether it was artificially produced
or preternatural. Explorer François Levaillant (also Le Vaillant) was the
first to theorise that the apron was an acquired, not natural, characteristic.[12] He likened 'that disgusting apron' to the enlarged prepuce that he
thought belonged to all Hottentot men, claiming, in support of accounts
purporting its existence, that the apron was 'still fashionable among a
certain horde', but that 'instead of being the gift of nature, it ought to
be considered as one of the most monstrous refinements ever invented
by I know not what coquetry'.[13] Another theory held that the apron was
not bodily skin but leather coverings that concealed the genitals, which,
according to Swedish naturalist Andrew Sparrman may have 'misled'
a traveller named Tackard, 'who, on his return to Europe, first propagated those stories concerning the natural veils or excrescences of the
Hottentot women'.[14]

From Kolbe through to Otto, the apron became an intense subject
of interest, exciting debate over whether it existed, and whether it was a
foreign physiological structure specific to Hottentot women or simply an
enlargement of the 'ordinary genitalia',[15] and whether it was natural or
acquired. By 1865, Johann Blumenbach, a notorious sceptic of anecdotal accounts, stated his belief that the 'apron' was merely a case of labial
elongation and that it should occupy the same category as 'men's tails'
to be considered 'like them, a fable'.[16]

SKETCHING SARAH BAARTMAN

The development of medical knowledge of the 'Hottentot apron' was probably most indebted to Georges Cuvier's influential post-mortem anatomical study of 1817, 'Faites sur le cadaver d'une femme connue à Paris et à Londres sous le nom de Venus Hottentotte' [Report on Observations Made on the Body of a Woman Known in Paris and London as the Hottentot Venus] (1817).[17] One of his aims, which he unquestionably achieved, was to settle the long-running disputes over the nature of the phenomenon, controversies that led him to proclaim: 'There is nothing more famous in natural history than the tablier of Hottentots, and, at the same time, no feature has been the object of so many arguments'.[18] Cuvier furnished the medical community with a report on his post-mortem examination of Saartjie 'Sarah' Baartman, a Khoi woman from the Cape of Good Hope who had been famously paraded around the European circus circuit as 'The Hottentot Venus'.

According to philosopher of the sciences Anne Fausto-Sterling, sources say Baartman was first taken in by a Boer family as servant girl and later brought to London in 1810 to be exhibited as a circus attraction.[19] She came to be widely known in Europe as the 'Hottentot Venus' and 'served as Europe's symbol of African sexuality'.[20] The 'Hottentot Venus' became part of the white popular cultural imagination, as visual representations of Baartman's body were displayed in all manner of media, from exhibition flyers to newspaper cartoons and works of art. It was through this image that 'the' African woman became defined, in the white colonial imaginary, by her protruding buttocks, which naturalists labelled 'steatopygia', and her anomalous genitals. Baartman was put on display not only for the European public, but also for men of science who were given the opportunity to 'examine' her, until her death in 1815, upon which her body was eagerly seized for post-mortem examination by Cuvier, the results of which were published in 1817.[21] These encounters would produce Baartman's body as one of the most visible and enduring examples of black femininity in the history of white colonial ethnography.

In March 1815, Sarah Baartman met Georges Cuvier and his assistant Henri de Blainville, and submitted to be drawn by a small team of artists in their employ, though she refused to let her genitals be inspected, and much to Cuvier's frustration, 'kept her apron concealed'.[22] De Blainville published his observations in 1816, aiming, among other things, to produce 'the most complete account possible of the anomaly of her reproductive organs'.[23] He failed in this endeavour, however, as, after the three days of being subjected to painstaking sketching, Baartman succeeded in keeping her genitals covered with a handkerchief. This did not prevent him from publishing an imagined account of her pudenda, replete with concocted sketches drawn, presumably, from the second-hand evidence of colonial explorers that he had already read.[24]

When Sarah Baartman died in the same year that Blainville and Cuvier first examined her, Cuvier jumped at the chance to perform an autopsy on her body. Unlike travellers' awkward attempts to gain visual access to women's bodies and then to redescribe body parts from memory or sketches—or his own attempts to persuade Baartman to reveal her genitalia to him—Cuvier had the luxury of unimpeded access to Sarah Baartman's cadaver, and was able to clarify, convincingly, that the *tablier* was indeed an enlargement of the labia minora.[25] In his article, Cuvier also clarified that Baartman was of the Bushman (also known as *Boschimans* and *Bosjesmans*), not Hottentot, race,[26] and that the apron was natural, rather than artificially produced; it could not be a product of culture because, by his rationale, it was neither beautiful nor a source of pride for the women, who, he presumed, bore it under sufferance.[27] Respected French anatomist and surgeon Alfred Velpeau paid special attention to Cuvier's clinical precision in noting that Baartman's nymphae were only three inches in length, and not six or eight as others before him had asserted.[28] It was perhaps in this that Cuvier paved the way for the beginnings of a measurable norm for the labia minora.

Cuvier took casts of Baartman's body, making a wax mould of her genitalia and preserving her skeleton. The cast and skeleton were housed at the Muséum nationale d'histoire naturelle and then the Musée de l'homme in France until the 1970s.[29] It is likely to this wax model that a student of Cuvier, Pierre Flourens, referred in a lecture on the internal and external sexual organs of females, in which he professed his belief in the correctness of Cuvier's account of the Hottentot apron: 'I now hold in my hands the sexual organs of the female … so generally known under the name of the Hottentot Venus, and you may easily convince yourselves of the justice of Cuvier's remark'.[30] Baartman's replicated genitals were hence accessible to other medical experts, ensuring Cuvier's enduring legacy as the pre-eminent scientific authority on the matter. His anatomical and intellectual coup signalled the coming of the end of intense debate over the puzzling status of the Hottentot apron and served to introduce the feature as an example of the condition that would become established in the medical literature as 'hypertrophy of the nymphae', such that in 1887, German gynaecologist Paul Zweifel could declare that 'all authorities are now agreed, as the result of autopsies ... that the Hottentot apron is due to great hypertrophy of the nymphae'.[31]

CHARLES ALEXANDRE LESUEUR AND THE CONSTRUCTION OF AN ARCHETYPE

Cuvier's opinion would eventually predominate, but it was also, importantly, a riposte to the findings of naturalist François Péron and illustrator Charles Alexandre Lesueur that had been presented to the Institute of France twelve years earlier. Péron and Lesueur argued that the Hottentot apron was inappropriately named, as it was a feature of Bushwomen, not Hottentots (a premise Cuvier accepted and incorporated into his own argument), and that it was 'a unique body, with nothing in common with the various parts of the ordinary sexual apparatus of women of other peoples' (this, Cuvier rejected).[32]

At the time he wrote his groundbreaking paper, Cuvier singled Péron's research out for critique; he argued, against Péron, that the apron was not a completely foreign appendage, but an enlargement of the labia minora, a genital structure belonging to all women of the human species, which loosely positioned him as a monogenist. Péron's contribution is an important part of the broader story anthropologists and anatomists were crafting about race and species through the figure of the Hottentot apron. In this period, the apron was embroiled in a debate between monogenists, who believed that all humans—and human races—were descended from a common origin, and polygenists, who thought that human races were originally separated. Creationist theories either traced the human races back to the pairing of Adam and Eve (monogeny) or held that the different races were put on the earth by God (polygeny). Secular theories—especially post-Darwin—proposed a prehistoric ape-like ancestor (monogeny) or suggested that human races had either evolved from an original pre-human ancestor to become distinct species of humans, or that they were derived from different species of prehistoric anthropoids (polygeny).

The existence of a genital structure unique to Bushwomen could be used by polygenists to prove that the races were different species, all ordered according to varying levels of perfection and imperfection. But for monogenists, the elongated labia of southern African women could be used to illustrate the effects of racial degeneration, according to the theory that the (perfect) humans descended from Adam and Eve had scattered the globe and degenerated into multiple races. In the secular view, the apron—whether a unique structure or an enlargement of an organ common to all women—could signify evidence of evolutionary atavism. What all of these explanatory models have in common is that they were part of a much larger scientific project that sought to explain blackness as degenerate, animal and uncivilised in order to justify white colonial domination and enslavement of black peoples. The Hottentot apron is a small but important part of this story, and its role in confirming the subordinate status of Khoisan women is implicated in the dispute between Péron and Cuvier and in the racial theories of their contemporaries.

Péron and Lesueur were French naturalists who were part of a four-year scientific expedition to the Antipodes, authorised by the French Government, from 1800 to 1804. Upon their return journey, on 3 January 1804, the two naturalists stopped at Table Bay at the Cape of Good Hope, spending three weeks there before sailing back to France. It was here that they compiled a study of the Hottentot apron, furnished with illustrations by Lesueur. Péron presented this memoire in 1805 to the Institute of France, at which Cuvier held a primary position as its Secretary.[33] However, despite Cuvier's assurances of publication, the co-authored memoire would not be published until 1883, many decades after Péron's death, when the manuscript and plates were unearthed by Gustave Lennier, Director of the Museum of Havre. Titled 'Observations sur le tablier des femmes hottentotes', the memoire appeared in the *Bulletin de la Société Zoölogique de France* (1883) and included sketches of the 'Hottentot apron' by Leseuer (Figs. 4.1a, b, c).[34] Péron and Lesueur were adamant that it was not 'a fold of skin from the belly', and although it protruded from the opening of the outer labia, they considered it entirely 'independent of the nymphae'.[35] It was an appendage belonging exclusively to Bushwomen and emerged from the 'upper commissure of the labia' supporting 'a narrow stalk descending into a larger body, which … is divided into two elongated lobes … roughly resembling a penis … [and is] about eight-and-a-half centimeters in length'.[36] After its publication, Plate 1 (Fig. 4.1a) would be reproduced in gynaecological texts as the prototypical case of

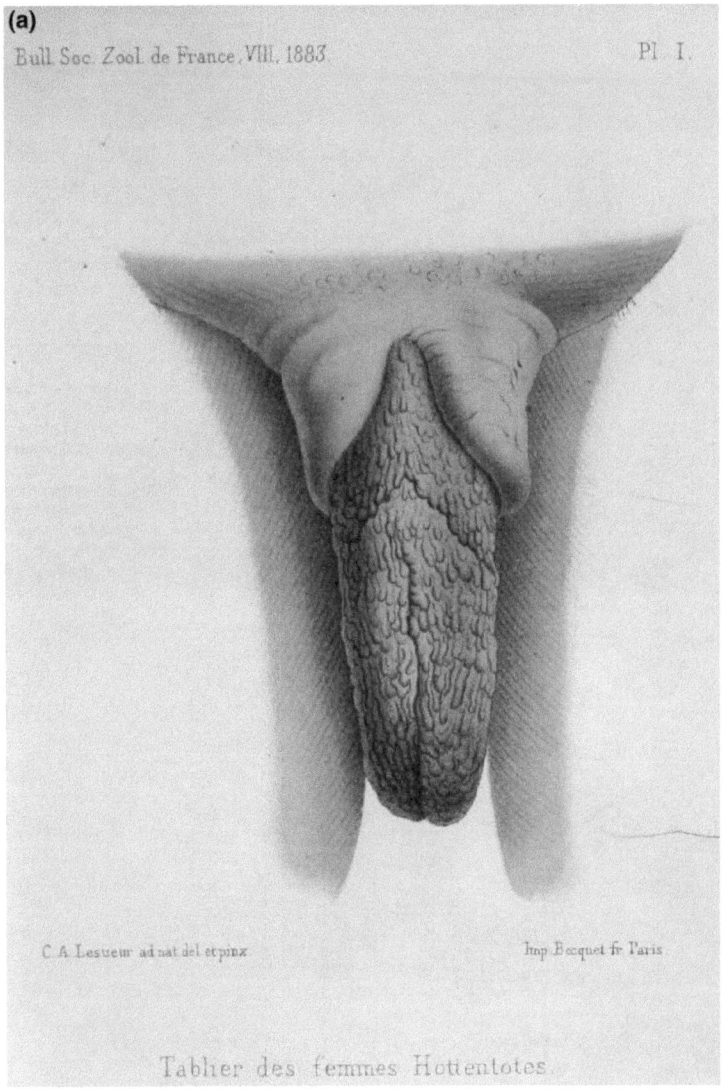

Fig. 4.1 Various illustrations of the 'Tablier des femmes Hotentotes'. François Péron and Charles Alexandre Lesueur, 'Observations sur le tablier des femmes hottentotes' [Observations on the Hottentot Apron], *Bulletin de la Société Zoölogique de France* 8 (1883). Courtesy Biodiversity Heritage Library. Digitised by Smithsonian Libraries

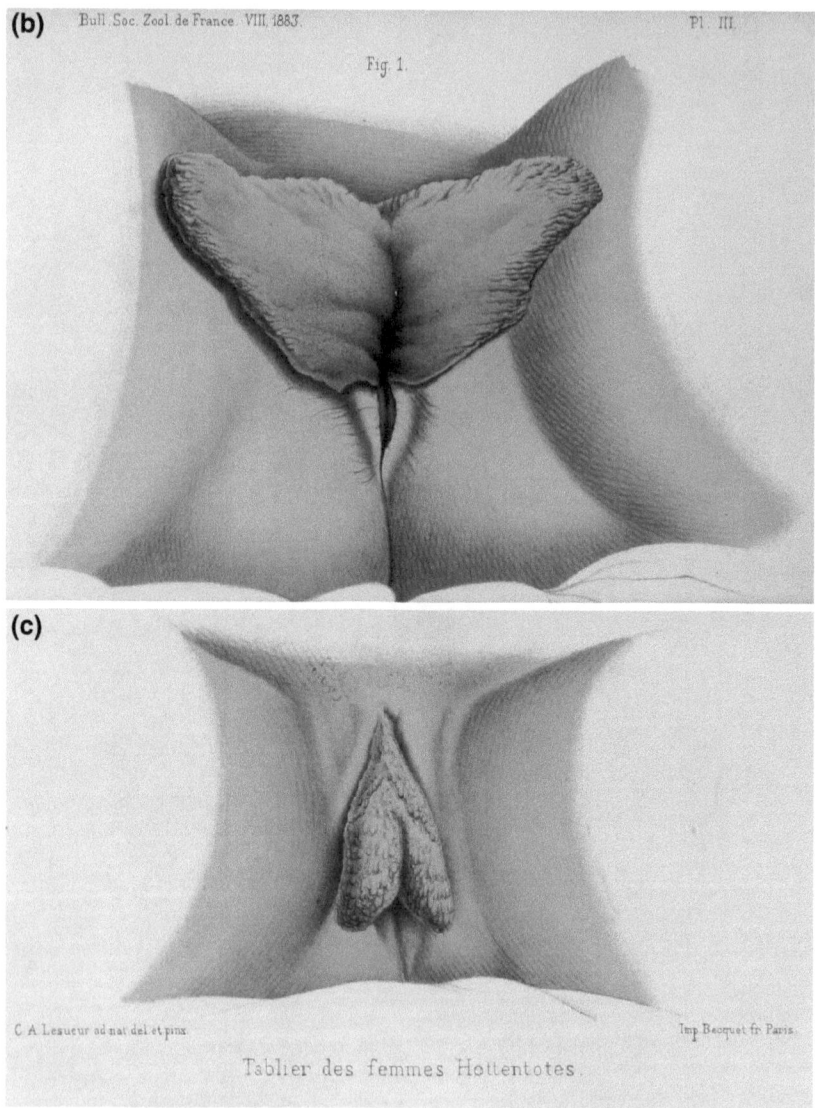

Fig. 4.1 (continued)

'hypertrophied' nymphae in the Hottenot apron.[37] Evidently, by the end of the nineteenth century, as a result of Cuvier's famous dissection, the apron was commonly understood to be a case of hypertrophy, and Lesueur's sketch could be used to illustrate this, regardless of its original context.

Prior to their publication in 1883, plates of Lesueur's illustrations had been restricted to private collections. One copy of the original drawings was held by George Ord, President of the Academy of Natural Sciences in Philadelphia, the celebrated centre of natural science research in the United States. Ord and Lesueur curated the academy's collections together, along with Thomas Say, and Ord became Lesueur's friend and biographer. In an extensive extract of his book, *A Memoir of Charles Alexander Lesueur*, reproduced in the *American Journal of Science and Arts* in 1849 (three years after Lesueur's death), Ord wrote of his 'ever-regretted' friend's 'drawings of the *Tablier*, the first, probably, that had ever been made by a competent artist'. Ord confessed he did not know whether the engravings had been published.[38] At that time, they had not, and the original illustrations remained in the hands of Lesueur's family until Lennier's recovery of as many of the original documents of the Péron and Lesueur's journey as he could find.[39]

Ord wrote that publication of the drawings in Péron and Lesueur's planned volumes on their travels—*Voyage de découvertes aux Terres Australes*—regrettably never came to fruition. He intimates that following the death of Péron, who had only completed and published one volume, Lesueur was too grief-stricken to complete the project. The task fell to Captain Louis Freycinet, who published the second volume in 1816, the Atlas of which, according to Ord, did not feature any of Lesueur's drawings. The revised 1831 edition included plates, but Ord claimed that those featuring the Hottentot apron were 'withheld from publication'.[40] An incensed associate of Ord alleged—much more bluntly—that 'the facts' about the Hottentot apron as representing species difference had been deliberately censored by Cuvier. In 1857, committed polygenist George R. Gliddon accused Cuvier of suppressing Lesueur's drawings by using his influence to prevent them from being published, supposedly because they disputed the monogenist position. Apparently, Ord had shown Gliddon the plates in his own personal collection.[41]

In his report on Sarah Baartman, Cuvier praised the accuracy of Lesueur's drawing (though he didn't include a copy of it in his paper), concurring that the 'apron' was 'a special attribute of her race', but not because it was a different organ entirely; rather, the illustration was, for him, a perfect replica of enlarged nymphae. For George Ord, however, Cuvier could not logically accept the truth of Lesueur's illustration and maintain that the apron was only an elongation of the nymphae. Such was his belief in Lesueur's illustrations as representing the truth of absolute racial difference, he was led to assert, rather hotly, that the illustrations in Cuvier's own published paper were so poor that they did not support his own case.

Péron stated that Lesueur's illustration, along with his own description, had represented this appendage 'with perfect accuracy'.[42] Though professed to be the proof of an empirically objective science, Lesueur's illustrations were in fact a visual reference for an imagined type. A number of women were brought to Péron and Lesueur, who selected from them the one whose pudenda best approximated the image of the 'Hottentot apron' that had already been composed in the anthropological literature: 'Several women of the same *species* [espéce] ... were brought; after they had been undressed, *we chose one that seemed to us the best shaped as such*.'[43] Not only did the naturalists select a particular body to be representative of racial type, but this wording suggests they thought that Hottentots and Bushwomen were separate species of woman, a polygenist position. As Bristol doctor (and known monogenist) James Prichard expressed it, Péron theorised a 'peculiar organ ... such as would afford some reason for imagining a specific diversity between them [the 'Bushman' race] and other human races'.[44] Although Péron and Lesueur clearly thought they had uncovered evidence to prove that races were essentially separate, they proposed—as an explanation for why this appendage only appeared in Bushwomen— that the apron disappeared through cross-breeding with Hottentot populations. The ambiguity of this definition, where races or 'species' are separate yet allow for hybridity, is emblematic of the immense uncertainty in this period around fixity and transformation, which, as historian Bronwen Douglas argues, 'often pivoted on the vexed question of racial crossing and its status in the unity or otherwise of the human species'.[45]

In the 1883 edition of the *Bulletin*, Péron and Lesueur's recovered memoire was immediately followed by an article by Raphael Blanchard, which introduced a similar, much expanded, theory on the apron. He drew attention to the importance of the rediscovery of Péron and

Lesueur's original research, but also sought to update their findings. Gesturing to Cuvier's opinion, he expressed surprise that an artist as conscientious as Lesueur misunderstood the character of the apron and that he and Péron came to the conclusion is was a unique organ, in spite of Laesueur's illustration, which clearly depicted the labia minora.[46] Nevertheless, Blanchard thought that this anomalous enlargement probably had an atavistic origin, since, he argued, it was also found in gorillas and in *Troglodytes Aubryi* (a species of chimpanzee).[47] By this stage, Darwinian theories of evolution could be used to explain the origins of the apron, which Blanchard duly did. He sought to address disagreement over the disputed kinship of the Bushwoman with apes or humans, suggesting that Bushwomen were indeed a human variant, though the least evolved, 'having barely crossed the threshold of humanity'.[48] Although he thought steatopygia—or fat buttocks, considered by naturalists of his time to be a defining characteristic of Bushwomen—was a sign of low development, the more convincing proof lay in the hypertrophied genital organs. These, he argued, also occured in orangutans and chimpanzees, which demonstrated that Bushwomen undoubtedly exhibited the signs of animality.[49] That these simian characters belonging properly to Bushwomen were also found among Hottentot women led him to conclude that they must be an atavism: Hottentots were more advanced than Bushmen, who were only barely advanced from anthropoid apes. This explained the appearance of hypertrophied genitals resembling those of simians in all Bushwomen and some Hottentots.[50]

Although Blanchard came down on the side of monogeny in claiming that Bushwomen were human, as did Cuvier, in reality, neither of their theories strayed very far from polygenism. The monogenist Prichard criticised Cuvier for 'erroneously' regarding the Bushmen 'to be of a different stock from the Hottentots', noting that he 'seems to have looked upon them as approximating very nearly to the Simiae'.[51] And in his report on Baartman, Cuvier's assistant de Blainville specifically stated his aim to provide a 'detailed comparison' of Baartman with 'the lowest race of humans, the Negro race, and with the highest race of monkeys, the orangutan'.[52] The white colonial understanding of the female Hottentot genitals was that they were both animal and anomalous; the labia functioned as the primary signifier for deviance from not only civilised humanity, but also femininity. Comparisons of Hottentot to animal, but especially simian, bodies are rife in early colonial accounts, which position the Khoi as the bestial intermediary between the animal and the human.[53] John Ovington, Chaplain of the ship *Benjamin* of the East India Company, wrote in 1689 that 'if there is any medium between a Rational Animal and a Beast, the Hotantot lays fairest claim to the Species',[54] and Robyn Wiegman records that in 1774, historian Edward Long wrote: 'Ludicrous as the opinion may seem, I do not think that an orang-utan husband would be any dishonour to the Hottentot female'.[55] The authors of *Anomalies and Curiosities of Medicine* (1901) make explicit the racial connection between labia size and evolutionary development, and suggest that it is because of the development of the Hottentot labia that a phylogenetic link to the orangutan can be assumed:

> Some of the lower African races have been distinguished by the deficiency in development of the labia majora, mons veneris, and genital hair. In this respect they present an approximation to the genitals of the anthropoid apes, among whom the orang-outang alone show any tendency to formation of the labia majora. The labial appendages of the Hottentot female have been celebrated for many years. Blumenbach and others of the earlier travelers found that the apron-like appearance of the genitals of the Hottentot women was due to abnormal hypertrophy of the labia and nymphae.[56]

Influential criminologist and anthropologist Cesare Lombroso wrote (with co-author and son-in-law William Ferrero) in 1893:

> Gratiolet and Alix (*Recherches sur l'anatomie des Troglodytes Aubryi*, 1886) demonstrated that in chimpanzees the outer labia are atrophied while the inner labia are highly developed. Hoffmann and Bischoff noted that in anthropoid monkeys the outer labia and mound of Venus are almost absent, while the clitoris is always highly developed and fluted on its inner surface. Moreover, the inner labia are highly developed, especially in the chimpanzee, less so in the other three species of monkey. Most of these traits are shared by Bushmen women. Anomalies of the female genitals can also be found among Europeans, although less distinctly.[57]

These studies and descriptions of the 'Hottentot apron' were generally geared towards proving, through 'scientific' methods of measurement and taxonomy, the phylogenetic difference between races and their position in the racial hierarchy, from semi-animal to civilised. They contributed to an overarching narrative among naturalists, zoologists, anthropologists, medical physicians and sexologists that the 'Hottentots' and 'Bushman' were more proximate to apes than they were to humans.

THE OTHER SEX

It was the difference between women, rather than between women and men, that so caught the imagination of nineteenth-century anthropologists and physicians writing about the Hottentot apron. As John Barrow put it in his *Account of Travels into the Interior of Southern Africa* (1801), the 'apron' was 'an extraordinary character that distinguished the other sex from the women of most nations'.[58] Hottentot women were not simply the other sex; they were the Other sex. This Otherness marked their bodies, like Africa itself, as territories to be explored, mapped out and understood. Those scientific activities that sought to denude and inspect the black female body were perversely and intimately entwined with a patriarchal colonial project that treated the land like a female body: that is, as mysterious yet open and submissive, and ultimately conquerable.

Men such as Lesueur, de Blainville and Cuvier were involved in a labour of the *imagination*: Péron and Lesueur selected a woman whose anatomy best suited their purposes, and de Blainville's portrait never arose from any visual contact he might have had with Baartman's genitalia. But let us not be deceived by Cuvier's unobstructed view and precise clinical description: he, too, contributed to the production of the Hottentot apron as a trope that could define and place the Hottentot body within a racial, and species, hierarchy. As I argued at the outset of this chapter, every account of the Hottentot apron is a product of the colonial sexual imaginary. Through empirical observation, an imaginary landscape of sex and animality emerged in the mountains of illustration and conjecture by which an image of the Hottentot Venus, and her invisible white counterpart, was drawn. What was *not* known about the apron, evidenced by its empirically contested status within the mounds of conflicting accounts, was vitally important to its construction as an indefinable *something* that excited in white observers both horror and fascination: it was 'abject', as the concept is described by psychoanalytic theorist Julia Kristeva. Abjection is the border between object and subject: alien, frightening, yet seductive. It is not Freud's uncanny, for that requires familiarity in doubling: the eerie quality of the uncanny is that we feel we have been there before. Rather, 'abjection is elaborated through a failure to recognize its kin'.[59] In the psychic landscape of the colonial sexual imaginary, the Hottentot or Bushman could not be further away from 'kin', or the human family; the 'apron' embodied, as Kristeva says of the abject, 'those fragile states where man strays on the territories of *animal*'.[60] It was the task of the sciences to confront this fear of the human animal—of the ecological ties that bound all human and animal life together—by discursive means, to populate the symbolic realm with images that could perform descriptive work in the most intimate detail while maintaining absolute separation. As Kristeva writes, the abject is the object of the phobic as that impossible body that evades linguistic representation, even as it continually forces language to speak it: 'Thus, fear having been bracketed, discourse will seem tenable only if it ceaselessly confront that otherness, a burden both repellent and repelled, a deep well of memory that is unapproachable and intimate'.[61] Although Kristeva is referring here to the mother's absent body, in the context of the colonial sciences, we may well speak of inaccessible human origins. The apron, both fearsome and compelling, encapsulated the deep anxieties that ran through the natural and medical sciences about the human in nature. It is a construct of a particular vision of the world and the place of the human in it within a distinctly European classificatory scheme that sought to explain and eject from the category of 'the human' the radically alien, black bodies with which it came into contact.

THE DIFFERENCE BETWEEN WOMEN

'Hottentot' and 'Bushman' women came to occupy the space of absolute difference between black and white, but the colonial mania for classification of type based on genital characteristics did not stop there. The difference between white, black and other races would be minutely examined in bountiful illustrations and exhaustive comparison and analysis in a major anthropological-sexological work on 'woman' by German anthropologists Heinrich Ploss, Max Bartels and Paul Bartels. Not long after the publication of Péron and Lesueur's hitherto buried memoires in 1883, the Hottentot apron became the subject of a lengthy analysis in Ploss, Bartels and Bartels's *Woman: An Historical, Gynaecological and Anthropological Compendium*.[62] With its first edition published in

German in 1885 and the eleventh published in 1927, *Woman* sold very well and served as a popular and respected authority for 'members of the medical profession, anthropologists, gynaecologists, and other men of science'.[63] By the time of its English translation in 1935, it had already become a 'well established source book of information on the anthropology, gynecology and ethnology of women'.[64] An abridged version of this book, saucily titled *Femina Libido Sexualis* (*Female Sexual Desire*), was published, somewhat surprisingly, in 1965, by the Medical Press.[65]

The 1935 edition of *Woman* provided an 'eclectic' sketch of 'the general "organism of woman" in its anthropological, psychological, and aesthetic aspects, and on the racial and ethnographical characteristics of the female genitalia'.[66] It contained detailed descriptions of female genital morphology organised by racial type, accompanied by images that are designed to illustrate pictorially racial and evolutionary difference. In *Woman*, Ploss, Bartels and Bartels explain that the 'labia minora, or nymphae, are of great importance to the anthropologist' because of racial variance, and they estimate the 'average length' to be three centimetres. Drawing upon the work of a twentieth-century French gynaecologist called Félix Jayle (see Chapter 5), they identify four types of labia: short, membranous, aleate and hypertrophic. The second type was regarded as 'normal' and the others as 'variations'.[67] It is the 'hypertrophic' type, however, that is almost exclusively attributed to 'African races', of which the Hottentot/Bushwoman is the prototypical case.[68] According to Ploss, Bartels and Bartels, the 'inner lips or nymphae in women of the Bushfolk and Hottentots are extremely and conspicuously long and pendant'.[69] They cite a post-mortem examination performed by English anatomists W. H. Flower and James Murie as having uncovered a 'defective' labia majora, in comparison to that of European women, and 'pendant flaps nearly 2 inches in length and very elastic, of so dark a red as to be almost black'. They noted, too, that Cuvier's model of the Hottentot Venus exhibited asymmetry.[70] In *Woman*, discussion and illustrations of deviant vulval morphology are restricted to non-white races, and those that fail to conform to the 'membranous' (read: white) type are considered aesthetically displeasing. Ploss, Bartels and Bartels refer to 'Japanese' genitalia as 'not aesthetically pleasing to European eyes, either in form or colour' and refer the reader to an illustration that supposedly demonstrates the offensiveness of the organ in the 'yellow races' due to 'the slightest possible development of the outer labia and a strong protuberance of the inner' (Figs. 4.2, 4.3).[71]

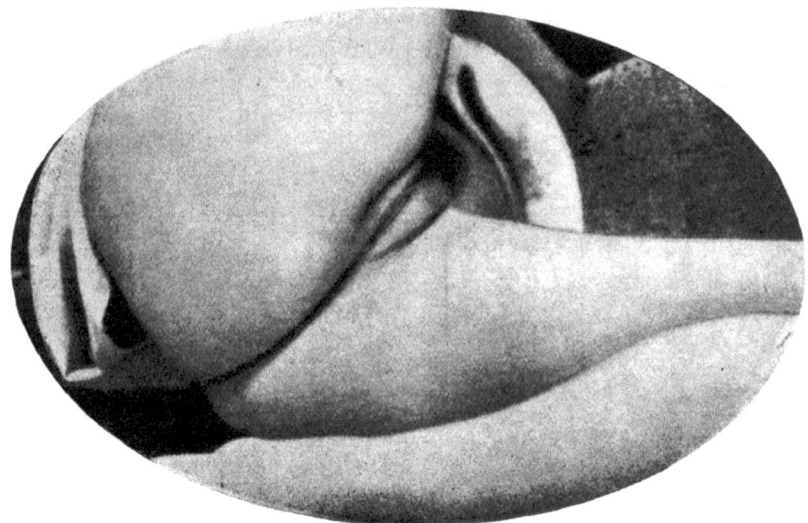

Fig. 4.2 'According to E. v. Baelz, the external genitalia of the Japanese women are not aesthetically pleasing to European eyes, either in form or colour; and this is specially the case in the aristocratic type.' Hermann Heinrich Ploss, Max Bartels and Paul Bartels, ed. and trans. Eric John Dingwall, *Woman: An Historical Gynaecological and Anthropological Compendium*, vol. 1 (London: William Heinemann, 1935), quote p. 322; fig. p. 317. Courtesy Matheson Library, Monash University, Melbourne

Woman is exemplary of what Irvin C. Schick calls 'ethnopornography' as the intersection of erotica and sexological ethnography.[72] The anthropological eye of the nineteenth century showed a fascination for the female nude, such that (female) nudity itself became an instrumental part of the Western epistemological gaze, and sexuality occupied a central role in 'shaping the form of the anthropological discourse on and of the inhabitants of Southern Africa'.[73] The ethnographic pictorial style allowed the viewer the pretence of looking at black women innocently, 'outside of the conventions of image possession and voyeurism by which [the heterosexual masculine gaze] looked at feminine spectacle'.[74] In other words, the sexualising gaze could hide its 'immoral' desires behind the veneer of legitimate scientific inquiry.

The female nudes featured in ethnographic photography offered an exotic sexuality available for the white male gaze in the conflation of

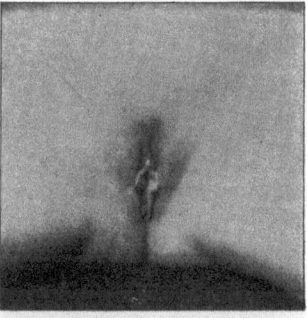

FIG. 290.—Vulva of a Korean.
(After Baelz.)

Fig. 4.3 'The illustration shows clearly the formation frequent among the yellow races, i.e., the slightest possible development of the outer labia and a strong protuberance of the inner.' Hermann Heinrich Ploss, Max Bartels and Paul Bartels, ed. and trans. Eric John Dingwall, *Woman: An Historical Gynaecological and Anthropological Compendium*, vol. 1 (London: William Heinemann, 1935), quote p. 322; fig. p. 318. Courtesy Matheson Library, Monash University, Melbourne

sexual and epistemological desire. The ethnographer's desire to know the female body was inextricable from the desire to possess it sexually. Ploss, Bartels and Bartels's *Woman* was 'reissued several times with ever increasing numbers of pictures' with each new edition 'augmented by large numbers of often explicit illustrations'.[75] The nudes in *Woman*, like those in traditional art, are conventionalised according to a visual code that makes explicit the colonial distinction between 'savage', aberrant black female sexuality and 'civilised', white beauty. Where white women are staged in classical poses against scenic shots of mountains, sea or forest, black women figure as 'natives' inhabiting the space in which they are photographed or are presented as specimens of nature for scientific study (Figs. 4.4–4.7). The labia minora are commonly depicted in the photographs in relation to their deviant, 'hypertrophic' form in the bodies of racial others: for example, in those of Japanese women and 'Bushwomen' (Figs. 4.8, 4.9). The relative paucity, in *Woman*, of photographic images of white, adult labia is a literal inscription of the invisible norm. In fact, the book's illustration of the 'normal' adult vulva is a rather artistic nude sketch (Fig. 4.10) taken from German gynaecologist Carl

Fig. 4.4 Blonde European. Hermann Heinrich Ploss, Max Bartels and Paul Bartels, ed. and trans. Eric John Dingwall, *Woman: An Historical Gynaecological and Anthropological Compendium*, vol. 1 (London: William Heinemann, 1935), 172. Courtesy Matheson Library, Monash University, Melbourne

Fig. 4.5 European Brunette. Hermann Heinrich Ploss, Max Bartels and Paul Bartels, ed. and trans. Eric John Dingwall, *Woman: An Historical Gynaecological and Anthropological Compendium*, vol. 1 (London: William Heinemann, 1935), 176. Courtesy Matheson Library, Monash University, Melbourne

Heinrich Stratz. Stratz was an early twentieth-century eugenicist who sought to provide an empirically accurate representation of female beauty through the scientific method of anthropometry (see Chapter 5).[76] It's no surprise that Stratz came to the conclusion that white women were aesthetically superior. He also understood women's central existential purpose to be the propagation of the (white) race—as opposed to men, whose duty was to themselves—and that this telos was embedded in the anatomical structure of the female body.[77] Female beauty was thus an 'expression of women's essence as reproductive creatures'[78] and racially determined. Today, the labia minora again serve as a privileged marker of bodily difference, although it is not, in the tradition of Stratz,

BEAUTY IN AMERICA

Fig. 4.6 Samoan Woman. Hermann Heinrich Ploss, Max Bartels and Paul Bartels, ed. and trans. Eric John Dingwall, *Woman: An Historical Gynaecological and Anthropological Compendium*, vol. 1 (London: William Heinemann, 1935), 192. Courtesy Matheson Library, Monash University, Melbourne

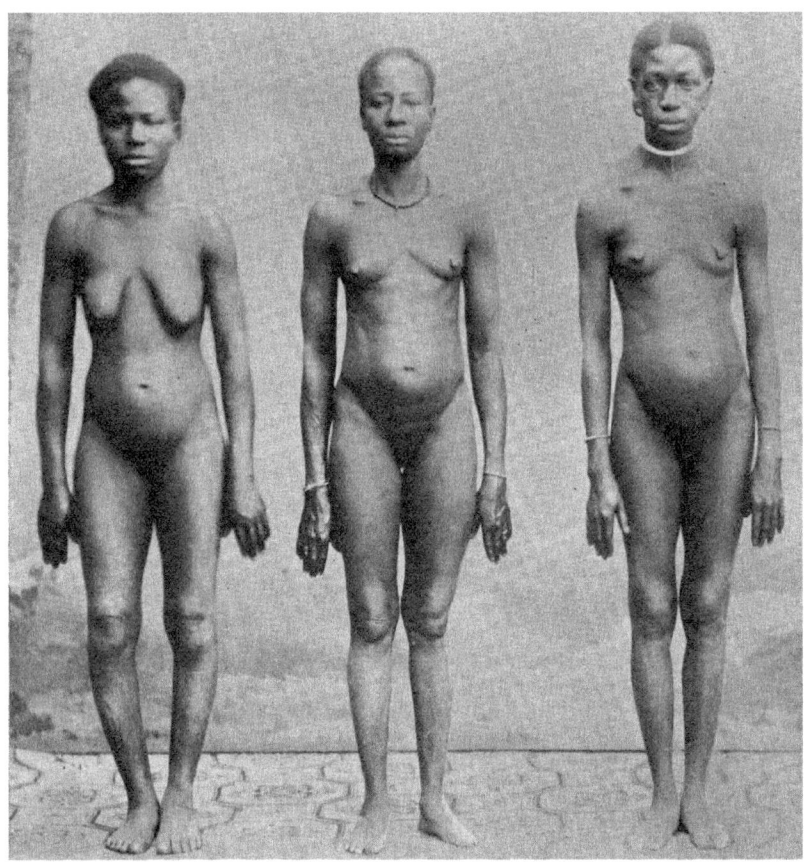

Fig. 4.7 Women from Bornu and Darfur. Hermann Heinrich Ploss, Max Bartels and Paul Bartels, ed. and trans. Eric John Dingwall, *Woman: An Historical Gynaecological and Anthropological Compendium*, vol. 1 (London: William Heinemann, 1935), 200. Courtesy Matheson Library, Monash University, Melbourne

woman's reproductive capacity that is deemed beautiful or considered the essence of femininity, rather the beautiful, feminine body is pre-pubescent and nulliparous. Figures 4.11 and 4.12 depicting nude pre-pubertal girls are particularly disturbing not just because of the evidently sex-ualised poses, but for the way in which race figures to distinguish the

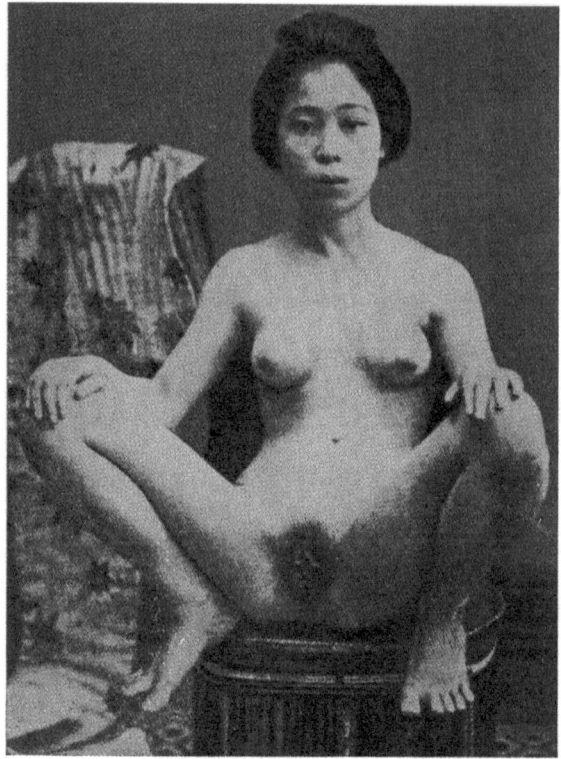

Fig. 4.8 Japanese woman with elongated nymphae. Hermann Heinrich Ploss, Max Bartels and Paul Bartels, ed. and trans. Eric John Dingwall, *Woman: An Historical Gynaecological and Anthropological Compendium*, vol. 1 (London: William Heinemann, 1935), 329. Courtesy Matheson Library, Monash University, Melbourne

pre-pubertal vagina. While the white girl stands modestly, in a stylised pose with a pet in a basket hanging from her arm, signalling the child at play, the 'Hottentot' nude is arranged upon plush fur, seductively posed with her open vulva clearly visible, in a manner reminiscent of, or perhaps foreshadowing, modern Western pornographic conventions. As feminist theorist Patricia Hill Collins has argued, 'the treatment of Black women's bodies in nineteenth-century Europe and the United States may be the foundation upon which contemporary pornography as the representation of women's objectification, domination, and control is based'.[79]

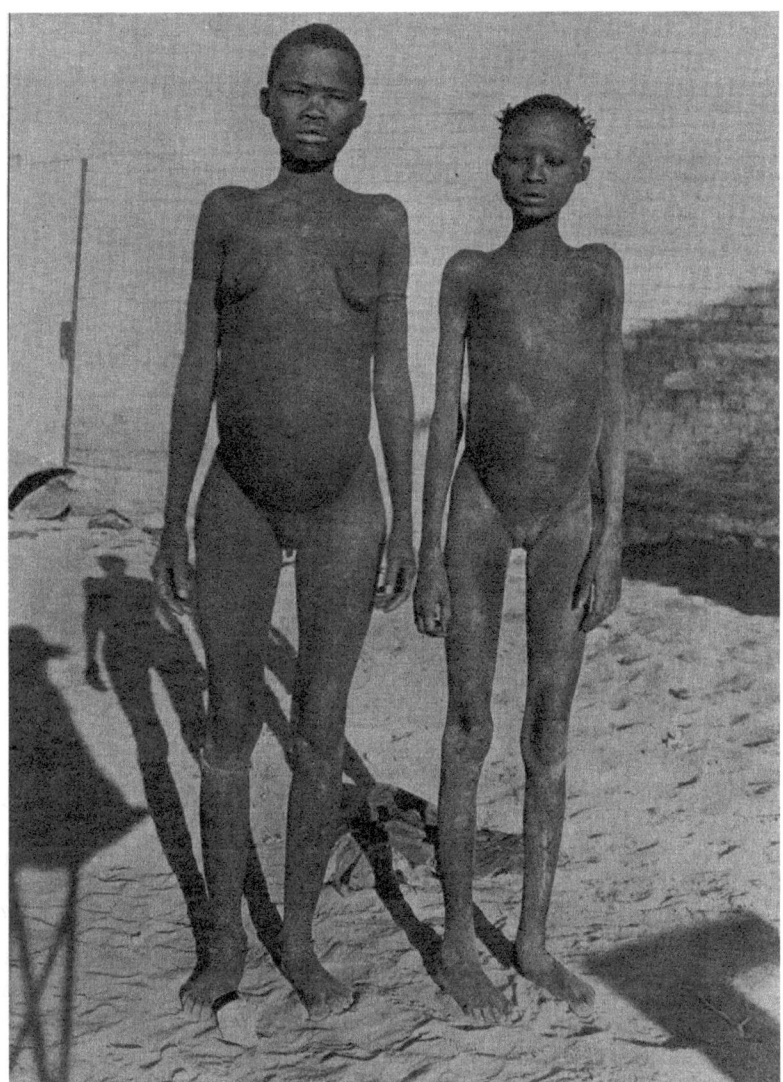

Fig. 4.9 Two Bushwomen. Hermann Heinrich Ploss, Max Bartels and Paul Bartels, ed. and trans. Eric John Dingwall, *Woman: An Historical Gynaecological and Anthropological Compendium*, vol. 1 (London: William Heinemann, 1935), 332. Courtesy Matheson Library, Monash University, Melbourne

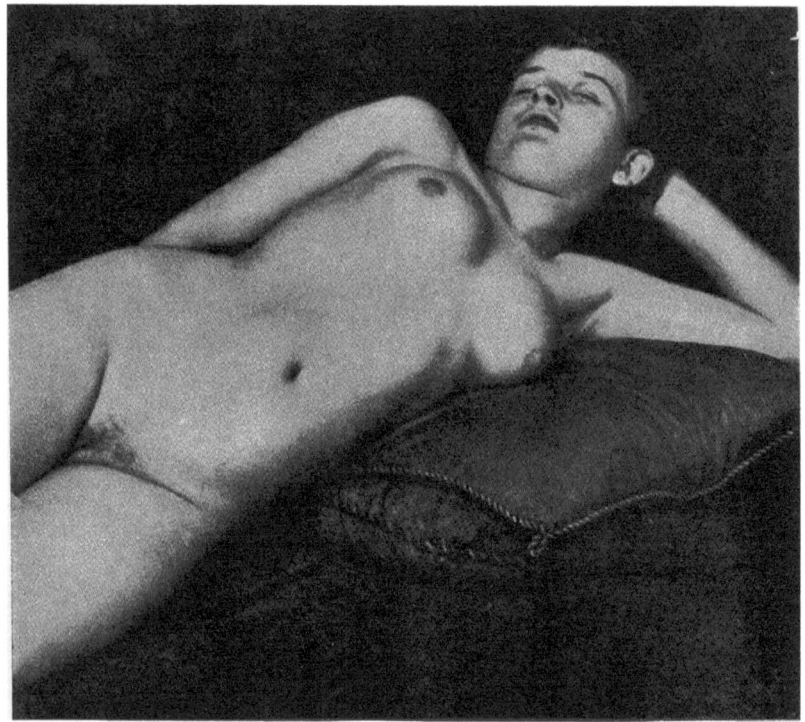

Fig. 4.10 The normal vulva with legs closed. Hermann Heinrich Ploss, Max Bartels and Paul Bartels, ed. and trans. Eric John Dingwall, *Woman: An Historical Gynaecological and Anthropological Compendium*, vol. 1 (London: William Heinemann, 1935), 6. Courtesy Matheson Library, Monash University, Melbourne

The racialised standards of female beauty and normality in *Woman* furnish us with a historical sense of the symbolic value of the labia (and the sexed body in general) in ordering types of bodies. With very few exceptions, the only 'normal' labia minora with which we are supplied is rendered through scientific illustrations (and in the Stratz illustration they are completely obscured from view), yet labia minora classified as aberrant or of a racial type are made visible in photographs of actual women, as well as through illustration. Hence, we see that the role of photography in the anthropological text is crucial to the verification and authorisation of racialised bodies. As Susan Sontag states,

Fig. 4.11 Anterior view of the vulva before puberty. Hermann Heinrich Ploss, Max Bartels and Paul Bartels, ed. and trans. Eric John Dingwall, *Woman: An Historical Gynaecological and Anthropological Compendium*, vol. 1 (London: William Heinemann, 1935), 318. Courtesy Matheson Library, Monash University, Melbourne

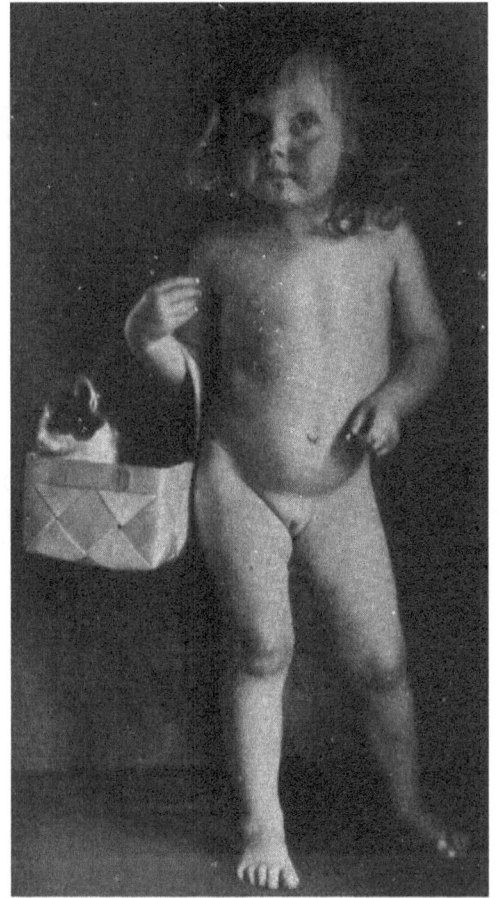

'Photographs furnish evidence'[80]; they appear to confirm that what we see in the image is a direct translation of the real, a miniaturised slice of the world. Stratz's sketch in *Woman* euphemises the naked female body by transforming it into a nude. Indeed, the romantic photographs of the Europeans and the exoticised beauty of the 'Samoan woman' emulate the conventions of the nude in art, whereas the photographs of the 'deviant' women (shown in Figs. 4.7–4.9) are stark in their attempt to portray a refusal of artifice.

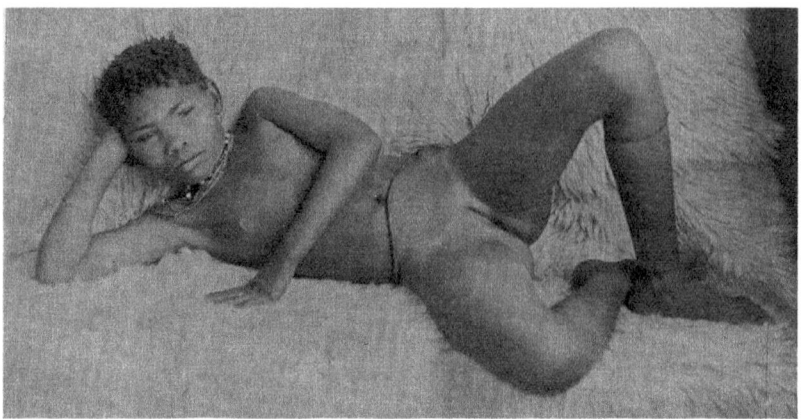

Fig. 4.12 Young Hottentot girl. Hermann Heinrich Ploss, Max Bartels and Paul Bartels, ed. and trans. Eric John Dingwall, *Woman: An Historical Gynaecological and Anthropological Compendium*, vol. 1 (London: William Heinemann, 1935), 323. Courtesy Matheson Library, Monash University, Melbourne

It is only with reference to this historical backdrop that it is possible to begin to understand some of the reasons for why the genital zone (in particular the labia) is so culturally significant in white Western nations. The very definition of labial hypertrophy as a condition cannot be separated from the racist discourses through which it came to attain its meaning as excessive, bestial or 'of nature', and beyond the bounds of that which was considered to be appropriate to the 'normal', white body.

DISPOSITION OR DISEASE?

By the turn of the twentieth century, as hypertrophy of the nymphae became more established as a medical condition, the dispute as to whether the apron was a separate structure or a case of elongated labia minora fell away and discussions of the Hottentot apron increasingly came under the sole definition of hypertrophy of the nymphae.[81] In the medical literature, post-Cuvier, doctors disagreed on the rarity of elongated labia in white populations, but what they did seem to agree on was that while hypertrophy among Hottentots/Bushwomen was normal because racially endemic, among whites it was not and therefore constituted a disease.

Army surgeon William Somerville, who was stationed at the Cape of Good Hope when the British took the colony from the Dutch, claimed that elongated labia was a natural feature belonging to Hottentot women, that the vaunted apron did thus not exist, and that it could not be considered a monstrosity or a disease because it was normal and common among these women.[82] But if this was not to be considered a health problem for Hottentot women, the same could not be said of white European women for whom elongated labia most assuredly constituted a problematic case of hypertrophy. As Zweifel flatly stated: 'Hypertrophy of the nymphae is met with among us [Europeans] as the result of disease.'[83] Gynaecologist Enoch Heinrich Kisch similarly explained: 'Hypertrophy of the nymphae, which, as the so-called *Hottentot Apron* has to be regarded as a racial peculiarity, is known also in Europe as a pathological condition which may at times constitute a hindrance to sexual intercourse.'[84] While the Hottentot apron was generally seen to be an ethnographic feature, it nonetheless served as an extreme case of a type of problem that could befall the white nymphae, though doctors disagreed on how rare it was. What was normal for Hottentot women was either unheard of in white women, or, if thought to cross racial borders, a problem of abnormal hypertrophy which could be solved, at the physician's discretion, by labial excision.

Naturalist John Barrow was adamant that the apron was a natural, yet shocking, elongation of the nymphae to a degree unthinkable in the white body: 'Nature seems to have studied how to make this pigmy race disgusting', he claimed of the Hottentots.[85] He asserted further that elongated nymphae could be found in all Hottentot women, though they were shorter 'in those of the colony' and did not appear in '*bastaards*' (mixed race offspring of slaves and Khoi women), proving, for him, that 'a connection with different nations counteracts the predisposition to such a conformation'. He also noted, likely referencing the medical literature on nymphotomia (see Chapter 3), that a similar elongation of the nymphae could be found in Egypt, which was 'situated under the same and opposite parallels of latitude as the Hottentot country'.[86] This assumption of a bodily type determined by geographic confluence brought together Classical tales of Egyptian genital deviance with newer accounts of the Hottentot anatomy. French naturalists Count de Buffon and Sonnini de Manoncourt, as well as German anatomist Adolph Wilhelm Otto, all directly compared the Hottentot apron to the vulvas of Egyptian women.[87] Otto went so far as to propose that the apron must be the same kind of genital growth cited in Classical gynaecological descriptions of circumcision in Egypt, asserting: 'It cannot be denied that this structure of the female organs of generation [among Hottentot women] is very similar to that of the Hottentot flesh-apron of the ancients ... and which presents a new and interesting form, beautifully corresponding with that already known.'[88] Elongated nymphae were commonly thought to be a problem among peoples from warmer climates generally, but particularly the Egyptians, 'Moors' and 'Copts', who were all known to practise female circumcision.[89] The assumption was that cultural rituals involving genital cutting had a rational cause: hereditary genital hypertrophies that impeded sexual congress. Mid-nineteenth-century anatomists Flower and Murie had concluded that 'the organisation is natural and congenital, and not produced, as has been supposed, by the degraded and filthy habits of the tribe'.[90] In this, they may simply have been referring to theories of ritualistic practices of manual elongation among some Indigenous South African peoples, such as the Basotho. But it is also possible that they were referring to emerging theories that labial elongation was the result of masturbation.

As I will discuss in Chapter 6, the racial explanation would be rivalled by the behavioural explanation promoted by influential twentieth-century American gynaecologist Robert Latou Dickinson, who declared that labial hypertrophy was unquestionably the result of masturbation and not biological inheritance. In 1938, an anthropologist by the name of Allan Worsley conflated the congenital and the acquired by suggesting that certain races were more disposed to masturbation: 'Among some peoples, notably the Hottentots and Abyssinians, excessive labial hypertrophy occurs as the result, it is said, of prolonged masturbation. The well-known Hottentot apron is an example.'[91] By 1948, the *British Medical Journal* had expressed scepticism at the evidence for masturbation as the cause of labial hypertrophy, with the suggestion that although labial stretching occurred 'among the women of some primitive tribes', the supposition of masturbation as an etiology was most likely exaggerated and 'impossible to prove, if only because a patient's denial of masturbation is not usually to be accepted, but it would appear that the condition is most often a developmental anomaly'.[92]

This etiological debate reflected a confusing lack of consensus as to whether the 'Hottentot apron' was a congenital racial characteristic or an acquired 'abnormality', which would continue well into the twenti-eth century. For instance, in *Obstetrics and Gynecology* journal in 1976, H. Melvin Radman attributed labial hypertrophy to both racial and sex-ual deviancy in connection with the Oriental woman:

> Most observers agree that the massive hypertrophy of the labia found in Oriental women is a post filarial condition engendered by a) blocking of the lymphatic return, b) prostitution or excessive intercourse, c) lack of cleanliness, or d) racial predisposition to skin hypertrophy.[93]

Radman went on to say that the Hottentot apron, by way of contrast, was a result of manual stretching.[94] Labial hypertrophy is not only understood to be a normal feature of the Oriental or Hottentot female body—and is thus, by implication, an abnormality among European women—but also a sign of prostitution, both of which are represented as forms of physical and moral degradation. Even as late as 1978, L. H. Honore and K. E. O'Hara would state that there are 'racial and genetic factors that determine the size and thickness of the labia minora and it is possible that these determinants are occasionally at fault, result-ing in excessively large labia minora, i.e. idiopathic labial enlargement'.[95] Contemporary articles of the last decade are still divided about the role of masturbation as a cause of labial hypertrophy, with one 2007 article stating that 'research shows no empirical evidence for an effect of sex-ual activity on labia length',[96] and another from 2011 listing 'mechan-ical irritation by excessive masturbation or intercourse' as one acquired cause.[97] Generally, the recent opinion on etiology varies: 'hypertrophy' is most likely congenital, but is also hypothesised to be caused by hor-mones, inflammation, infection, chronic stimulation, manual stretching, recurrent dermatitis, and stretching following multiple pregnancies.[98] Genetics still appears as an etiology, but explicit references to race, as well as the suspected role of masturbation appear, thankfully, to have mostly disappeared from the discussion.

Conclusion

While racial and sexual deviancy are no longer readily apparent in the medical literature—presumably because they are recognised as belong-ing to a flawed scientific explanatory model—it doesn't mean that they do not still resonate in what we might call the 'white cultural uncon-scious' as a central motivating force in the desire for labiaplasty. In this respect, I follow psychoanalytic theorist John Cash's concept of a 'politi-cal/cultural unconscious'[99] as the congealment of a discursive repertoire made available to us by the processes of a history within which we are all subjectively situated. Such a repertoire consists of 'racial imagery'[100] embedded within concrete practices of identity formation. The trick of whiteness is in the ubiquity of its visual representations which none-theless pretend to be representing everything but racial difference. Whiteness signifies itself everywhere, yet conceals its traces with the priv-ilege of historical amnesia. I suggest that the contemporary practice of cosmetic labiaplasty surgery is the resignification of an old colonial fear—of white femininity threatened by racial contamination—that refuses to show itself, except as the expression of body shame.

It is significant that contemporary cosmetic surgery websites detail-ing labiaplasty procedures usually feature images of white bodies either nude with hands obscuring the genitals or pictured in white underwear. Whiteness as a visual theme is all-pervasive—from the colour of bodies and clothing to the pale pink tint of genital skin and the idealised labia minora 'neatly' tucked away behind the labia majora, hidden from sight. The spectre of Sarah Baartman's body is uncannily recapitulated in the 'before' and 'after' photos of 'successful' labiaplasties publicly available on the internet. The historical legacy of Baartman's public display is that 'the presentation of the exotic requires a definition of the normal',[101] which is exactly what before-and-after photos are specifically designed to produce. Feminist theorists Virginia Braun and Leonore Tiefer affirm that with 'the numerous before-and-after photos on surgeon websites or occasional clinical case reports of labiaplasty … we are expected to natu-rally agree that the "after" shot is an improvement on the "before"'.[102] What is most striking about these pictures is that the eye is drawn to the exotic, unsightly pre-surgery vagina, the abhorrence of which is visually attested through its opposition to the 'normal', neat vagina, with its invisible labia minora. There is a double comparison at work here: one between the abnormal and the normal ('this looks nicer than that'), and the other between image and viewer ('does mine look like that?'). It's difficult not to be seduced by the alluring representation of difference offered up by the image in the fascinated consumption of a disgusting, *abject*, Other. With the assistance of technological 'progress', the white vagina has 'evolved' to be even more compact and devoid of that which the white colonial imagination, a cultural imaginary that is with us still, represents as 'animal'. The growing demand for labiaplasty procedures is only 'new' insofar as it resurrects, albeit in a different fashion, historically entrenched narratives in the colonial sexual imaginary that make the female body a border object: a historical and cultural artefact situated between human and animal, white and black.

NOTES

1. Sander L. Gilman, 'Black Bodies, White Bodies: Toward an Iconography of Female Sexuality in Late Nineteenth-Century Art, Medicine and Literature', *Critical Inquiry* 12, no. 1 (1985): 216.
2. Dylan Evans, *An Introductory Dictionary of Lacanian Psychoanalysis* (London and New York: Routledge, 1996), 28–9.
3. Pheng Cheah, 'The Material World of Comparison', in *Comparison: Theories, Approaches, Uses*, ed. Rita Felski and Susan Stanford Friedman (Baltimore, Johns Hopkins University Press, 2013), 189n24.
4. Frantz Fanon, *Black Skin, White Masks* (London: Pluto Press, 1967), 190.
5. Ruth Frankenberg. 'Introduction: Local Whitenesses, Localizing Whiteness', in *Displacing Whiteness: Essays in Social and Cultural Criticism*, ed. Ruth Frankenberg (Durham: Duke University Press. 1999), 9.
6. Frankenberg, 'Introduction', 11.
7. Isaac Schapera and B. Farrington, ed. and trans., *The Early Cape Hottentots Described in the Writings of Overt Dapper (1668), Willem ten Rhyne (1686), and Johannes Gulielmus de Grevenbroek (1695)* (Cape Town: Van Riebeeck Society 1933), 45. http://www.dbnl.org/tekst/ dapp001earl01_01/dapp001earl01_01.pdf. Citations refer to the web edition.
8. Ten Rhyne, in Schapera and Farrington, *The Early Cape Hottentots*, 115.
9. Peter Kolbe, *The Present State of the Cape of Good Hope and the Hottentots*, trans. Mr Medley (London: W. Innys, 1731), 118. Originally published in German as *Caput Bonae Spei Hodiernum, das ist vollständige Beschreibung des Afrikanischen Vorgebürges der Guten Hoffnung* (Nürnberg, 1719). According to Velpeau, the apron became a subject of interest from Kolbe onwards. See Alfred Velpeau, *An Elementary Treatise of Midwifery; Or, the Principles of Tokology and Embryology*, trans. Charles D. Meigs (Philadelphia: Lindsay and Blakiston, 1845), 89–90.

10. Cook, cited in Robert J. Gordon, 'The Venal Hottentot Venus and the Great Chain of Being', *African Studies* 51, no. 2 (1992): 186–7.

11. Adolph Wilhelm Otto, 'Anatomical Description of the Organs of Generation in a Hottentot Female', *The Lancet* 19, no. 478 (1832): 148.

12. Hermann Heinrich Ploss, Max Bartels and Paul Bartels, ed. and trans. Eric John Dingwall, *Woman: An Historical Gynaelogical and Anthropological Compendium*, vol. 1 (London: William Heinemann, 1935), 327.

13. Francois Levaillant, *Travels into the Interior Parts of Africa*, vol. 2, translated from the French (London: Printed for G. G. J. and J. Robinson, 1790), 112–13.

14. Quotation in Andrew Sparrman, *A Voyage to the Cape of Good Hope*, vol. 1, translated from the Swedish original (London: Printed for G. G. J. and J. Robinson, 1785). His opinion on the 'apron' was reproduced in the *Encyclopaedia Britannica*, vol. 8, 3rd ed. (Edinburgh: Printed for A. Bell and C. Macfarquhar, 1797). For debate over its artificial or natural status, see Paolo Mantagazza, *The Sexual Relations of Mankind*, trans. Samuel Putnam (Honolulu: University Press of the Pacific, [1935] 2001), 117.

15. Stephen Jay Gould, *The Flamingo's Smile: Reflections in Natural History* (New York and London: W. W. Norton and Company, 1985). Kindle Edition, loc. 3949–3951.

16. Johann Blumenbach, *The Anthropological Treatises of Johann Friedrich Blumenbach*, ed. and trans. Thomas Bendyshe (London: Longman, Green, Longman, Roberts and Green, 1865), 143.

17. Georges Cuvier, 'Extrait d'observations faites sur le cadaver d'une femme connue à Paris et à Londres sous le nom de Venus Hottentotte' ['Report on observations made on the body of a woman known in Paris and London as the Hottentot Venus'], *Mémoires du Musée nationale d'histoire naturelle* 3 (1817): 259–74. For a full account of Cuvier and his assistant de Blainville's influential contributions to medical discourse on the 'Hottentot Apron', see Anne Fausto-Sterling, 'Gender, Race, and Nation: The Comparative Anatomy of "Hottentot" Women in Europe, 1815–1817', in *Deviant Bodies*, ed. Jennifer Terry and Jacqueline Urla (Bloomington and Indianapolis: Indiana University Press, 1995), 19–48. Cuvier is cited as an authority by Alfred Velpeau, Pierre Flourens and American Charles D. Meigs. See Alfred Velpeau, *Velpeau's Anatomy of Regions*, trans. Henry Hancock (London: Printed for Longman, Orme, Brown, Green, and Longmans, 1838), 337; Alfred Velpeau, *An Elementary Treatise on Midwifery*, 90; Pierre Flourens, 'Lectures on Human Embyology', in *The Lancet for 1834–35. In Two*

Volumes. Volume the Second, ed. Thomas Wakley (London: Mills and Son, 1835), 565; Charles D. Meigs, *Woman: Her Diseases and Remedies* (Philadelphia: Blanchard and Lea, 1859), 99–100.

18. Cuvier, cited in Gordon, 'The Venal Hottentot Venus', 187.
19. Fausto-Sterling, 'Gender, Race, and Nation', 28.
20. Robyn Wiegman, *American Anatomies: Theorizing Race and Gender* (Durham and London: Duke University Press, 1995), 58.
21. Gilman, 'Black Bodies, White Bodies', 213.
22. Fausto-Sterling, 'Gender, Race, and Nation', 32–3; Clifton Crais and Pamela Scully, *Sara Baartman and the Hottentot Venus: A Ghost Story and a Biography* (Princeton: Princeton University Press, 2009), 135.
23. de Blainville, cited in Fausto-Sterling, 'Gender, Race, and Nation', 33.
24. Allison P. Coudert, 'From the Clitoris to the Breast: The Eclipse of the Female Libido in Early Modern Art, Literature, and Philosophy', in *Sexuality in the Middle Ages and Early Modern Times: New Approaches to a Fundamental Cultural-Historical and Literary-Anthropological Theme*, ed. Albrecht Classen (Berlin and New York: Walter de Gruyter, 2008), 851.
25. Gould, *The Flamingo's Smile*, loc. 3955–3958.
26. Flourens, 'Lectures on Human Embryology', 565; Fausto-Sterling, 'Gender, Race, and Nation', 35–6.
27. Denean Sharpley-Whiting, 'Writing Sex, Writing Difference: Creating the Master Text on the Hottentot Venus', in *Gender Relations in Global Perspective: Essential Readings*, ed. Nancy Cook (Toronto: Canadian Scholars' Press, 2007), 312–13.
28. Velpeau, *An Elementary Treatise on Midwifery*, 90.
29. Peter Wade, *Race: An Introduction* (Cambridge: Cambridge University Press, 2015), 70.
30. Flourens, 'Lectures on Human Embryology', 565.
31. Paul Zweifel, 'Diseases of the External Female Genitals; lacerations of the Perineum', in *Cyclopaedia of Obstetrics and Gynecology*, vol. 12, ed. Egbert H. Grandin (New York: William Wood and Company, 1887), 228.
32. François Péron and Charles Alexandre Lesueur, 'Observations sur le tablier des femmes hottentotes' [Observations on the Hottentot Apron], *Bulletin de la Société Zoölogique de France* 8 (1883), 21, my translation.
33. Gustave Lennier, 'Note sur l'expédition française des terres australes pendant les années 1802 a 1804' ['Note on the French Expedition to the Southern Lands in the years 1802 to 1804'], in *Bulletin de la Société Zoölogique de France* 8 (1883).

34. Péron and Lesueur, 'Observations sur le tablier'. For information on the delayed publication of the memoire, see E. A. Hooten, 'Some Early Drawings of Hottentot Women', in *Varia Africana II*, ed. Oric Bates (Cambridge: The African Department of the Peabody Museum of Harvard University, 1918), 84; C. Plug, 'Peron, Francois', S2A3 Biographical Database of Southern African Science, http://www.s2a3.org.za/bio/Biograph_final.php?serial=2176.
35. Péron and Lesueur, 'Observations sur le tablier', 21, 28, my translation. See also David D. Davis, *Elements of Obstetric Medicine* (London: Printed for Taylor and Walton, 1841), 56.
36. Péron and Lesueur, 'Observations sur le tablier', 17, my translation.
37. See for example Zweifel, 'Diseases of the External Female Genitals', illustration located opposite page 226; John Bland-Sutton and Arthur E. Giles, *The Diseases of Women: A Handbook for Students and Practitioners* (London: Rebman Publishing Co., 1897), 78; Enoch Heinrich Kisch, *The Sexual Life of Woman in Its Physiological and Hygienic Aspects*, trans. M. Eden Paul (New York: Rebman Company, c. 1910), 329.
38. George Ord, 'A Memoir of Charles Alexander Lesueur. Read before the American Philosophical Society, at the stated meeting, on the 6th of April, 1849', in *The American Journal of Science and Arts*, second series, vol. 8 (1849): 205.
39. Gustave Lennier, 'Note sur l'expédition française des terres australes pendant les années 1802 a 1804' ['Note on the French Expedition to the Southern Lands in the years 1802 to 1804'], in *Bulletin de la Société Zoölogique de France* 8 (1883): 7.
40. Ord, 'A Memoir of Charles Alexander Lesueur', 210.
41. George R. Gliddon, 'Commentary upon the Principal Distinctions Observable among the Various Groups of Humanity', in *Indigenous Races of the Earth*, ed. Alfred Maury, Francis Pulszky, J. Aitken Meigs, J. C. Nott and Geo. R. Gliddon (Philadelphia and London: J. B. Lippincott and Co., Trubner and Co., 1857), 628.
42. Péron and Lesueur, 'Observations sur le tablier', 17, my translation.
43. Péron and Lesueur, 'Observations sur le tablier', 17, my translation and emphasis.
44. James Cowles Prichard, *Researches into the Physical History of Mankind*, 3rd ed., vol. 2 (London: Sherwood, Gilbert and Piper, and J. and A. Arch, 1837), 329.
45. Bronwen Douglas, 'Climate to Crania: Science and the Racialization of Human Difference', in *Foreign Bodies: Oceania and the Science of Race 1750–1940*, ed. Bronwen Douglas and Chris Ballard (Canberra: ANU E Press, 2008), 58.

46. Raphael Blanchard, 'Etude sur la steatopygie et le tablier des femmes boschimanes' [Study on the steatopygie and the apron of the Bushman women], *Bulletin de la Société Zoölogique de France* 8 (1883): 54.
47. Cesare Lombroso and Guglielmo Ferrero, *Criminal Woman, the Prostitute, and the Normal Woman*, trans. Nicole Hahn Rafter and Mary Gibson (Durham and London: Duke University Press, [1893] 2004), 53.
48. Blanchard, 'Etude sur la steatopygie et le tablier des femmes boschimanes', 67, my translation.
49. Blanchard, 'Etude sur la steatopygie et le tablier des femmes boschimanes', 73.
50. Blanchard, 'Etude sur la steatopygie et le tablier des femmes boschimanes', 74. See also Zweifel, 'Diseases of the External Female Genitals, 228–9.
51. Prichard, *Researches into the Physical History of Mankind*, 329.
52. de Blainville, cited in Fausto-Sterling, 'Gender, Race, and Nation', 33.
53. Fausto-Sterling, 'Gender, Race, and Nation', 36.
54. Ovington, cited in Margaret T. Hodgen, *Early Anthropology in the Sixteenth and Seventeenth Centuries* (Philadelphia: University of Pennsylvania Press, 1964), 422.
55. Long, cited in Wiegman, *American Anatomies*, 57.
56. George M. Gould and Walter L. Pyle, *Anomalies and Curiosities of Medicine* (Electronic Text centre, University of Virginia Library. [1901] 1997), 306–7, http://etext.lib.virginia.edu/toc/modeng/public/GouAnom.html.
57. Lombroso and Ferrero, *Criminal Woman*, 53–55.
58. John Barrow, *An Account of Travels into the Interior of Southern Africa* (London: Printed by A. Strahan, 1801), 278.
59. Julia Kristeva, 'Powers of Horror', in *The Portable Kristeva*, ed. Kelly Oliver (New York: Columbia University Press, 2002), 233.
60. Kristeva, 'Powers of Horror', 239, emphasis in original.
61. Kristeva, 'Powers of Horror', 234.
62. Ploss, Bartels and Bartels, *Woman*.
63. M. F. Ashley-Montagu, review of *Woman: An Historical Gynaecological Compendium*, by Hermann Heinrich Ploss; Max Bartels; Paul Bartels; Eric John Dingwall; William Heinemann, *Isis* 25 no. 1 (1936): 169.
64. Unsigned review of *Woman: An Historical Gynaecological and Anthropological Compendium*, by Hermann Heinrich Ploss, Max Bartels and Paul Bartels, ed. Eric John Dingwall, *JAMA* 106, no. 9 (1936): 733.

65. Herman Heinrich Ploss, Max Bartels and Paul Bartels, ed. Eric John Dingwall, *Femina Libido Sexualis: Compendium of the Sexual Characteristics of the Woman* (New York: The Medical Press, 1965).

66. Unsigned review of *Woman: An Historical Gynaecological and Anthropological Compendium*, by Hermann Heinrich Ploss, Max Bartels and Paul Bartels, ed. Eric John Dingwall, *BMJ* 1, no. 3913 (1936): 17.

67. Ploss, Bartels and Bartels, *Woman*, 312.

68. Ploss, Bartels and Bartels, *Woman*, 323.

69. Ploss, Bartels and Bartels, *Woman*, 327.

70. Ploss, Bartels and Bartels, *Woman*, 327–8.

71. Ploss, Bartels and Bartels, *Woman*, 322.

72. Irvin C. Schick, *The Erotic Margin: Sexuality and Spatiality in Alterist Discourse* (London and New York: Verso, 1999).

73. Gordon. 'The Venal Hottentot Venus', 185.

74. Liz Conor, *The Spectacular Modern Woman: Feminine Visibility in the 1920s* (Bloomington and Indianapolis: Indiana University Press, 2004), 203.

75. Schick, *The Erotic Margin*, 79–80.

76. Michael Hau, *The Cult of Health and Beauty in Germany* (Chicago: University of Chicago Press, 2003), 42.

77. Hau, *The Cult of Health and Beauty*, 69.

78. Hau, *The Cult of Health and Beauty*, 70.

79. Patricia Hill Collins, *Black Feminist Thought: Knowledge, Consciousness, and the Politics of Empowerment* (New York and London: Routledge, 2000), 147.

80. Susan Sontag, *On Photography* (London and New York: Penguin, 1971), 5.

81. For example, see John Burns, *The Principles of Midwifery* (London: Longman, Orme, Brown, Green and Longmans, 1837), 67; Velpeau, *Velpeau's Anatomy of Regions*, 337 and *An Elementary Treatise on Midwifery*, 89–90; Jean Cruveilhier, *The Anatomy of the Human Body*, ed. Granville Sharp Pattinson (New York: Harper and Brothers, 1844), 471; Charles D. Meigs, *Females and Their Diseases* (Philadelphia: Lea and Blanchard, 1848), 81 and *Obstetrics: The Science and the Art* (Philadelphia: Lea and Blanchard, 1849), 78; Wooster Beach, *An Improved System of Midwifery* (New York: Charles Scribner, 1851), 36; John King, *Women: Their Diseases and Their Treatment* (Cincinatti: Longley Brothers, 1858), 22; Franz Winckel, *Diseases of Women*, trans. J. H. Williamson and Theophilus Parvin (Philadelphia: P. Blakiston, Son and Co., 1887), 31; J. M. Baldy, ed., *An American Text-Book of Gynecology, Medical and Surgical, for Practitioners and Students* (Philadelphia: W. B. Saunders, 1894), 164; Sutton and Giles, *The*

Diseases of Women, 78; Barton Cooke Hirst, *A Text-Book of Diseases of Women* (Philadelphia: W. B. Saunders and Company, 1903), 72; Kisch, *The Sexual Life of Woman*, 328.

82. William Somerville, 'Observationes Quaedam de Hottentotis, Paesertim de Structura Genitalium Peculiari Hottentotarum', *Medico-Chirurgical Transactions*, vol. 7 (London: Printed for Longman, Hurst, Rees, Orme and Brown, 1816), 154–60. This account is republished in English translation in *William Somerville's Narrative of His Journeys to the Eastern Cape Frontier and to Lattakoe 1799–1802* (Cape Town: Van Riebeeck Society, 1979).

83. Zweifel, 'Diseases of the External Female Genitals', 230.

84. Enoch Heinrich Kisch, *The Sexual Life of Woman*, 328.

85. Barrow, *An Account of Travels*, 279.

86. Barrow, *An Account of Travels*, 280–1.

87. Count de Buffon, *Natural History, General and Particular*, vol. 3, trans. William Smellie (London: Printed for Strahan and T. Cadell, 1786); C. S. Sonnini, *Travels in Upper and Lower Egypt*, vol. 2, trans. Henry Hunter (London, Printed for John Stockdale, 1799); Otto, 'Anatomical Description'.

88. Otto, 'Anatomical Description', 148.

89. See for example W. Lawrence, *Lectures on Physiology, Zoology and the Natural History of Man* (London: Benbow, 1822), 366; Beach, *An Improved System of Midwifery*, 36.

90. C. W. D., 'Flower and Murie on the Dissection of a Bushwoman', *Anthropological Review* 5, nos. 18/19 (1867): 322.

91. Allan Worsley, 'Infibulation and Female Circumcision: A Study of a Little-Known Custom', *BJOG* 45, no. 4 (1938): 690.

92. 'Enlarged Labia Minora', *BMJ* 1, no. 4540 (1948): 85.

93. H. Melvin Radman, 'Hypertrophy of the Labia Minora', *Obstetrics and Gynecology* 48, no. 1 (1976): 79s.

94. Radman, 'Hypertrophy of the Labia Minora', 79s.

95. L. H. Honore and K. E. O'Hara, 'Benign Enlargement of the Labia Minora: Report of Two Cases', *European Journal of Obstetrics and Gynecology and Reproductive Biology* 8, no. 2 (1978): 63.

96. R. Bramwell, C. Morland and A. Garden, 'Expectations and Experience of Labial Reduction: A Qualitative Study', *BJOG* 114, no. 12 (2007): 1493.

97. Mayer Horacio, Maria Elizalde, Natalia Duh and Hugo Loustau, 'Bidimensional Labia Minora Reduction', *European Journal of Plastic Surgery* 34, no. 5 (2011): 345.

98. Costas H. Pappis and Philip S. Hadzihamberis, 'Hypertrophy of the Labia Minora', *Pediatric Surgery International* 2, no. 1 (1987): 50–1;

H. Sakamoto, G. Ichikawa, Y. Shimizu, A. Kikuchi and T. Yamamoto, 'Extreme Hypertrophy of the Labia Minora', *Acta Obstetricia et Gynecologica Scandinavica* 83, no. 12 (2004): 1225–6; Amiria Lynch, Mohan Marulaiah and Udaya Samarakkody, 'Reduction Labioplasty in Adolescents', *Journal of Pediatric and Adolescent Gynecology* 21, no. 3 (2008): 147–9; Oren M. Tepper, Marcelo Wulkan and Alan Matarasso, 'Labioplasty: Anatomy, Etiology, and a New Surgical Approach', *Aesthetic Surgery Journal* 31, no. 5 (2011): 511–18.

99. John Cash, 'The Political/Cultural Unconscious and the Process of Reconciliation', *Postcolonial Studies* 7, no. 2 (2004): 166.
100. Richard Dyer, *White* (London and New York: Routledge, 1997), 1.
101. Fausto-Sterling, 'Gender, Race, and Nation', 30.
102. Virginia Braun and Leonore Tiefer, 'The "Designer Vagina" and the Pathologisation of Female Genital Diversity: Interventions for Change', *Radical Psychology: A Journal of Psychology, Politics and Radicalism* 8, no. 1 (2009).

CHAPTER 5

Sexual Anthropometry

In 2015, American Law graduate and sex toy manufacturer Brian Sloan devised and ran the 'Autoblow Vaginal Beauty Contest', garnering the interest of 182 female entrants aged 18 and over who submitted photos of their vulvas via an online recruitment page. Monetary prizes of US$5,000, US$2,500 and US$1,250 were offered to first, second and third place. The photos were then voted on by 134,707 people (81 per cent of them men) from 191 countries. The three winners were white women from European countries ('Nell', Scotland; 'Jenny', Bavaria; and 'Anita', Hungary), who were subsequently flown to Berlin to have their vulvas 3D-scanned to feature as 'vagina sleeves' for the Autoblow2 oral sex simulator for men.[1] When the three winners met with Sloan in Berlin, their vulvas were copied in fine detail and digitally translated by a 3D scanner for a faithful replication. The video of the process shows a painfully awkward transaction: 'Jenny' said during the process, 'I'll just pretend that I'm not here anymore', as if wishing to erase herself. While one woman's vulva is being 'arranged' by male assistants, Sloan remarks with a grimace that 'It's like waiting at the bank'—he clearly just wants the messy human ethics to be over before turning the flesh into saleable silicone divorced from the means of its production. 'Anita' revealed that 'I was very uncomfortable. It was like being at the doctor's'.[2]

What is most intriguing about this story of American capitalist ingenuity is that Sloan commissioned a 'scientific' study of the data he had collected.[3] The result was a parodic—or, perhaps more appropriately, ironic—self-published paper produced by an anonymous 'group of data

C. Nurka, *Female Genital Cosmetic Surgery*,
https://doi.org/10.1007/978-3-319-96490-4_5

scientists',[4] who coded the vulvas and sorted them into distinct types and also determined which of the types was most desired by the voters. Of the 182 submissions, 110 photographs from 21 countries were selected for the 'Vulva Paper'. Photos were only included if clitoral hood size, labia size, labia minora protrusion and rugosity (how smooth or wrinkled the labial surface is) could be measured or otherwise adequately assessed by the researchers from the photograph. Using statistical clustering methods, the researchers arrived at six types, which ranged from 'simple' to 'complex', beginning with non-protuberant and soft labia minora and ending with those most wrinkled and protuberant. The purported aim of the 'Vulva Paper' was to 'assess the diversity in vulval morphology and voters' preference for different morphologies'.[5] It found, unsurprisingly, that of the six 'styles', the 'simple' type was preferred. Bizarrely, it included in its three citations two legitimate feminist studies on labial diversity published in *BJOG* and *Medical Humanities*, both of which suggest that representations of labia minora in the sex industry, specifically pornography, conform to a current patriarchal ideal (small, pink and non-protuberant) and do not reflect the broad range of vulval varieties among women.[6]

Sloan's beauty contest and statistical study together produce an idea of what constitutes the most beautiful vulva, and therefore what is most desired by straight men: this then becomes the measure of a woman's bodily worth, both to those appraising her and to herself. The measure of vulval beauty is literalised in the pains Sloan's 'scientific' observers took to measure the length and protrusion of the labia minora in the photos using an on-screen ruler. Sloan's social scientists used anthropometry (measurement of the human body) to establish a vulval beauty norm. In the institutional practice of the beauty pageant, the 'norm'— Beauty—is the image of what is assumed to be the most desirable for the most people. Michel Foucault explains normalisation as an organising force which takes bodies as its target and submits them to ranking systems and models of inclusion and exclusion. Normalisation, Foucault explains, is a rule that can function 'as a minimal threshold, as an average to be respected or as an *optimum towards which one must move*'.[7] It is a measure that 'compares, differentiates, hierarchizes, homogenizes, excludes'.[8] If anthropometry is a disciplinary technique that has been used by Sloan to establish a norm of female beauty, then we can say that the women's body parts are ranked from most to least desirable and that the criteria for inclusion into the optimum category (The Vulva Paper's 'class 1' type) are small, non-protuberant labia minora encased within pinkish-white labia majora.[9]

It is not hard to see how this contest produces a beauty norm so that Sloan can capitalise on female submission to a heterosexual male gaze; and it is easy enough to link this particular porn ideal (non-protuberant labia) to incidence of labiaplasty. Yet I begin with the Autoblow beauty contest not to confirm this hypothesis, but to suggest that we turn our attention to the submerged history of anthropometry that re-emerges in this contemporary example, where science and desire meet in a clinical process that submits the female body to an authoritative male gaze. As I will show in this chapter, the science of measurement that Sloan used for the 'Vulva Paper' has its roots not in the sex industry or in pornography, but in early-twentieth-century medicine. We catch a glimpse of this vestigial disciplinary presence in participant Anita's comment that the process of having her vulva scanned was 'like being at the doctor's'.

This chapter departs from the statistical calculation of vulval types for commercial profit in the contemporary sex industry to cut a path that winds back to earlier mathematical genital typologies developed in the interests of expanding medical knowledge of health and illness. In what follows, I explore how scientific practices of anthropometry produced ways of identifying and classifying 'normal' female embodiment which were a distinctive part of early-twentieth-century eugenic medicine. Specifically, I draw on the genital taxonomy of a French gynaecologist by the name of Félix Jayle, who, in his book *La Gynécologie* (1918), produced highly detailed categories of vulval types from measurements taken from his female patients, devoting thirty pages to the *Nymphes*, or labia minora, alone. This text is noteworthy for the empirical attention Jayle paid to the size and shape of the external female genital structures, and for his novel method of categorising the labia minora into four distinct 'principal types': 'short' (small and hidden), 'membraniform' (leaf-shaped), 'aliform' (wing-shaped) and 'hypertrophic' (enlarged).[10] Importantly, Jayle proposed that the hypertrophic type was specific to black women and that its appearance in white women was a sign of racial degeneration.

This chapter will show how Jayle produced a white bodily norm in making sense of his own measurements by applying a deeply racialised interpretive framework that attributed disease to hereditary causes. Jayle's genital typologies formed part of a larger ambitious project of providing a comprehensive set of measurements of the 'normal' female body.

This broader taxonomy sought to provide a mathematical picture of bodily diversity with the aim of extinguishing those morphological features that indicated abnormality, degeneration and disease. The key to this was in finding out what made the body normal. Jayle thought that anthropometry could reveal the precise form of the perfectly healthy human body, which was also a beautiful one, being structurally well-proportioned and hormonally balanced. Like many other anthropometrists of his time, Jayle drew his ideal of perfect health and beauty in woman from Classical art—as I will show, the ancient Greeks had a very particular influence on European theories of health, beauty and vitality in early-twentieth-century anthropometry. Jayle's ultimate goal was to uncover the measurements of the perfectly normal, or average, white French female body: for him, normality held the secret to the eradication of disease through the cultivation of healthy practices and habits, which could then be passed down to subsequent generations, building a stronger, healthier white French nation.

THE NORMAL AND THE BEAUTIFUL

In the introductory lecture to his 1918 book *La Gynécologie*, Félix Jayle lamented that unlike previous centuries, where doctors collaborated with artists to produce magnificently illustrated volumes, doctors of the nineteenth century had lost their taste for the 'Beautiful' and the 'True'.[11] One purpose of Jayle's book was to introduce his theory that the ovaries, and not the uterus, were the true source of female health and illness; but the other aim was that it should bring the arts and the sciences together to restore respect for beauty to the practice of science. Quoting literary luminary Anatole France, Jayle wrote: 'Pour ma part, s'il me fallait choisir entre la Beauté et la Vérité, je n'hésiterais pas; c'est la Beauté que je garderais, bien certain qu'elle porte en elle une Vérité plus profonde que la Vérité même; J'oserai dire qu'il n'y a de Vrai au monde que le Beau.'[12] (For my part, if I had to choose between Beauty and Truth, I should not hesitate; it is Beauty I should keep, in the certainty that it bears a Truth more profound than Truth itself; I will dare to say that there is nothing True in the world except the Beautiful.) *La Gynécologie* was the result of a collaboration with artist Henri Bellery-Desfontaines, who had strong ties to the Parisian medical community: he had decorated the interior of the Charity Hospital; worked on various projects for the gynaecological clinic at Broca Hospital for Samuel

Pozzi; and carved furniture for the home of Pasteur Institute bacteriologist Dr. Henri Tissier (bizarrely, Bellery-Desfontaines would die in 1909 from typhoid fever after eating bad oysters at Tissier's home).[13] Bellery-Desfontaines designed the typeface for the book and its decorative elements, and authored some of its illustrations. His student Henri Rapin and the illustrator Gabriel Reignier took over after he died. Jayle's elevation of the Beautiful reflected his appreciation of the fine arts, as did his antipathy for medical photography. By the early twentieth century, photography had become well established in medical centres across Europe, yet Jayle felt that illustrations offered a greater degree of accuracy, while photographs could only represent the appearance of truth. In his view, photographs revealed more than they needed to, they magnified unimportant elements, they were not pleasurable to look at, and nor could they reveal the vital essence of their object.[14]

The medical philosophy of female health and illness espoused in *La Gynécologie* was underpinned by Jayle's conviction that Beauty and Truth were the essential principles that brought the arts and sciences together. The healthy body was de facto a beautiful one, and beauty held the secret to human health and vitality: 'The study of the nude shows rapidly, both to the doctor and to the artist, that a healthy and regular body is proportional in its parts, which cannot be altered without destroying the harmony of the whole: "Things of true proportions are usually beautiful" (Albert Dürer).'[15] Jayle believed that physicians could read the signs of health or illness, especially hereditary predisposition to types of illness, in the shape of the body, and that there were laws of morphological anatomy with which physicians were obliged to acquaint themselves. He wrote that it was the physician's task to examine 'the development of the perfect body, in order to understand the body's relationship to both health and beauty'.[16] He believed that if modern physicians could determine the morphological qualities of the perfect, beautiful body using the combined methods of scientific anthropometry and artistic measurement, then it would be possible to cultivate healthy, strong, disease-resistant bodies and minds. In Jayle's opinion: 'Nature inspires adoration of the beautiful body, in which is preserved physical and moral health: *mens sana in corpore sano* [a sound mind in a sound body].'[17]

Jayle heralded *La Gynécologie* as the first medical book to combine gynaecology with the artistic canon and its study of 'morphological anatomy': that is, the study of the 'laws of proportions' of the body, both as a whole, and in relation to its parts.[18] Yet while his application of anthropometry to gynaecology may have been original, Jayle's synthesis of art and science was borrowed from the French anthropological tradition founded by Paul Broca, who established the Société D'Anthropologie (Society of Anthropology) in 1859. From its inception, the discipline of anthropology in France was closely tied to medicine, as, according to historian David Lomas, the Society of Anthropology was mainly composed of medically trained professionals. Lomas also explains, importantly, that its methods of data collection through taking exhaustive measurements of human bodies and body parts, particularly skulls, 'were derived from artistic canons of proportion'.[19] Indeed, eminent French physician and anthropologist Paul Topinard wrote: 'The first attempt at anthropometry for the purpose of determining the proportions of the human body, and craniometry, for analysing the physiognomy, are [sic] due to artists.'[20]

Accordingly, Jayle argued that the value of the artistic canon was its attempt to establish a mathematical system of proportion, which could serve as the ideal female bodily norm. Crucially, the bodily vitality that could be inferred from the well-proportioned shape implied *normality*. Although he conceded that the artistic canon had changed over time according to the tastes of the epoch, what did not change was the artist's desire to calculate the dimensions of the perfect human form. It was important for physicians to study the artistic canon, he argued, 'because they [artists] give, in simple formulas, an average of sufficient truth'.[21] The anthropological canon could make the artistic canon more reliable. As science was more rigorous than art, it could perfect the basic foundations of human measurement that were established by artists. Jayle asserted that by combining the collective research of the arts and sciences, one could 'make a sufficiently precise conception of the average, normal, ideal Type of the European woman'.[22] Hence, he sought to study the qualities of the normal healthy body, rather than the pathological one, arguing that medicine had not paid enough attention to morphological anatomy because 'pathological descriptions are aimed more at the disease than at the patient'.[23] Medicine, he felt, should not restrict itself to the identification and diagnosis of disease, and nor should anatomy be concerned solely with the study of dead bodies. Rather, physicians needed to consider the living body as a functioning whole. The artistic canon could light the way for the physician in showing the 'normal' body as it should be: without imperfections.

Jayle saw himself as filling a significant gap in anatomical knowledge and was highly critical of post-mortem anatomy on the grounds that most measurements had been taken from urban working-class populations suffering diseases that had impaired, in the living person, bodily structure and function. Thus, he argued, these were measurements of pathological bodies and skewed the data. He suggested instead that 'to have a normal anthropometric [or scientific] canon, it would be necessary to measure only normal subjects'.[24] While the artistic canon could be used as a baseline, scientific anthropometry was able to show the proximity of actual, lived bodies to the perfectly proportioned ideal. Hence, Jayle introduced classes of female 'Types' to sort the range of individual bodies into 'normal' and 'variant' categories, according to elements such as rib-cage and pelvic size (Slender, Heavy, Round types); apparatus (Regular, Thoracic, Abdominal, Cerebral, Mixed types); fat distribution (Regular, Thin, Fat, Steatopygic types); endocrine functioning (Ovarian, Thyroid, Pituitary, Adrenal, Mixed types) and race (White, Yellow and Black).[25] He also organised female body types according to age. Ever the scientist, and not one to content himself with an abstract artistic representation of a single female ideal, Jayle pointed out that there are, in fact, multiple female body norms according to age, and these are outlined in five stages: nulliparity, parturity, menopause, old age and senility. Unlike the artist, he wrote, the doctor 'must know the normal aspect of the female body at all ages'.[26]

In general, Jayle arranged types of bodies according to a hierarchical scale of normal or degenerative. He believed that both artists and doctors could only arrive at an accurate image of the 'normal' body if pathological bodies were eliminated entirely from the field of measurement.[27] For Jayle, only the regular, or normal, body was considered healthy: variations of this type were degenerative and showed signs of illness. In developing the concept of the 'normal' body, Jayle restricted himself to the study of white Parisian women, stating that 'the Normal Woman, like the Normal Man, is a being of regular proportions, possessing well-balanced apparatuses, with harmoniously developed osseous, muscular and endocrine systems'.[28] Fig. 5.1 is an illustration of the Regular, or Normal, apparatus type. This 'Regular' type has 'regularity of proportions' in the torso and limbs, and is neither too thin (where the musculature is too visible) nor too fat (where the musculature is entirely concealed). The figure that best represents the Regular type, Jayle asserts, is the Venus de Milo.[29] In spite of his discussion of the influence of age, Jayle chose to use a nulliparous nineteen-year-old subject to represent the normal female body type.

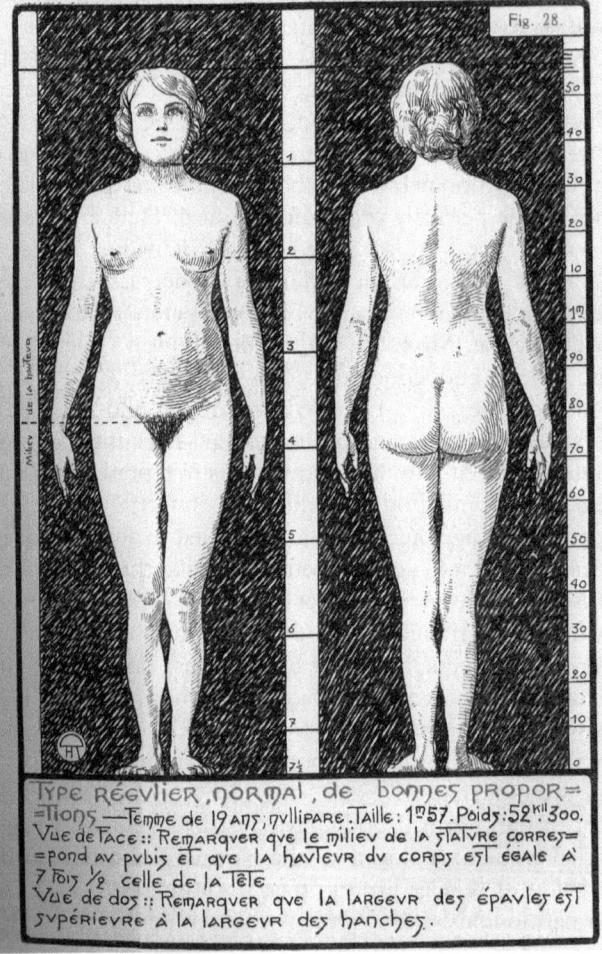

Fig. 5.1 'Regular type, normal, good proportions. Female of 19 years; Nulliparous. Height: 1 m 57. Weight: 52 kgs. 300. Front View: Note that the pubis is situated at mid-height, and that the height of the body is equal to 7 ½ times that of the head. Rear View: Note that the width of the shoulders is greater than the width of the hips.' Félix Jayle, *La Gynécologie. Tome 1: L'Anatomie Morphologique de la Femme* (Paris: Masson & Cie., 1918), 105. Courtesy Matheson Library, Monash University, Melbourne

APPROACHING NORMALITY

Jayle's concept of normality was envisaged as a perfect and truthful mathematical average, and it was indebted to the concept of the 'average man' developed by the influential nineteenth-century Belgian statistician Adolphe Quetelet (1796–1874). In Quetelet's method, an average type could be deduced from a large pool of measurements by calculating clustering and divergence. By eliminating extreme divergences or individual variations from the calculation of a sufficient number of people, the statistician could isolate that which was the most common among the most people.[30] As Quetelet expressed it, 'those who are closest to the average are greatest in number; those who are furthest away from it are fewest in number'.[31] Those considered to be on the extreme outer edges had to be excluded from the measurable field; they therefore set the limit for any calculation of the perfect average. Quetelet held that the truth lay between extremes or limits 'defined by nature', which meant that the average had to be a product of real populations (rather than, say, an artist's imagination), which were bounded by historical and geographical limits. The average was not supposed to be an abstract universal, but a calculation based on real living populations that, as Peter Cryle and Elizabeth Stephens explain, 'pointed to an ontological reality'.[32] Nevertheless, as a distillation of difference resolved into a single figure, the average man represented a certain kind of ideal purity, with qualities 'developed in due proportion, in perfect harmony, alike removed from excess or defect of every kind, so that, in the circumstances in which he is found, he should be considered as the type of all which is beautiful—of all which is good'.[33]

As far as medicine was concerned, Quetelet's average man could be considered to be a 'perfect' type, 'and everything differing from his proportions … would constitute deformity and disease; every thing found dissimilar, not only as regarded proportion and form, but as exceeding the observed limits, would constitute a monstrosity'.[34] As Cryle and Stephens have observed, Quetelet was convinced of the utility of statistics for the medical sciences, against the backdrop of opposition from doctors who insisted that patients could not be averaged; doctors felt that they treated patients in their specificity based on their professional expertise and judgement.[35] Nevertheless, Cryle and Stephens argue, Quetelet's theory of the 'average man' was significant for its intervention in the medical field and the novel way it conjoined the 'average' and the 'normal' in the figure of the patient.[36] The physician was already working with a conception of the average man, Quetelet argued, because illness always presented itself to the physician as a deviation from a 'normal state'. The doctor needed a concept of what was normal, or average, to know what was pathological.[37] Quetelet stated that 'in order to recognise whatever is an anomaly, it is essentially necessary to have established the type constituting the normal or healthy condition'.[38]

Quetelet's influence on Jayle is apparent in the latter's quest to divine the qualities of perfectly proportioned body. As Cryle and Stephens note, in his 1871 essay *L'Anthropométrie*, Quetelet had taken an interest in the dimensions of the 'normal' human body in order to chart bodily defect, with reference to the defects that afflicted the bodies of the urban poor, particularly child factory-workers. If the statistician 'could establish just what those normal proportions were', Cryle and Stephens write, then it fell to therapeutic medical science 'to do all that it could to reduce the gap between the actual and the normal/ideal'.[39] Similarly, like Quetelet, Jayle asserted that to arrive at a 'normal' figure, one had to take bodies considered excessive or defective out of the equation, which, of course, was not an entirely objective process, as the statistician had to use his judgement to decide who would be included in the range of normal human variety.[40] Jayle was surely inspired, in his endeavour to identify perfect health, by Quetelet's claim that the exemplary beautiful and proportionate 'human type, in our climates, is identical with the one that can be deduced from the observation of the most regular ancient statues'.[41] Importantly, Quetelet also developed what we might call a humoral model of the average man that Jayle would elucidate within his own theory of health and illness. Quetelet's model of graded averages is composed of a mix of species, race and individual characters, the differences between which all bear on the shape of the perfectly average human, which narrows to an average race, and is further attenuated to an average individual:

> The constitution of the average man serves as a type to our [human] kind. Every race has its peculiar constitution, which differs from this more or less, and which is determined by the influence of climate, and the habits which characterise the average man of that particular country. Every individual, again, has his particular constitution, which depends also on his organisation and his mode of existence.[42]

Quetelet's attention to the individual, the racial and the human was not lost on Jayle in his elaboration of a human female type (qualities that are specifically female), a racial type (qualities that belong to the 'three great human branches'), and an individual type (qualities derived from the family line and environmental influences). Jayle's general theory was that the body's humoral qualities which determine its proximate relationship to the normal or regular type are formed by hereditary and environmental influences that act on the ovary. The hereditary influences come from the family line and racial type, while the environmental influences may be factors such as climate, family habits, living conditions and the acquisition of diseases that are then transmitted hereditarily.[43] Every body experiences morphological changes which move it away or bring it closer to the normal type. Thus, writes Jayle, 'the variant types, distinguished from the average type, are determined by characters sufficiently marked to permit their individualisation'.[44] In other words, the variant type must be sufficiently distanced from the average to be considered outside the scope of the normal ideal. Further, the only way one could hope to arrive at a true measurement of the normal was to eliminate entirely from the field of measurement bodies that displayed signs of obvious pathology, such as rickets and inherited malformations caused by parental syphilis, tuberculosis and alcoholism.[45]

Difficulties in Quetelet's thinking carried over to Jayle, especially regarding the question of change over time. Perhaps the greatest problem for Jayle's 'normal' woman was the application of a fixed mathematical ideal to a changing body. The ageing process complicated the beautiful norm, especially if the latter was exemplified, as Quetelet had asserted, in 'the most regular ancient statues'.[46] Jayle realised that the female body in the Artistic Canon really only represented a single age-type—the adult Nulliparous type. He thus added the caveat that because the body changed constantly, the doctor needed to consider the stability of the Canon against the constant cellular changes in the body. If beauty signalled health, then age indicated bodily decline, which, for Jayle, began around forty years of age (the period of post-partum maturity before menopause), though he noted that the mature woman's fading beauty could be found in the alluring fat deposits in her hips and thighs.[47] But the average was always going to be a static concept, no matter how many types into which it could be divided, which meant that ageing bodies had a proximate relationship to a fixed point of perfection in time. Beauty had a chronological end point. Jayle tried to calculate what was normal for different ages of women, but if beauty was part and parcel of normality, then the ageing body itself had to be considered a divergence from a Nulliparous norm. In this case, Jayle's different age-based types (with their different humoral constitutions) returned back to a concept of perfect health embedded in the youthful body. As I will go on to show, racial types would also appear in Jayle's taxonomies of normality, which inevitably swung back to a conception of perfection embedded in the white body. Ultimately, the state of health that Quetelet's 'average man' represented—and which involved value judgements about whom to include and exclude—turned out to provide a very narrow template indeed. It enabled Jayle to view physical diversity as gradations of deformity and to assert a highly problematic causal connection between beauty and health. As Cryle and Stephens have astutely observed of Quetelet's statistical method, 'the average acted as a vehicle for implicit judgements about the normal' and was the theoretical site at which 'the average and the normal came effectively to coincide'.[48]

THE NORMAL VULVA

It is apparent that Jayle struggled to reconcile the arts and the sciences because he was highly aware of the discrepancy between a formal ideal and the bodily diversity of his actual patients, which is why that discrepancy needed to serve as an indicator of how close his patients were to the norm and to perfect health. Thus, he wrote, 'medicine must understand the real as well as the ideal'.[49] He applied the same principle to the female genitals, finding a 'variability of dimensions of nymphae, hymen, vagina and cervix',[50] though he also insisted on normal and variant types.

Jayle's illustration of 'the normal vulva' (Fig. 5.2) represents the genital phenotype of the human woman. In his view, medical men needed to know what the 'normal' vulva looked like if they were to assess pathological changes correctly. He came up with four main types, while noting that individuals may display mixed intermediary versions of these: short, membraniform (leaf-shaped), aliform (wing-shaped) and hypertrophied. He concluded that there was one type, the membraniform type (Fig. 5.3), that was both normal and healthy in white women. Using a plant analogy, he compared the membraniform nymphae to a lily leaf, with the petiole (stalk of the leaf blade) extending into the clitoris, the midrib corresponding to the adherent edges, and the leaf point ending at the perineum. He wrote that there is 'as in the leaf, a widening in

Fig. 5.2 'The Normal vulva, in the standing position. Female 25 years old (the pubic hair has been cut).' Félix Jayle, *La Gynécologie. Tome 1: L'Anatomie Morphologique de la Femme* (Paris: Masson & Cie., 1918), 340. Courtesy Matheson Library, Monash University, Melbourne

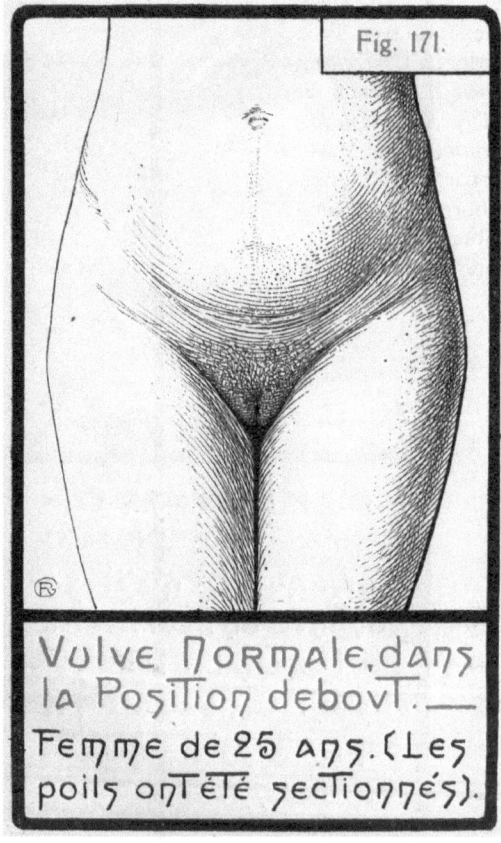

the middle and a tapering at the anterior and posterior ends'.[51] The lily, for Jayle, would have served as a symbol of nature at her finest, and the healthy vulva reflected nature in the full bloom of her beauty.

Although Jayle was writing in the twentieth century, his plant analogy stemmed from the botanical sciences of the eighteenth century. As Londa Schiebinger has argued, early modern botanical understandings of plant reproduction were structured through human models of gender and sexuality.[52] She notes that Carl Linnaeus, the father of modern taxonomy, described the female plant with reference to the human reproductive system, equating the various parts of the plant to the vulva, vagina, Fallopian tube, ovary and eggs.[53] Schiebinger argues that both

Fig. 5.3 The membraniform type. Félix Jayle, *La Gynécologie. Tome 1: L'Anatomie Morphologique de la Femme* (Paris: Masson & Cie., 1918), 367. Courtesy Matheson Library, Monash University, Melbourne

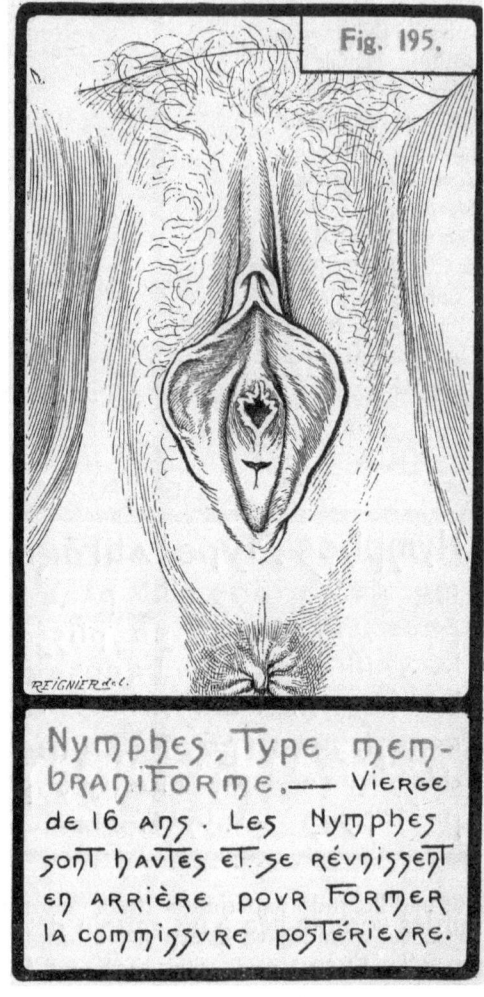

botany and anatomy were instrumental in defining the modern science of sexual difference, which replaced an ancient Greco-Roman humoral model with a 'materialistic' one that sought to find the evidence of sex in every part of the body, from bones to organs to sex hormones. Jayle's book was a curious mix of an ancient humoral model of the body and a modern one. In his anatomical approach, the shape of the genitals (and the body generally) was important in diagnosing imbalances in the systems of the body, but particularly the endocrine system. Jayle specialised in endocrinology, having conducted experimental opotherapy on more than 400 women with 'utero-ovarian troubles', whom he injected with glandular extracts from ox ovaries.[54] For Jayle, the ovarian gland organised the 'hereditary and acquired humors of the organism', and governed the entire female reproductive system. The state of the ovary determined the health of the reproductive system and its regularity in form and function.[55]

In this medical framework, the all-powerful ovary governed the appearance of the nymphae. The membraniform type, Jayle asserted, 'is found in women of good constitution, whose ovarian glands are perfectly healthy, that is to say, in the great majority of subjects'.[56] He wrote that the normal adult nymphae measured between 2 and 4 cm, and that the short type, which is concealed to varying degrees by the labia majora, was normal infants, but abnormal in adults. While the normal labia was pigmented, scalloped and often furnished with extra folds, the short type was smooth on its surface and edges. Quite against the conventional wisdom that the nymphae should be small and entirely concealed by the labia majora, as discussed in Chapter 3, Jayle drew on his own anthropometric data to assert that this was not, in fact, ideal, as the 'short type' indicated a degree of atrophy and ovarian insufficiency (Fig. 5.4). The aliform (or wing-shaped) type was the white woman's version of hypertrophy (Fig. 5.5). Jayle claimed that the enlargement of the nymphae among white women was anomalous and could be 'considered to be of atavistic [*reversive*] character'.[57] Unlike the majestic contours of the lily, the aliform labia were very pigmented, veiny and folded in upon themselves and gave the appearance of 'the wings of a large moth, with the vestibular organs corresponding to its body'.[58] Lastly, the hypertrophied type was specific to African women, including 'Abyssinians', 'Negresses' and 'Bushman' women (Fig. 5.6).[59] Jayle's illustration is a reproduction of Charles Alexandre Lesueur's drawing from his visit to the Cape of Good Hope in a state-sponsored colonial expedition to Australia from 1800 to 1804 (see Chapter 4). Jayle explains that the hypertrophied nymphae can reach a length of twenty centimetres or more, and that they are peculiar for the way they 'form, at the vaginal orifice, a sort of drooping cover'.[60] He regarded the hypertrophic type as being 'racial in character' and 'commonly observed in certain countries of Africa where it is characteristic among some tribes'.[61] For Jayle, hypertrophied labia

Fig. 5.4 The short type. Félix Jayle, *La Gynécologie. Tome 1: L'Anatomie Morphologique de la Femme* (Paris: Masson & Cie., 1918), 366. Courtesy Matheson Library, Monash University, Melbourne

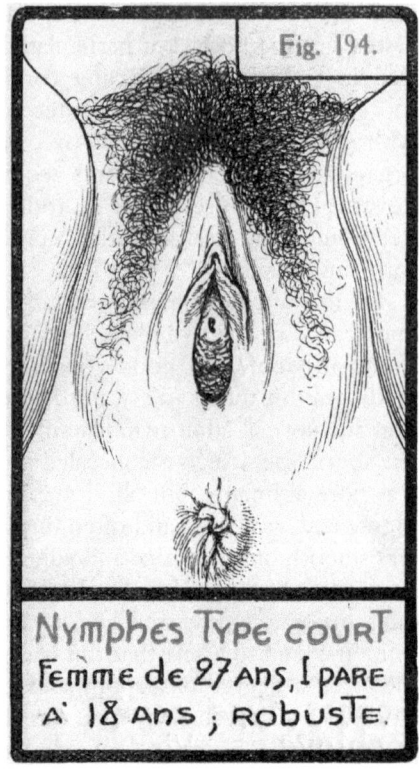

minora were evidence of tribal consanguinity, or interbreeding, and marked the evolutionary limit of race. It was the characteristic expression of a primitive human body type belonging to a 'lower' race: 'Its origin is undoubtedly very remote, like the steatopygia which accompanies it so often.'[62] As has been well established by historian Sander Gilman, labial hypertrophy and steatopygia came to be synecdoches for a black female type,[63] which was the case for Jayle, as for Cuvier before him. Jayle followed Raphael Blanchard's theory of atavism (see Chapter 4), in reasoning that their appearance in white women indicated racial degeneration and inherited deformity.

Jayle's postulation about the degenerative character of labial hypertrophy was but one element in a larger theory of race, evolution and heredity. He fashioned his theory of heritability through enquiries taking place in nineteenth-century France about how heredity worked, what was fixed

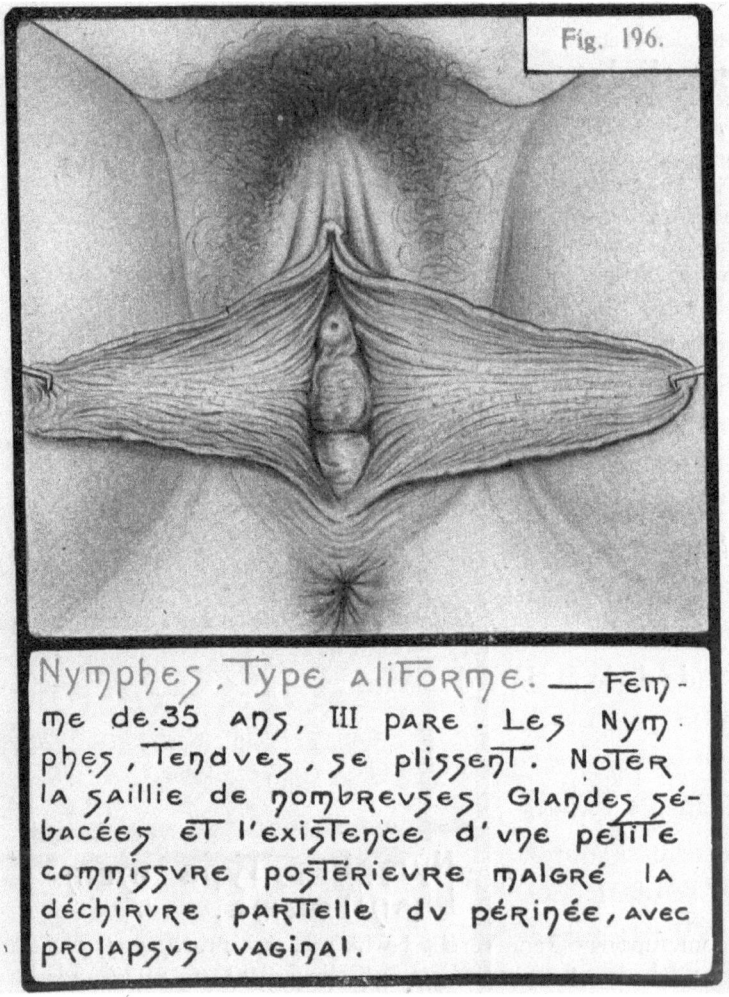

Fig. 5.5 The aliform type. Félix Jayle, *La Gynécologie. Tome 1: L'Anatomie Morphologique de la Femme* (Paris: Masson & Cie., 1918), 368. Courtesy Matheson Library, Monash University, Melbourne

or constitutional, and what was changeable.[64] Jayle argued that the one thing religious monogenists and anthropologists (whether monogenists or polygenists) could agree upon was that the races were shaped by different 'milieus', or environments. His view was influenced, in part, by

Fig. 5.6 The hypertrophic type. Félix Jayle, *La Gynécologie. Tome 1: L'Anatomie Morphologique de la Femme* (Paris: Masson & Cie., 1918), 370. Courtesy Matheson Library, Monash University, Melbourne

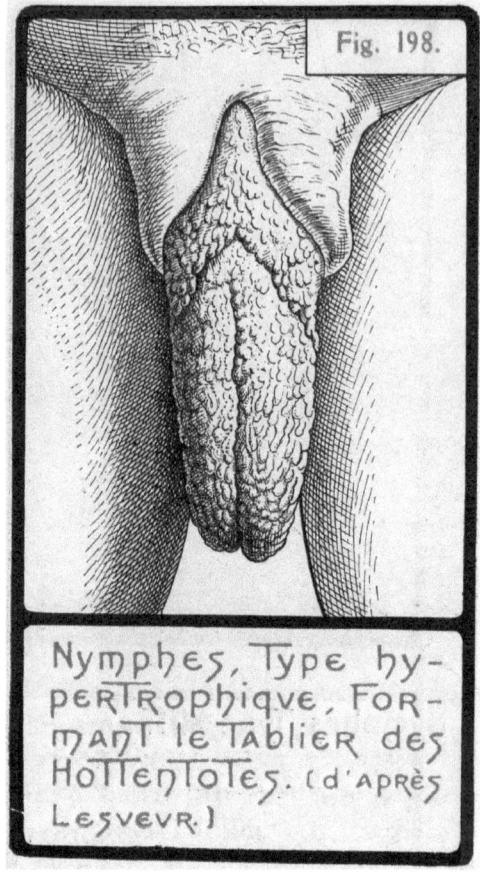

his contemporary René Verneau, who was the anthropology chair at the Muséum national d'histoire naturelle from 1909 to 1927 and the editor of the journal *L'Anthropologie* from 1894 to 1930. Quoting Verneau, Jayle explained that environmental change induced evolutionary progress. For Verneau, Europeans were more evolved than 'primitive' races because they had undergone greater change:

> The human being is subject to all the laws that govern other living organisms; and, like them, it varies when the milieu changes. The Australian, for example, who has evolved so little, lives in an archaic environment; some

of the plants and animals surrounding him represent forms that existed in the Tertiary period. The life of most of the tribes of Australia continues to be most primitive. It is therefore easy to imagine that the human type subjected to conditions which have changed so little, has stabilised more and more. In Europe, on the contrary, everything has changed since our first ancestors walked beside the great hippopotamus, the ancient elephant and Merck's rhinoceros [an extinct genus]. Each change in the climate, the flora, the fauna, and the way of life corresponded to a more or less marked change in the physical type of man.[65]

Verneau thought that each racial type corresponded to a stage of human evolution, equating Australian Aboriginal people with Neanderthals[66] and placing Europeans at the top of the evolutionary hierarchy. Figure 5.7 visually depicts this racial theory of evolution.

Like Verneau, Jayle believed that the environment influenced the formation of the human races. For Jayle, the human racial types were largely fixed, having been adapted to their local 'milieus', or environments. He suggested that races would degenerate and die off if transplanted to new environments (for example, from temperate climates to tropical ones) because they were not adapted to them. The few individuals who survived would eventually acquire new humoral properties that would then be passed on genetically to form new racial types. Theoretically, he suggested, if the three main races (White, Yellow, Black) were all to be transplanted from their original milieus, they would disappear and resolve into a new race.[67]

Importantly, Jayle believed that heredity and environment were not diametrically opposed but mutually reinforcing: 'The environment exerts a preponderant action, so that through the generations it may succeed in modifying heredity, that is to say, imprinting a race with a new character, which, by its transmission, becomes itself hereditary.'[68] While the racial types were relatively stabilised, recently acquired characteristics could be transformed or eradicated by the influence of exercise, diet and dress, or 'physical culture'.[69] Jayle thus concluded that healthy habits of living could mould a normal European body type that would gradually become biologically fixed through the influence of heredity. Jayle's rationale was that if the races had formed according to the influence of different environments, then it was reasonable to assume that the body could be perfected by exerting 'positive' environmental influences upon it. After all, he had already explored the potential of opotherapy in restoring balance

Fig. 5.7 Frontispiece from Edmond Perrier and René Verneau, *La femme. Dans la nature, dans les moeurs, dans la légende, dans la société*, book 1 (Paris: Bong & Cie, 1908). Courtesy BIU Santé, Paris

to the endocrine system. His hope was that even if parents possessed defects themselves, they could produce superior children by raising them 'according to perfect principles of hygiene', by which they would 'approach the regular type and, in turn, create an absolutely normal [i.e., unblemished] line [*lignée*]'.[70] Jayle argued that body morphology provided the physician with visual information about a body's predisposition toward disease, and was a crucial diagnostic tool in the identification and eradication of 'abnormality' and the cultivation of 'normality' through physical culture. Jayle was brutally decisive on this point: 'The regular type constitutes, in my opinion, what is normal. All others are abnormal, and physical culture should erase them from the morphological table if it is applied methodically to the raising of man.'[71]

Jayle's Eugenics

Jayle was working with theoretical models that were a distinctive part of early-twentieth-century national anxieties over population health, at a time of acute national panic over population decline following French defeat in the Franco-Prussian war in 1871 and stagnant birth rates. Medical aspirations to cultivate healthy bodies were also entwined with the pursuit of white racial perfection and purity as French elites worried about the effects of colonial rule, especially in North Africa, with the proliferation of racial mixing and reverse migration.

To French physicians like Jayle, medical specialists could help restore the white population of France through prescribing exercises that would prevent bodily decay and abnormalities, and through eugenic sexual selection. For Jayle, breeding out irregularity was the secret to cultivating disease resistance in the white body, which was a key goal of eugenic medicine. 'Eugenics' (*l'Eugennétique*) was famously coined in 1883 by British anthropologist Sir Francis Galton, who proposed that mental and physical characteristics were genetically heritable. Galton drew on Darwin's theory of natural selection to propose that racial perfection could be obtained through selective breeding. Hence, eugenics encouraged reproduction in people who were deemed to be of more value than others, and discouraged the same in those considered morally, mentally, or physically, including racially, unfit.

However, like other French eugenicists of his day, Jayle was influenced more by Lamarck than Darwin. In keeping with French eugenicists' preference for Lamarckian theories of heredity, Jayle believed that physical exercises and dietary regimes could change the qualities of the living body (for instance, to be taller or shorter), which would then be inherited by offspring. By contrast, Darwinian theory held that changes in an organism in its lifetime had no effect on natural selection, by which some organisms with certain traits became dominant simply because they were useful in the environmental context, while organisms without those traits died off. In spite of these differences, both neo-Lamarckian and Darwinian eugenicists had as their common goal racial betterment through reproduction.

Jayle was a member of the French Eugenics Society, which was formed in 1912, only a few months after the First International Eugenics Congress was held in London.[72] The president of the French Eugenics Society was neo-Lamarckist biologist Edmond Perrier, who was also the Head of the Museum of Natural History,[73] and the society's mission was to research and apply knowledge about

> the reproduction, preservation and the improvement of the species, and the study of questions of heredity and selection in their application to the human species, and questions relating to the influence of environment, economic status, legislation and customs on the quality of successive generations and on their physical, intellectual and moral aptitudes.[74]

With these goals in mind, eugenicists like Jayle made use of the concept of degeneration, introduced by the French-Austrian psychiatrist Benedict Morel in his influential publication *Traité des Dégénérescences*, in 1857.[75] Morel defined degeneration as a 'morbid variation from an original type'[76] and a heritable physical and mental constitutional weakness that, for him, represented individual, social and national decline.[77] Jayle argued that gynaecological diseases were essentially degenerative and caused by both newly acquired and hereditary ovarian abnormalities, leading him to conclude that the 'degeneration of the ovary and hereditary predisposition are ... causes of the majority of gynaecological disorders'.[78] He was most concerned about the degenerative effects of displacement of the acclimatised body into 'foreign environments',[79] both at home, with the shift from agricultural to urban labour, and abroad, with colonies in the African tropics deemed unsuitable for white bodies acclimatised to temperate European climates.[80] In the local white population, he warned of the degenerative influence of the social conditions of working-class urban families who lived in darkened houses, were susceptible to microbes and pollution, and had diets that were too rich in meat and alcohol.[81] At this time, eugenicist doctors like Jayle were engaged in promoting 'social hygiene' to try to eradicate the inherited effects of alcoholism, tuberculosis, venereal disease and rickets as environmental, or social, causes of infant disease.[82] On an imperial scale, he worried about the effects of travel and racial mixing on French populations, for, in his view, certain human races, as with animals or plants, 'are not accustomed … to certain climates: the crossing of a foreign race that is not acclimatisable with an indigenous race gradually degenerates or dies out'.[83] In his belief that transplanted races would degenerate and die off, Jayle probably followed de Gobineau, the progenitor of the theory of Aryan superiority, who held that racial degeneracy caused by the 'influx of foreign elements' would bring about the destruction of the French nation.[84] Jayle's thinking in this area is particularly evident in the work of eighteenth-century naturalist Comte de Buffon, who had argued that human varieties, or types, were largely shaped by climate. Buffon was also interested in the effects of racial mixing on degeneration, arguing that geographic dislocation (or, in Jayle's phrasing 'transplantation') would eradicate the dislocated race, using 'Negroes' transported to America as his example. In this case, black reproduction with native whites hastened the process of whitening among black people, which, he said, would have taken environmental conditions alone a far longer period to achieve.[85]

Jayle's theory of transplantation and degeneration implied that *any* race transplanted from its native climate would degenerate; but the language of degeneration was steeped in the racial and class hierarchies of his day. That is, within the framework of Galtonian eugenics, the problem of degeneration was a *white* one: degeneration could only go one way—from white perfection to black imperfection. A similar principle held for mobile local populations. The urban poor degenerated because their bodies were not accustomed to urban conditions, which was why they were affected by rickets from lack of light. Again, degeneration went one way—from country to city. Urban conditions were degenerative because bodies were formed in 'nature'. Bodies ruined by urban life, then, could potentially be restored by 'natural' living, a philosophy that formed the basis of the German life reform movement and the uptake of natural therapies, nudism and vegetarianism as healthy practices.[86] But if white urban civilisation was so destructive of health and if natural living was consonant with the body's needs, then why did it not follow that white bodies were the most degenerative and therefore inferior? Why did eugenicists like Verneau and Jayle believe that the 'uncivilised' Indigenous peoples of Australia, for instance, were degenerate, rather than healthy, strong and genetically superior? The trick of whiteness is that it can turn rationality into knots. White populations were perceived to be advanced yet vulnerable, and herein lies the heart of eugenics.

The reason why the eugenic race sciences make no sense is that they were inherently contradictory, in that scientists used whatever explanation came to hand to cobble together theories that usually led back to white superiority. The science of heredity and evolution was concocted through a belief system that held class, race and gender inequality to be biologically intrinsic.

HEREDITY AND BEAUTY

Anxieties around birth rates and national degeneration also dominated political and scientific discourses among France's neighbouring European imperial powers such as Germany, Britain and Italy. The assumed natural relationship between health and beauty was not restricted to France; it was part of a cross-pollination of ideas among European eugenicists generally. Jayle's theories notably intersected with those of the 'life reform movement' in Germany, which created a popular hygienic culture that prescribed natural therapies for maintaining a healthy body.[87] His contemporary Carl Heinrich Stratz had earlier claimed to have produced a definitive anthropometrics of the normal, healthy and beautiful white female body. Ten years prior to the publication of *La Gynécologie*, in 1908, Stratz had come to exactly the same conclusion that the only way to measure healthy, normal bodies would be to exclude abnormal or degenerate ones from the field of measurement. In his *Die Schönheit des weiblichen Körpers* (*The Beauty of the Female Body*), Stratz, like Jayle, had praised himself for being the first to bring the anthropometric tools of physician to the artistic canon, and for conducting observations on living bodies, rather than corpses.[88] He, too, argued that 'accomplished beauty and perfect health are one and the same',[89] and that physical culture, especially for children, would promote good health and a beautiful body.[90] Stratz took the Classical Medici Venus to be the ideal female body, as did Verneau in the four-volume work on woman that he co-wrote with Edmond Perrier, *La femme. Dans la nature, dans les moeurs, dans la légende, dans la société* (*Woman: in Nature, in Mores, in Legend, in Society*), also published in 1908.[91] For Stratz, Classical statues were a true representation of female beauty that could be found in real women, though he admitted there were few women who could compare. However, like Jayle, he felt that the perfect beauty exemplified by Greco-Roman statuary was something to strive for.[92] Like Jayle, Stratz argued that to understand the laws of beauty demonstrated in the artistic canon, one first needed to exclude abnormal bodies exhibiting 'deformities' caused by corsetry, heredity, diet, lifestyle and disease.[93] Once these 'abnormal' bodies were excluded from the field of measurement, one then had access to the 'normal' body, which was also beautiful due to the harmony of its proportions. Historian Michael Hau points out that Stratz's method was tautological because he argued (as did Quetelet and Jayle) that both physicians and artists needed to select normal bodies to arrive at normal measurements. That is, they had to use their judgement to select 'normal' individuals to measure, to arrive at the scientifically precise measurements that indexed perfection.[94] Yet while Jayle grappled with the problem that the ageing body posed to identifying a single norm, Stratz proposed that the norm would manifest itself at a particular time in a woman's life, asserting that the 'normal physique' would appear when the body reached its 'fullest bloom'.[95] The body in full bloom could be determined by the state of the breasts. The mature, full and high breast was the sign of the body in full flower; its 'wilting is the first sign that the bloom is over'.[96] Like Jayle, Stratz excluded from his norm bodies affected by rickets and other 'disturbances' that interrupted bodily symmetry. Stratz suggested, following Quetelet's theory of the average, that while no one could ever be perfectly symmetrical, and that while individual deviations could exist within the 'normal' range, 'disturbances' that noticeably interrupted the symmetry of the body could be considered signs of abnormality.[97] Stratz fixed his average type in anthropologist Gustav Fritsch's canon[98]: 'The more a body correlates to the canon,' he wrote, 'the more it may make a claim to beauty.'[99] Hence, anything that fell outside the limits of Fritsch's model could be classed as deviant.

Stratz combined his statistical methodology with the artistic canon to pin the beautiful norm to Classical Greek statuary. He would also use Darwinian evolutionary theory to argue that 'among the different kind of human races, the white race is the most civilised and is therefore the most beautiful'.[100] Hence, among white women, abnormalities in the body's symmetry may be attributable either to a reversion to an earlier type or to inherited irregular morphological characteristics passed down by parents who carried the same defect.[101] Like many other physicians before him, Stratz classed protuberant labia as a significant defect in European women, particularly because it was characteristic of Hottentots. As Hau argues, Stratz projected a 'vulgar sexuality' onto women from other nationalities and races in order to contrast civilised, bourgeois beauty with animal sensuality.[102] Like Jayle, Stratz adhered to the three-race theory and, as Hau writes, he claimed that white female proportions came the closest to those of Fritsch's canon.[103] In Stratz's reasoning, whiteness was the default signifier for a species norm because white women represented a species ideal of Woman more than did 'black' or 'yellow' women. He considered white women to be unreservedly the most beautiful of all the races. For him, beauty embodied white racial strength, vitality and superiority.

> It seems unquestionable to me that the white race and its descendants claim justifiably the first rank … The most striking proof is that the white race, not only in Europe but also in other parts of the world, is gradually eradicating the rest. In America, the Redskins are already numbered [i.e., dwindling], and in a few hundred years, one will read with a shudder, as in old fairy tales, that there were once people with black skin.[104]

Stratz's Darwinism was aggressively assimilationist and assumed that evolution would inevitably end with the complete dominance of the white body, whether through murder or breeding. The norm was, then, for Stratz, a thoroughly material ideal that constituted the violent assertion of authority and domination consistent with colonial efforts to settle foreign lands and eliminate indigenous populations. It could be said that Stratz's racial Darwinism was fuelled by what historian Patrick Wolf has famously termed 'the logic of elimination' of settle r colonialism.[105]

Conclusion

Brian Sloan's search for the most beautiful vagina to develop a sex toy he could market to heterosexual men in many ways replicated the clinical approach to the female body of eugenic anthropometry. The nation-oriented scientific research of early-twentieth-century eugenics is perversely recapitulated in the modern late-capitalist context, where heterosexual male consumer preference guides the sorting of vulvas into types, arranged from unattractive to attractive. For Sloan, as for Jayle, the average could be measured in terms of what was the most common for the most people, though Sloan was measuring frequency of voter preference, which settled on 'class 1 vulvas'.[106] Yet Sloan's competition could not have been held without female participation, and women also made up 19 per cent of voters. Likewise, Jayle could not have produced such meticulous measurement without the participation of his female patients. 'Nell', the woman who won Sloan's beauty contest, argued that the contest was benign: 'I honestly think it's harmless ... if there's something out there creating standards for vagina beauty, it's mostly porn, where you get a lot of women undergoing labiaplasty. That's absolutely more harming'. She also emphasised that her own body should not be treated as a standard to which other women should aspire because 'each one of us is different ... It would be extremely boring if it were all the same'.[107] Nell considered herself to have a normal, average or everyday, yet individual, vagina, which she compared to the surgically altered vaginas that she believed were to be found in porn. For Nell, the normality of her own body in its unique difference and her averageness as a member of the public marked her own participation in the sex industry as different to that of professional porn performers. Yet Nell's vagina would lose its individuality in becoming a type, and she would not have any control over the coding or voting process that transformed her anatomy it into a replicable 'class 1' prototype.

With the rise of contemporary medical reality television, we see the flipside of the beauty contest, as media audiences are made privy to the private body-shame of ordinary fellow citizens for commercial profit but also for the social benefits of destigmatisation that public sharing can bring about. This media space, however, is arguably more appealing to female consumers than pornography, and is, in that sense, an important site of information about body norms. In the present-day British reality TV show *Embarrassing Bodies*, for example, GP Dr. Pixie McKenna advised her patient that although her labia looked healthy from a gynaecological point of view, she did have 'quite a lot of excess skin', that her labia were 'sticking right down', and that '*normally* you wouldn't get that appearance'.[108] McKenna concludes with this appraisal: 'What you've got is a *normal variant* ... I think we could be able to help you with this ... I'm not thinking a gynaecologist here, I'm thinking more a cosmetic surgeon. They can do a fairly minor procedure and remove that excess skin for you'.[109] While some medical specialists may pay lip service to normality, what they are in fact promoting is the idea that protruding inner labia are excessive and abnormal.

This language of the 'normal variant' may well have come straight from Jayle's *La Gynécologie*, with its implicit assumption that despite falling within the limits of human variation, the 'variant' is at variance with the normal ideal and needs correction. Jayle's statistical investigations of bodily normality were remarkable for how they attempted to represent the diversity of vulval morphology in ways that had not been attempted before; typically, medical texts provided a single picture of female genital anatomy, except where 'anomalies' such as intersexual embodiment or the Hottentot apron were concerned. The 'variant' in this vocabulary is not a neutral term referring to the simple fact of human difference. While Jayle's eugenics sought to approach normality through reshaping the body through disciplinary exercises, over generations, contemporary cosmetic surgery enables female consumers to obtain a 'normal' vulva through surgical excision. I will address the history of female genital cosmetic surgery and the question of gender norms in greater detail in Chapter 7, but I cite the example of the celebrity doctor here to highlight the cultural pervasiveness of the normal in enforcing sexual conformity: cosmetic surgery works to reassure women that they can become perfectly feminine.

In their history of normality, Cryle and Stephens argue that our modern concept of the normal has been shaped more by 'the emergent self-improvement and consumer cultures of the mid-twentieth century' than by the large disciplinary institutions of the nineteenth century.[110] They turn to the US, citing the example of public health initiatives that used anthropometric data against which individuals could measure themselves to improve their health. At the same time, mass public surveys designed to unmask the tastes and practices of 'average Americans' supported the design of products for consumers. The modern conception of normal, the authors argue, is not primarily a repressive site of violence and exclusion but a productive space of 'self-cultivation and self-improvement'.[111] They clarify that 'this sphere is not inhabited primarily by discipline but by commerce. It is focused not on standardization, but on the individual consumer', where individual variation is prioritised over conformity.[112] Rather confusingly, they oppose the 'productive or individuating' functions of normality to 'repressive and standardizing' ones,[113] as though individuating productions could not also be repressive or standardising. Jayle's range of bodily 'types' is an excellent example of the production of distinct individuals within a broader standardising taxonomy distinguishing between perfect normality and the deviations that he thought should be erased from the 'morphological table' in the interests of racial progress.

I hope to have shown in this chapter that the strategies of self-improvement deployed even by 'positive' eugenic models such as those of the French Eugenics Society, which focused on strengthening and fortifying the health of the white population (as opposed to implementing state-based sterilisation programs, as would happen in the US and Germany), were part of an evolving epistemology of repressive colonialism because they served to justify white supremacy and its violent excesses.

This was a sphere of self-improvement that was grounded in state-based anxieties about the possibilities for *too much* variation posed by the spectre of white racial degeneration. In other words, the desire for self-improvement is as much tied to the demands of citizenship as it is to the solicitations of consumer capitalism.

Normality is Janus-faced in its power to produce social identities and effects: on the one hand, it possesses the power to reduce what is considered extraordinary, alien and 'wrong' to the ordinary and the unremarkable, and is therefore a crucial tool in advancing political struggles for social acceptance of people, bodies or acts considered deviant and unacceptable. But it also has the power to establish the limits of what can be counted as human or monstrous, and what is alien, wrong, unfamiliar, lacking and in need of correction. Hence, it is not so easy to distance the normal from the perfect or the desirable. Although women have varying degrees of sexual agency, what we desire for ourselves is enmeshed with the desires of others in ways that reproduce and reinforce powerful cultural fantasies of bodily perfection, which fuel the cosmetic surgery industry. The biopolitical regulation of individuals and populations in the administration of the state—'the administration of bodies and the calculated management of life',[114] as Foucault terms it—cannot be divorced from the question of how desire is lived, and its relationship to the shifting discursive limits of what it is socially possible to desire. What we desire for, with and through our bodies is intimately bonded to the social institutions, discourses and disciplinary regimes, especially gender and race, through which biological being is experienced and realised. This is why I suggest that the commercial availability of female genital cosmetic surgery in late-capitalist consumer culture should not be detached from the normalising, disciplinary purposes of eugenic medicine because it is in this sphere that the patient and the consumer converge.

NOTES

1. Sophie Kleeman, 'Meet the Woman with the Most Beautiful Vagina in the World', *Mic*, 31 July 2015, https://mic.com/articles/123110/nell-vagina-beauty-contest-winner#.W6u3KIgad; Samatha Rogers, 'The "World's Most Beautiful Vagina' Winners, as Explained by Scientists', *Daily Dot*, 24 July 2015, https://www.dailydot.com/irl/vulva-paper-worlds-most-beautiful-vagina/; castitty, 'World's Most Beautiful Vagina Contest', Porn.com, 22 June 2015, https://www.porn.com/blog/worlds-most-beautiful-vagina-contest/.

2. Marisa Kabas, 'Meet the Winners of the "World's Most Beautiful Vagina" Pageant', *Daily Dot*, 13 November 2015, https://www.daily-dot.com/irl/most-beautiful-vagina-video/.
3. Autoblow 2, 'The Vulva Paper: A Scientific Analysis of the Autoblow Vaginal Beauty Contest's Data', accessed 28 June 2017, http://vulva-paper.com/.
4. Rogers, 'The "World's Most Beautiful Vagina" Winners'.
5. Autoblow 2, 'The Vulva Paper'.
6. Helena Howarth, Volker Sommer and Fiona M. Jordan, 'Visual Depictions of Female Genitalia Differ Depending on Source', *Medical Humanities* 36, no. 2 (2010): 75–9; Jillian Lloyd, Naomi S. Crouch, Catherine L. Minto, Lih-Mei Liao and Sarah M. Creighton, 'Female Genital Appearance: "Normality" Unfolds', *BJOG* 112, no. 5: (2005): 643–6.
7. Michel Foucault, *Discipline and Punish*, trans. Alan Sheridan (Harmondsworth: Penguin, 1977), 183, emphasis mine.
8. Foucault, *Discipline and Punish*, 183.
9. See 'The Vulva Paper' to view an example of the favoured 'class 1' vulval type. There are also pictures of winning vulvas on the Autoblow2 website at http://www.vaginacontest.com/winners: these are not all 'class 1' vulvas, however. Sloan perhaps wants to appear to be in support of vulval diversity by using these photographs. His 'Vulva Paper' emphasises that although the 'class 1' vulva was the most popular of the six classes, there were more voters who preferred protuberant labia (classes 2 to 6) to non-protuberant labia (class 1). The labial diversity pictured here might be a positive representation of normal bodily diversity were it not for the glaring problem that the worth of these body parts is entirely dependent on judgements of beauty.
10. Félix Jayle, *La Gynécologie. Tome 1: L'Anatomie Morphologique de la Femme* (Paris: Masson & Cie., 1918), 367–71, my translation.
11. Jayle, *La Gynécologie*, 2.
12. Jayle, *La Gynécologie*, 2, my translation.
13. Xavier Chardeau, 'Biographie de l'artiste', accessed 12 October 2017, http://www.bellerydesfontaines.com/biographie.html.
14. 'La Photographie met tout sur le même plan, déforme à Plaisir, grossit ce qui est inutile et omet souvent de faire ressortir le principal caractére de l'objet.' Jayle, *La Gynécologie*, 9.
15. Jayle, *La Gynécologie*, 37, my translation.
16. Jayle, *La Gynécologie*, 17, my translation.
17. Jayle, *La Gynécologie*, 17, my translation.
18. Jayle, *La Gynécologie*, 33, my translation.
19. David Lomas, 'A Canon of Deformity: *Les Demoiselles D'Avignon* and Physical Anthropology', *Art History* 16, no. 3 (1993): 428.

20. Topinard, cited in David Lomas, 'A Canon of Deformity: *Les Demoiselles D'Avignon* and Physical Anthropology', *Art History* 16, no. 3 (1993): 428.
21. Jayle, *La Gynécologie*, 37, my translation.
22. Jayle, *La Gynécologie*, 96, my translation.
23. Jayle, *La Gynécologie*, 31, my translation.
24. Jayle, *La Gynécologie*, 95, my translation.
25. For a discussion of the variant types, see Jayle, *La Gynécologie*, 96–156.
26. Jayle, *La Gynécologie*, 212, my translations.
27. Jayle, *La Gynécologie*, 95–6.
28. Jayle, *La Gynécologie*, 153, my translation.
29. Jayle, *La Gynécologie*, 108.
30. See Georges Canguilhem, *The Normal and the Pathological*, trans. Carolyn R. Fawcett (New York: Zone Books, 1991), 156–7. For a more detailed discussion of Quetelet's statistical method, see Peter Cryle and Elizabeth Stephens, *Normality: A Critical Genealogy* (Chicago and London: University of Chicago Press, 2017), chap. 3.
31. Quetelet, cited in Cryle and Stephens, *Normality*, 126.
32. Cryle and Stephens, *Normality*, 139.
33. Adolphe Quetelet, *A Treatise on Man and the Development of His Faculties*, trans. R. Knox (Edinburgh: William and Robert Chambers, 1842), 100.
34. Quetelet, *A Treatise on Man*, 99.
35. Cryle and Stephens, *Normality*, 16–17.
36. Cryle and Stephens, *Normality*, 108.
37. Cryle and Stephens, *Normality*, 109.
38. Quetelet, *A Treatise on Man*, vi.
39. Cryle and Stephens, *Normality*, 134.
40. Stephens and Cryle also make this point. See Cryle and Stephens, *Normality*, 137.
41. Quetelet, cited in Cryle and Stephens, *Normality*, 135.
42. Quetelet, *A Treatise on Man*, 99.
43. Jayle, *La Gynécologie*, 3, 96.
44. Jayle, *La Gynécologie*, 96, my translation.
45. Jayle, *La Gynécologie*, 95.
46. Quetelet, cited in Cryle and Stephens, *Normality*, 135.
47. Jayle, *La Gynécologie*, 215, 218.
48. Cryle and Stephens, *Normality*, 140–1.
49. Jayle, *La Gynécologie*, 524, my translation.
50. Jayle, *La Gynécologie*, 524–5, my translation.
51. Jayle, *La Gynécologie*, 369, my translation.
52. Londa Schiebinger, *Nature's Body: Sexual Politics and the Making of Modern Science* (Hammersmith: Pandora, 1993), chap. 1.

53. Schiebinger, *Nature's Body*, 21.
54. Wm. H. Carey, 'Jayle, M. F.: The Employment of Hypophysary Opotherapy in Gynecological Practice; Its Immediate Results', *International Abstract of Surgery Supplementary to Surgery, Gynecology and Obstetrics*, vol. XIX, ed. Franklin H. Martin, August Bier, Paul Lècene and B. G. A. Moynihan (Chicago: Surgical Publishing Company of Chicago, 1914), 647. See also Mary Lynn Stewart, *For Health and Beauty: Physical Culture for French Women 1880s–1930s* (Baltimore and London: Johns Hopkins University Press, 2001), 49.
55. Jayle, *La Gynécologie*, 2, my translation.
56. Jayle, *La Gynécologie*, 369, my translation.
57. Jayle, *La Gynécologie*, 395, my translation.
58. Jayle, *La Gynécologie*, 369, my translation.
59. Jayle, *La Gynécologie*, 370, my translation.
60. Jayle, *La Gynécologie*, 370, my translation.
61. Jayle, *La Gynécologie*, 525–6, my translation.
62. Jayle, *La Gynécologie*, 526, my translation.
63. Sander Gilman, 'Black Bodies, White Bodies: Toward an Iconography of Female Sexuality in Late Nineteenth-Century Art, Medicine, and Literature', *Critical Inquiry* 12, no. 1 (1985): 204–42.
64. See for example Carlos López-Beltrán, 'In the Cradle of Heredity: French Physicians and L'Hérédité Naturelle in the Early 19th Century', *Journal of the History of Biology* 37, no. 1 (2004): 39–72; Martin Staum, 'Nature and Nurture in French Ethnography and Anthropology 1859–1914', *Journal of the History of Ideas* 65, no. 3 (2004): 475–95.
65. Verneau, cited in Jayle, *La Gynécologie*, 153, my translation.
66. Lomas, 'A Canon of Deformity', 432; Staum, 'Nature and Nurture', 486.
67. Jayle, *La Gynécologie*, 3, 6.
68. Jayle, *La Gynécologie*, 102, my translation.
69. Jayle, *La Gynécologie*, 154.
70. Jayle, *La Gynécologie*, 156, my translation.
71. Jayle, *La Gynécologie*, 154, my translation.
72. Marius Turda and Aron Gillette, *Latin Eugenics in Comparative Perspective* (London: Bloomsbury, 2014), 47.
73. Turda and Gillette, *Latin Eugenics in Comparative Perspective*, 48.
74. French Eugenics Society, cited in Turda and Gillette, *Latin Eugenics in Comparative Perspective*, 48.
75. Benedict-Auguste Morel, *Traité des dégénérescences physiques, intellectuelles et morales de l'espèce humaine* (Paris: J. B. Baillière, 1857).
76. Morel, cited in Susan Y. Najita, *Decolonizing Cultures in the Pacific: Reading History and Trauma in Contemporary Fiction* (New York and London: Routledge, 2006), 48.

77. Mitchell Bryan Hart, *Social Science and the Politics of Modern Jewish Identity* (Stanford: Stanford University Press, 2000), 79.
78. Jayle, *La Gynécologie*, 7, my translation.
79. Jayle, *La Gynécologie*, 154, my translation.
80. Jayle, *La Gynécologie*, 3–4.
81. Jayle, *La Gynécologie*, 3–4.
82. See, for example, Joanne Woiak, 'Drunkenness, Degeneration, and Eugenics in Britain, 1900–1914' (PhD thesis, University of Toronto, 1988), 22; William H. Schneider, 'The Eugenics Movement in France, 1890–1940', in *The Wellborn Science: Eugenics in Germany, France, Brazil, and Russia*, ed. Mark B. Adams (New York and Oxford: Oxford University Press, 1990), 94–5.
83. Jayle, *La Gynécologie*, 6, my translation.
84. Arthur de Gobineau, *The Inequality of Human Races*, trans. Adrian Collins (London: William Heinemann, [1853] 1915), 25. On degeneration and de Gobineau, see François Vergès, *Monsters and Revolutionaries: Colonial Family Romance and Métissage* (Durham: Duke University Press, 1999), 95–6.
85. Comte de Buffon, *Buffon's Natural History*, vol. 9 (London: H. D. Symonds, 1797), 318; see also Susanne Lettow, 'Improving Reproduction: Articulations of Breeding and "Race-Mixing" in French and German Discourse (1750–1800)', in *The Secrets of Generation: Reproduction in the Long Eighteenth Century*, ed. Raymond Stephanson and Darren N. Wagner (Toronto: University of Toronto Press, 2015), 127.
86. See Michael Hau, *The Cult of Health and Beauty in Germany: A Social History, 1890–1930* (Chicago and London: University of Chicago Press, 2003).
87. See Hau, *The Cult of Health and Beauty in Germany*.
88. Carl Heinrich Stratz, *Die Schönheit des weiblichen Körpers* (Stuttgart: Verlag von Ferdinand Enke, 1908), 2.
89. Stratz, *Die Schönheit des weiblichen Körpers*, 2, translation by Christiane Kühling.
90. Stratz, *Die Schönheit des weiblichen Körpers*, 3.
91. Lomas, 'A Canon of Deformity', 432, 444n39.
92. Stratz, *Die Schönheit des weiblichen Körpers*, chap. 2.
93. Stratz, *Die Schönheit des weiblichen Körpers*, 2.
94. Hau, *The Cult of Health and Beauty in Germany*, 41–2.
95. Stratz, *Die Schönheit des weiblichen Körpers*, 144–5, translation by Christiane Kühling.
96. Stratz, *Die Schönheit des weiblichen Körpers*, 144, translation by Christiane Kühling.
97. Stratz, *Die Schönheit des weiblichen Körpers*, 71.

98. Stratz, *Die Schönheit des weiblichen Körpers*, chap. 4. See also Hau, *The Cult of Health and Beauty in Germany*, 43–4.
99. Stratz, *Die Schönheit des weiblichen Körpers*, 67, translation by Christiane Kühling.
100. Stratz, *Die Schönheit des weiblichen Körpers*, 75, translation by Christiane Kühling.
101. Stratz, *Die Schönheit des weiblichen Körpers*, 75.
102. Hau, *The Cult of Health and Beauty in Germany*, 91.
103. Hau, *The Cult of Health and Beauty in* Germany, 88.
104. Stratz, *Die Schönheit des weiblichen Körpers*, 77, translation by Christiane Kühling.
105. Patrick Wolfe, 'Settler Colonialism and the Elimination of the Native', *Journal of Genocide Research* 8, no. 4 (2006): 387–409.
106. Autoblow 2, 'The Vulva Paper'.
107. Kabas, 'Meet the Winners of the "World's Most Beautiful Vagina" Pageant'.
108. *Embarrassing Bodies*, 'Enlarged Labia', television program, Channel 4, website transcript, accessed 10 January 2018, http://cms.channel4embarrassingillnesses.com/video/embarrassing-bodies/consultation-enlarged-labia/, emphasis mine.
109. *Embarrassing Bodies*, 'Enlarged Labia', emphasis mine.
110. Cryle and Stephens, Normality, 14.
111. Cryle and Stephens, *Normality*, 327.
112. Cryle and Stephens, *Normality*, 14.
113. Cryle and Stephens, *Normality*, 9.
114. Michel Foucault, *The History of Sexuality*, vol. 1, trans. Robert Hurley (Penguin: London and New York, 1978), 140.

CHAPTER 6

Deviant Desires

Félix Jayle was not the only gynaecologist at the turn of the twentieth century who desired to understand what genital shape said about female health. Across the Atlantic, eminent American obstetrician and sex reformer Robert Latou Dickinson provided detailed measurements and illustrations of 'hypertrophied' labia minora in a paper titled 'Hypertrophies of the Labia Minora and Their Significance', published in the journal *American Gynecology* in 1902.[1] In this paper, Dickinson strenuously disagreed with the common belief that hypertrophy of the labia minora was mainly found in Bushman tribes, criticising the moniker 'Hottentot apron' as a 'gross error'. He claimed that he himself had documented many cases in which the labia minora were three to five centimetres in projection, 'as long as those of most of the carefully recorded cases among Hottentots',[2] and dismissed Charles Alexandre Lesueur's illustration of the tablier (see Fig. 4.1) as 'a fleshy exaggeration, badly drawn'.[3] Dickinson argued instead that hypertrophy of the labia minora was not a racial or biological feature, but acquired through masturbation. Combining his observations of women's vulvas with their own confessions of their sexual histories, he concluded that hypertrophy of the labia minora and surrounding structures indicated the presence of a masturbatory habit, either in the past or ongoing.

This chapter draws on Dickinson's anatomical studies to argue that the Freudian twentieth century nurtured the growth of psychiatric theories correlating abnormal genital anatomy and abnormal desire. A new and sophisticated science of the mind shifted the medical gaze

© The Author(s) 2019
C. Nurka, *Female Genital Cosmetic Surgery*,
https://doi.org/10.1007/978-3-319-96490-4_6

away from the archetypal 'Hottentot apron' toward a theory of sexual perversion. Félix Jayle and Robert Latou Dickinson represented two competing explanations for labial hypertrophy. One was *evolutionary*, the other *behavioural*. For Jayle, labial hypertrophy was decidedly racial and appeared as an atavism among white women; Dickinson, on the other hand, attributed labial enlargement to masturbation. But this did not mean that race disappeared. After all, Dickinson claimed that 'in some tribes low in the scale it [masturbation] is universal among the women'. In white women, 'primitive instincts' reinforced by neurotic heredity provided favourable conditions for immoderate masturbation.[4] However, when white neurosis was the main model of explanation for genital abnormality, anthropological studies of black women were pushed to the periphery.

By the beginning of the twentieth century, gynaecological medicine looked increasingly towards psychiatry to understand female-specific mental illness. From around the eighteenth century, the 'nervous woman', or the 'hysteric', was the most visible example of a science of sex that saturated female biology with sexual pathology. Historian and philosopher Michel Foucault termed this process the 'hysterization of women's bodies'.[5] For modern clinicians, the body revealed clues not just about disease and how it worked, but also about the nature of sex. Because women were considered to be the representatives of sex itself (women were sometimes referred to in medical books as '*the* sex'), their bodies and desires became conspicuous targets of medical interrogation and analysis. As Sigmund Freud famously wrote in his meditation on female sexuality, femininity was a riddle to be deciphered.[6] According to Foucault, the modern sciences which Freud helped to define produced sexuality as 'an obscure speech (*parole*) that had to be ferreted out and listened to'.[7] The modern, secular sexual sciences adapted 'the ancient [Christian] procedure of confession to the rules of scientific discourse'[8] in producing sex as a problem of truth that spoke itself through bodies, symptoms and nosologies. As Dickinson wrote of the process of treatment for masturbation, 'confession, however fragmentary, is a long first step toward recovery'.[9]

Gynaecology played an important role in locating the 'obscure speech' of sex and the means for its decipherment in the female genitals. In this chapter, I look at how Dickinson solicited the 'truth' of sex through consulting the individual's body to scrutinise her distance from 'normal' female sexuality. Dickinson was quite convinced that the shape of the vulva revealed the female patient's masturbatory habits and believed that the patients who showed signs of hypertrophy and freely admitted masturbating provided the evidence to prove that his theory was correct. Hence, if a woman with 'marked enlargements' denied having masturbated, she was assumed to be lying.[10] Female reticence had to be overcome by careful and sensitive questioning. Unlike boys, girls were considered to be so pathetically ignorant as not to comprehend that the good feeling aroused by masturbation was sexual, which made it all the more urgent for doctors to identify and stop the practice. The influential British sexologist Havelock Ellis suggested, for example, that in hysterics, the sexual instinct was so repressed that even though masturbation gave them pleasure, they were 'quite innocent of any knowledge of the erotic character of the experience'.[11] Similarly, Dickinson argued that while the male sex drive was well understood, in girls the masturbation problem was more difficult to address because 'the secretiveness of the girl lessens the chances of detection or confession of a solitary indulgence that is self-taught'.[12]

From the late nineteenth century, it was not uncommon for medical guides and textbooks to portray women as wilfully ignorant of sex to the point of stupidity or as shrewd dissemblers who wantonly deceived well-meaning doctors. Doctors commonly shared and believed stories of cunning female patients who deliberately incited physicians to inspect their genitals for the perverted purpose of sexual gratification.[13] In some instances, doctors themselves produced the erotic responses they were looking for, as in the case related by Dr. A. J. Bloch, who claimed to have detected signs of sexual perversion in a nine-year-old girl. After touching the entrance to her vagina and the labia minora with no sign of excitement from the girl, he then proceeded to the clitoris, whence 'the legs were thrown widely open, the face became pale, the breathing short and rapid, the body twitched from excitement', and the girl emitted 'slight groans'. Bloch performed a clitoridectomy.[14] Girls and women were deceptive and secretive, but their genitals could tell the doctor if they had a venereal disease or were virgins or masturbators.

Dickinson saw himself as a sexual detective in taking 'detailed entries on anatomical findings ... as a matter of confirmation or contradiction of the patient's story',[15] especially in cases where he suspected masturbation was the cause of pelvic congestion or pain. Although Dickinson was a sexual liberal and ardent proponent of sex education, he dedicated over four decades to uncovering the secrets of the female genitals and the story they could tell about a woman's fantasy life, her femininity and her sexual health. His lifelong interest in female sexuality began with the hypertrophied labia minora and that which he perceived to be their cause.

AN ACQUIRED DEFORMITY

Dickinson's research was based on clinical data taken from the mostly white, middle-class women who had attended his practice in Brooklyn. He began his paper on 'Hypertrophies of the Labia Minora and Their Significance' with the revelation that in four recent American gynaecological textbooks what the authors were calling 'normal' virgin vulvas were in fact abnormal hypertrophied types. The paper presented detailed descriptions and illustrations drawn from Dickinson's own observations of 427 cases of various hypertrophies, including of the labia minora, the prepuce (clitoral hood), urethral glands, veins, clitoris, and areolae and breasts. His description of the hypertrophied labia minora is as follows:

> The type, or full development, of the deformity consists in a finely wrinkled and deeply pigmented enlargement of the labia minora and hypertrophy of some adjacent structures. Thickened, elongated, curled on themselves, thrown into tiny, close-set, irregular folds that cross at all angles, as in a cock's comb, the lesser labia protrude in all positions through the larger labia … One labium is sometimes greater than its fellow.[16]

An avid illustrator, Dickinson provided his own drawings showing the typical style of elongation, wrinkling and corrugation of hypertrophied labia minora. To stake his claim that masturbation was a cause, he had to counter the pregnancy hypothesis in arguing that the effects of parturition were not enough to produce the sorts of changes he was describing.[17] Using the rhetorical device of an imaginary case history, Dickinson relayed a tale of how the vulva of the masturbator changed over time. In the beginning, the prepuce and labia minora are smooth, with the latter hidden behind the labia majora. After a few months, the labia minora then grow larger, thicker and darker, developing ridges and folds. Within years, they become corrugated and asymmetrical, and project 1/4–1/2 an inch below the outer lips; the prepuce wrinkles. They continue to grow, acquiring a 'weatherbeaten' appearance and 'hanging down in folds like curtains'; the vulva is desensitised. Finally, they shrink and atrophy with age.[18] He provided three illustrations to show the stages of increase, archetypal hypertrophy, and then 'flabbiness and atrophy found years after friction or pressure has been abandoned'.[19]

Dickinson reproduced these findings in greater illustrative detail in his book *Human Sex Anatomy: A Topographical Hand Atlas* (1933). Although Jayle had not mentioned Dickinson's 1902 paper at all, Dickinson referenced Jayle's work in the *Hand Atlas*, calling his *Gynécologie* 'a much neglected volume' that 'should be included in every reference collection or well equipped gynecological library'.[20] In fact, Dickinson had attempted to collaborate with Jayle, but his invitation was rebuffed. Dickinson wrote: 'To Jayle we owe a large debt for his extensive, varied and lucid drawings and text, but when I begged him to carry the work further he declared other investigations were more engrossing to him'.[21] This must have come as a blow to Dickinson, whose passion for illustration and scientific exactitude led him to dedicate four decades of his life to sketching his patients' vulvas.

In spite of his praise of Jayle's vulvar studies, Dickinson disagreed that hypertrophy of the labia minora was congenital and caused by ovarian problems. He also disagreed with Jayle about what was average, or most frequent: the membraniform or 'leaf-shaped' type of labia minora which Jayle had defined as normal Dickinson had described in his 1902 paper as deformed. Yet Jayle's work influenced Dickinson to change his view that hypertrophy of the labia could be called a deformity. In the *Hand Atlas*, Dickinson dispensed with the distinction between the 'normal virgin vulva' and the 'abnormal forms' that he had established in the 1902 paper.[22] Instead, he chose to call 'the average shape with average measurements ... a *basic* form to which the others can conveniently be referred without any claim that it constitutes the *normal* anatomy of the parts'.[23]

However, this careful relabelling did not do much to shift the basic distinction between the prototypical virgin vulva and its enlarged counterpart. In Dickinson's illustration, the labia minora in the 'basic' form of the virginal vulva are completely hidden. Yet even though Dickinson changed his language from deformity to variation, he was quite consistent in his view that habitual masturbation could cause both physical and nervous disorders. In the 1902 paper, he associated masturbation with endometritis (inflammation of the endometrial lining of the uterus), vaginal catarrh (mucous) and trigonitis (inflammation of the bladder).[24] In 1931, he had added cervicitis (inflammation of the cervix), mastitis (inflammation of the breast), ovaritis (inflammation of the ovaries), dysmenorrhea (menstrual cramps), menorrhagia (heavy menstrual flow) and eye strain.[25]

In his 1902 paper, Dickinson also proposed that vulval hypertrophy exhibited 'a very close relationship' to neurasthenia, citing Ellis's opinion that neurasthenics were 'especially predisposed to masturbation'.[26] Neurasthenia was a vague term for nervous illness which encompassed an impossibly large array of symptoms including dizziness, tinnitus, headaches and migraines, back pain, fatigue, nerve pain, dyspepsia, nausea, flatulence, abdominal distension and pain, irregular bowel movements, vaginal discharge, irregular or heavy menstruation and menstrual pain, and sexual excitability.[27] Cause and effect depended on the individual case: either masturbation stressed the nervous system causing neurasthenia or neurasthenic women were hypersexual and predisposed to 'the danger of sexual excess'.[28] Referring to masturbation as a 'mental misery',[29] Dickinson described in passing the unfortunate cases of two nymphomaniac patients who had 'wrecked their nerves with impossible excesses'.[30] Dickinson considered habitual masturbation an abnormal sexual behaviour indicating uninterest in or dislike of 'normal' heterosexual sex. Upon finding that 10 per cent of his patients had complained of apathy or disgust of the sex act, he surmised that this 'lack of feeling' was 'in direct proportion to the previous excesses'.[31] 'Revulsion of feeling after marriage' may partly be due, Dickinson suggested, to an exhaustion of sexual energy through premarital masturbation, but more often to a distaste for the 'male caress'.[32] In this opinion, he followed Ellis, who had proposed that excessive prepubertal masturbation led, especially in women, 'to an aversion for normal coitus in later life'.[33] For Dickinson, masturbating women were physically and mentally abnormal, occupying a sexual spectrum with frigidity and aversion to men at one end and nymphomania at the other. His early-twentieth-century views, however, came out of a longer medical discourse that associated masturbation with physical disease and mental disorder, dating back to the eighteenth century.

MASTURBATORS AND NYMPHOMANIACS

As documented by historian Thomas Laqueur in his excellent book *Solitary Sex*,[34] the modern *medicalised* discourse of masturbation began around the first decade of the eighteenth century with the publication of a pamphlet titled *Onania*, by a Swiss physician named Samuel-Auguste Tissot. *Onania* portrayed masturbation as an evil that induced horrible physical and mental diseases, and a grisly death.[35] Female masturbators were vulnerable to 'hysterical fits', 'incurable jaundices', 'violent cramps in the stomach and back', 'acute pains in the nose', *fluor albus* (leukorrhea), 'descents and ulcerations' of the womb and 'extension ... of the clitoris'.[36] According to Laqueur, this was when the story of Onan travelled from the pulpit to the clinic. But masturbation did not just cause physical disorder; it also interfered with the sexual order. Dickinson's argument that masturbation turned women away from heterosexual sex can be found in Tissot. A common symptom in women, Tissot wrote, was 'the indifference which this infamous practice leaves for the lawful pleasures of Hymen, even when their inclinations and powers still remain; an indifference which does not only induce many to embrace a life of celibacy, but even accompanies the nuptial bed'. The pleasures of masturbation induced women to remain unmarried and, if they did marry, to feel no pleasure from penetrative sex. At worst, a woman 'detested' it.[37] In 1739, a medical guide aimed at ordinary women titled *The Ladies Dispensatory or Every Woman Her Own Physician* asserted that a most grievous effect of masturbation was barrenness because it caused 'an Indifferency to the Pleasures of *Venus*, and in Time a total Ineptitude to the Act of Generation itself'.[38] It is a tormenting situation for a woman, the *Dispensatory* asserted, if 'she feels in herself no Inclinations to the Enjoyment of it [heterosexual intercourse] ... and is thereby not only insensible, as to her own Particular, but makes imperfect to her Husband, that exquisite Pleasure, which ought to result from their mutual Embraces'.[39] Women were not only bound to the natural law of procreative power, but if they masturbated, they were at risk of ruining the heterosexual pleasures that natural law also decreed. As Laqueur has shown, Tissot and his contemporaries did not believe masturbation to be a crime against God's law as laid out in the Bible, but a vice that contravened the natural laws of the physical body.[40] That is, visible decay of the body was a reliable sign of immoral acts: masturbation was immoral because it violated the laws of nature, and any organism that violated natural law was bound to suffer. Marriage law was, then, thought to reflect a natural law that endorsed monogamous heterosexuality as the only legitimate form of sexual pleasure.

Masturbation had unique consequences for women. According to Tissot, it could lead to a most disastrous female-specific illness called *Furor Uterinus*, or what we now recognise as 'nymphomania'. Tissot wrote that *Furor Uterinus* 'deprives them [women] of decency and reason, and puts them upon a level with the most lascivious brutes, till a desperate death snatches them from pain and infamy'.[41] *Furor Uterinus* would come to be known as 'nymphomania' through the work of medical writers such as Johann Dolaüs, Jean Astruc and William Cullen.[42] But it was in 1771 that French doctor M. D. T. Bienville would bring 'nymphomania' into the public domain in his widely distributed pamphlet *Nymphomania, or, a Dissertation concerning the Furor Uterinus* (published in English in 1775). In this pamphlet, Bienville fleshed out the character and various miseries of the unfortunate nymphomaniac, issuing grave warnings that female indulgence in sexual pleasure would lead to gynaecological ailments, madness and death. In the final stage of the disease, the incurable nymphomaniac's reproductive system was afflicted with abscesses, ulcers and cancerous tumours.[43] As a disease of the brain, it inflamed in women excessive passion, causing sexual aggression, frenzied desire, delirium, rage and madness. Nymphomania was the curse of unrequited or withheld love and the consequence of novels that set the passionate mind afire with lascivious thoughts; it caused women to think and speak of nothing but sex; and it befell widows and 'debauched' women (presumably prostitutes) who had suddenly been deprived of regular sex, as well as married women whose husbands were cold lovers or impotent. In short, nymphomania arose from unfillable sexual frustration that drove women literally mad with desire. Importantly, Bienville also declared that nymphomaniacs were chronic masturbators who 'perpetually dishonor themselves in secret by habitual pollutions'.[44] By the nineteenth century masturbation and nymphomania had become mutually reinforcing diagnoses.[45]

That Faithful Mirror

With the rise of the 'diseases' of masturbation and nymphomania in the eighteenth and nineteenth centuries, doctors began to look for the symptoms of disordered desires and sex practices in the characteristics of the body. As Tissot wrote, the appearance of the body was the 'faithful mirrour' of the state of health of the body as well as the soul.[46] Both masturbation and nymphomania were thought to reveal themselves in the abnormal size of the female sexual organs. In his 1711 treatise on venereal disease, British surgeon John Marten related that post-mortem examinations had shown that women with *Furor Uterinus* had enlarged ovaries.[47] According to the *Ladies Dispensatory*, the protrusion of the clitoris common to masturbators caused women to be mistaken for 'Hermaphrodites, who were equally qualified for both Actions of Generation'.[48] Bienville thought that nymphomania was accompanied by a generalised inflammation of the vagina and womb, and localised swelling of the clitoris 'larger than in discreet women'.[49]

Nineteenth-century proto-psychiatrists, or 'alienists', as they were then called, came to the conclusion that the genital organs and the brain were connected by a sympathetic nervous system. The director of the Indiana Hospital for the Insane and president of the Indiana State Medical Association Dr. Wilson Lockhart had said in 1866 that diseases of the mind were first and foremost diseases of the body.[50] This thinking was also apparent in the gynaecological medicine of the time. In 1838, French gynaecologist and speech therapist Colombat de L'Isère wrote that nymphomaniacs bore in their bodies 'some of the characteristics of Sappho', whereupon, among other signs, 'the clitoris and the nymphae, which are generally of anormal length, are endowed with exquisite sensibility'.[51] Ten years later, British physician Samuel Ashwell asserted that the physical cause of nymphomania could be put down to 'an excited, enlarged, and sensitive clitoris', usually occurring in women of 'an irritable, excitable temperament',[52] while in 1880, his compatriot David D. Davis observed that women predisposed to nymphomania possessed 'a more than ordinary development of the sexual organs'.[53]

In the nineteenth century, it was not uncommon for doctors to recommend clitoridectomy as a treatment for masturbation and nymphomania. For instance, German physician Cristoph Wilhelm Hufeland recommended removal of the clitoris and nymphae for the most severe case of nymphomania,[54] which was also recommended by American doctor John Kellogg (of breakfast cereal fame) and British gynaecologist Heywood Smith.[55] The British surgeon Isaac Baker Brown gained particular notoriety for his penchant for resorting to clitoridectomy to 'cure' masturbation.[56] In 1867 Baker Brown was expelled from the Obstetrical Society of London for carrying out many such operations. It had by then become evident to the majority of physicians and specialists that clitoridectomy did nothing to relieve the symptoms of hysteria, though some members of the British Gynaecological Society had expressed the opinion in 1886 that clitoridectomy 'held out the best prospect of curing masturbation' and had only fallen out of favour due to 'sentimental objections'.[57] In the same year, German gynaecologist Franz Winckel had declared clitoral amputation to be 'a dark page in the history of our progress' and that 'the majority of gynaecologists are firmly convinced that it is quite useless in epilepsy, hysteria, or masturbation'.[58]

By 1880, American physician Morton Monroe Eaton asserted that he had never seen a case of an enlarged clitoris accompanying a case of nymphomania, and that hypertrophy of the nymphae was, in fact, more common. He thought that women with enlarged labia minora 'were more than ordinarily passionate',[59] and that their appendages caused such great friction as to 'excite sexual passion, and give rise in some cases to nymphomania'.[60] He strongly discouraged amputation of the clitoris, but advised that in cases where the labia were a source of irritation and annoyance, they could be removed 'easily and safely', using surgical scissors.[61] As with Tissot's theory that physical appearance was a mirror for the state of health of body and mind, Eaton associated enlarged organs with excessive passions (Figs. 6.1, 6.2).

For much of the eighteenth and nineteenth centuries, enlarged sex organs were usually spoken of as a result of nymphomania, which was generally thought to be a product of some kind of physical cause embedded in the body's humoral constitution, such as a congenitally large clitoris; genital swelling, sensitivity and excitability; or a nervous morbidity of the brain. But by the close of the nineteenth century, doctors were inclined to view the act of masturbation itself as responsible for female genital enlargement.

A landmark book compiling every conceivable disease arising from masturbation was *Excessive Venery, Masturbation and Continence* by Joseph W. Howe, Professor of Clinical Surgery at the Bellevue Medical College in New York.[62] First published in 1883, Howe's authoritative work on sexual excess and its diseases contained a detailed account of the effects on the vulva of masturbation. By 1888, the latest reprint of the book was hailed by a reviewer in the American *Lancet* as 'the most advanced professional knowledge upon these subjects',[63] and it continued to be reprinted into the next century, even after Howe's death in 1890. Howe wrote:

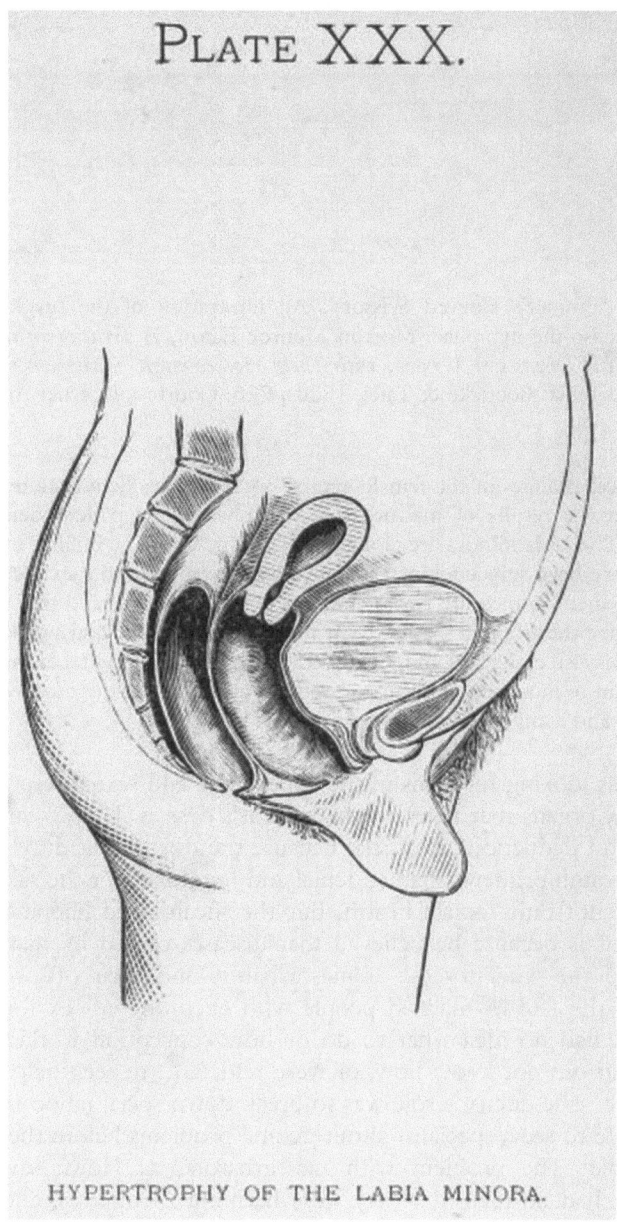

Fig. 6.1 Plate XXX, 'Hypertrophy of the Labia Minora'. Morton Monroe Eaton, *A Treatise on the Medical and Surgical Diseases of Women, with Their Homeopathic Treatment* (New York and Philadelphia: Boericke & Tafel, 1880). Courtesy Internet Archive, San Francisco

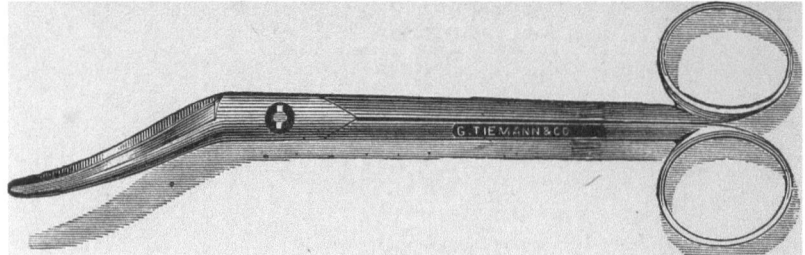

Fig. 6.2 'Emmet's Curved Scissors'. An illustration of the surgical scissors used to excise the nymphae. Morton Monroe Eaton, *A Treatise on the Medical and Surgical Diseases of Women, with Their Homeopathic Treatment* (New York and Philadelphia: Boericke & Tafel, 1880), 726. Courtesy Internet Archive, San Francisco

> The local changes in the female genital organs always demonstrate plainly enough the results of masturbation, even when the patient denies the habit. The labia minora are elongated. In some cases the pulling to which they have been subjected increases their size to an enormous extent. I have known them to measure two inches and a half in breadth and to look very much like the ears of a spaniel ... At the base they are red and swollen. The clitoris is also elongated and thicker than in health ... A digital examination is certain to increase the normal secretions, and produce turgescence of the clitoris and nymphae.[64]

Howe was looking for signs in the appearance and sexual responsiveness of the sex organs that revealed the patient's desires. He saw such observations and deductions as crucial because the doctor was duty-bound to break through prudery, shame, denial and ignorance for the sake of safe-guarding not only female health, but the 'health and happiness of the race'. This is because he believed that diseases caused by masturbation could sap the 'vital forces' of masturbators and their offspring.[65] He spoke of the fate of married people who encountered sex for the first time and had no idea what to do or how conception worked, and of those who did not know how, or were reluctant, to seek help for geni-tal disease. The doctor's role was to break down social taboo to encourage people to see a specialist about genital problems before they became untreatable. The problem with masturbators, as Howe saw it, was that they had no idea that they were harming themselves, and because they were secretive about it, the doctor's responsibility was to force a confession for the sake of sexual hygiene. Hence, Howe stressed the necessity of inquiring into the private sexual lives of his patients.

The evidence suggests that Dickinson derived his theory of labial hypertrophy directly from Howe, as Dickinson had only just graduated with a medical degree from Long Island College Hospital a year before Howe, a professor, published *Excessive Venery, Masturbation and Continence*. Like Howe, Dickinson saw elongated labia minora as a telling sign of masturbation. By the time of his scientific publication on 'Hypertrophies of the Labia Minora and Their Significance' in 1902, Dickinson had already amassed 1,000 gynaecological cases. Although he never acknowledged Howe in his 1902 paper, Dickinson had the same aim of peering into the sex lives of his patients to extract confessions so that he might help married couples better understand their sexed biology and sexual intimacies.

THE CONJUGAL VULVA

It was with this aim in mind that he wrote, with Lura Beam, *A Thousand Marriages*, which was published in 1931.[66] *A Thousand Marriages* drew upon an impressive 1,098 cases, 900 with extensive notes on the patients' sex histories, collected over Dickinson's forty-two years in practice as a general practitioner and gynaecological specialist (from 1882 to 1924).[67] Through his many consultations, he came to believe that women's health 'was bound up with their happiness', which, in women, was instinctually directed toward love.[68] This book could be considered a result of the many accounts of sexual unhappiness by married women that had been revealed to him in his consultations.

The book was part of a series issued by the Committee on Maternal Health, which Dickinson had formed in 1923 with the backing of female philanthropists. According to the committee, the practical goal of *A Thousand Marriages* was 'conjugal hygiene', which meant that its chief social value lay in its understanding of marital disharmony and how to prevent it for the benefit of social harmony, particularly with regard to reducing divorce, adultery and prostitution.[69] 'A hygiene of marriage', the committee wrote, 'can do its part in training people in sane choice of mates, can lend aid in adjustment to marriage and, above all can further stability of union'.[70] The discourse of marital 'hygiene' grew out of eugenic philosophy and referred to preventive social-reform measures that would eradicate degenerate people and bodies from the population and encourage the propagation of the 'fit'. Like many of the sex reformers of his time, Dickinson was a eugenicist who saw heterosexual reproduction as a *social*, and not simply a biological, phenomenon.

Dickinson's sexological research took place in a social climate beset by anxieties over the decline of white middle-class birth rates, as was also the case in Europe. In the 1920s, the white middle-class birth rate in the United States dropped significantly, with Dickinson expressing concern, in 1925, that one in five marriages in New York were childless.[71] Most of the women who attended his practice had sought him out because they were afflicted with what he termed 'involuntary sterility': that is, they wanted children but had problems conceiving.[72] He wanted white middle-class couples to be both healthy and fertile, and in his findings on sterility in married couples, he warned that 'imperfect sexual adjustment' was a 'positive deterrent' to fertility.[73] Dickinson was also actively involved in promoting birth control as a key foundation for the happy marriage and healthy children. Successful fertility was about encouraging the right kind of (white, middle-class) people to have the right number of children—and it would also promote healthy sexuality. Dickinson's psychoanalytic view was that regular penetrative sex was healthy for couples and that the contraceptive methods of sexual abstinence and withdrawal were psychologically damaging. While birth control could foster 'healthy' and 'normal' heterosexual sex for couples, it could also limit overpopulation among the poor and prevent the reproduction of undesirables. As historian Jane Carey argues, a key platform of the eugenic approach to fertility 'was to limit the "over-fertility" of dysgenic groups', such as the 'feebleminded', the 'mentally defective' and the 'poverty-stricken'.[74] Dickinson had formed the Committee on Maternal Health in 1923 because he felt that the activist birth control movement, led by Margaret Sanger, was not scientific enough and that only empirical research undertaken by trained medical professionals could form the basis of sound arguments in favour of contraception.[75] At this time, sex reformers like Sanger argued that birth control could 'prevent the birth of diseased or defective children' and limit 'the fertility of the feebleminded, the mentally defective, the poverty-stricken'.[76] Likewise, Dickinson fully supported the sterilisation of 'the defective and the criminally insane' because it could prevent 'the degenerate and the criminal … from propagating their kind'.[77] For Dickinson, 'marital hygiene' meant creating the optimal conditions for marriage and reproduction that would create model citizens and eliminate undesirables.

Dickinson's sex research was necessarily bound up with fertility on the one side and sterility on the other. In between, there was sexual pleasure and marriage. But in the end, any question put to sex research needed to address itself to the achievement of normality. As Dickinson put it: 'No one aspect of human fertility or sex life can be properly investigated by itself alone. This holds good whether that aspect be sex education or marriage; control of conception or sterility; premarital instruction or conjugal maladjustment; abortion or sterilization of the unfit; or the dual considerations that are focal and ultimate, namely, the normal and the ideal'.[78] In his desire to build the foundations for the normal and the ideal in marriage, Dickinson combined the well-established framework of eugenics with the newly developed analytic tools of psychoanalysis. He thus developed a system of practice that could promote *social* happiness and stability through *individual* psycho-sexual interventions.

In *A Thousand Marriages*, Dickinson appears as a proto-psychoanalyst, even though he insisted that when he began taking case notes or sex histories (from 1890), he had no knowledge at all of psychoanalysis.[79] In this book, he attempts to understand gynaecological problems in the context of a woman's sexual relationship to herself and others. After his first few years in practice, Dickinson came to believe that female gynaecological complaints should not be isolated to the genitals, but examined in relation to a woman's social relationships, a holistic approach that he ridiculously termed 'pelvic social problems'.[80] He had found that a woman's sexual history usually revealed itself in the midst of a major life change such as pregnancy and childbirth, as this was usually the time at which the patient 'suddenly bursts into speech'.[81] For Dickinson, the appearance of the vulva when probed by the doctor was crucial to the consultation because it expressed a woman's attitude to heterosexual intercourse. When a gynaecological problem is a sexual one, he asserted, 'there are not two but three participants in pelvic examination—the patient, the doctor and the problem'.[82] Some patients he marked in his records as 'erotic at examination'.[83] These were women who were interpreted as harbouring unconscious erotic desire, which manifested in vaginal secretion, clitoral-bulb swelling and flushing, and the occasional clitoral erection. Dickinson would deliberately hurt such 'passionate' women to stop these reactions. Alternatively, a woman may shrink from examination, and to her may be assigned the problem of frigidity: 'The vulva stands for emotional experience and the emotions appear automatically as the vulva is approached, but in the form of fear, or resentment and anger against the doctor.'[84]

In his meditations on sex in marriage, Dickinson divided female experience into categories of 'adjusted' and 'maladjusted', while noting that these were fluid states that shifted with changes in the couple's life experiences and circumstances. Sexual shame or disgust, presence of venereal disease, infertility, abstinence, male impotence, lack of orgasm and unequal levels of sexual desire could all make women unhappy and maladjusted. Adjusted women, on the other hand, achieved a satisfying sexual balance. The main difference between sexually adjusted and maladjusted women, Dickinson explained, was that adjusted women were mentally unconflicted and accepted their situation. All marriages went through trouble, but the woman's response to the trouble was what determined her level of adjustment. The happiest women desired their husbands, enjoyed sexual intercourse, experienced mutual orgasm, and were more fertile than maladjusted women. They understood their bodies, told their husbands what they liked sexually, and worked through sexual difficulties with their husbands to enrich their sex lives. But the maladjusted woman struggled against marriage, and miserably repressed was the woman who refused, endured or loathed marital sex.

The book's feminist contribution is that it represented heterosexual women as having sexual needs, and it reproduced a great variety of female sexual experience in women's own words. The book presented rich qualitative sociological data, providing a sympathetic overview of the variety of women's experiences of sexual pleasure and pain, childbirth, abortion, birth-control methods, and their feelings of resentment at sexual inequality in their marriages. In his foreword to *A Thousand Marriages*, Havelock Ellis wrote of his pleasure at reading a work 'so scientific and so sane in its recognition of the real facts, so wise and tolerant in its attitude towards the variations which come within the range of normality'.[85] By this he meant that it was only by discussing sex in detail that it became possible to grasp the complexity and diversity of sexual experience, and to return sex to the status of a natural fact, rather than a shameful secret. In confronting the troubles of marriage truthfully, the empathetic gynaecologist could 'lift a weight of suffering from an unfortunate patient who for years has been befooled by some false notion of "sin" or "abnormality"'.[86] Ellis stressed the urgency of dispelling 'ignorance and superstition' among women, who were the greatest victims of 'the troubles of marriage and of the perils of sex'.[87]

There is no doubt that Dickinson believed that it was vital that women needed to be taught about sex and men needed to be taught how to please their wives sexually. He also encouraged women to take an active part in sexual negotiation and coitus. He did not believe that it should be normal for women to be left unsatisfied sexually, quite against social and religious custom, which held that women were, or ought to be, passionless. Consider the following passage, for example:

> Let it be noted that if a doctor asks the wife the mere question whether sex relations are 'normal' the answer is usually affirmative, although it develops later that what she meant by 'yes' was that the husband can enter and finish. Therefore nothing short of a specific query whether the woman herself has pleasurable excitement, or a definite climax or finish, and the relative frequency and completeness of satisfaction will give evidence in this matter. She may think that excitement or desire is all there is to 'normalcy'. She may have a rare orgasm and suppose this natural. She may need for detumescence [Havelock Ellis's term for discharge of sexual energy] two or more orgasms, yet think one is the normal.[88]

Yet while Dickinson sought to expand the ambit of sexual normality by championing active female sexuality and detaching sex from sin, his sexual liberalism was reliant on the boundary between the normal and the perverted. Dickinson was conducting his research in an era marked by the flourishing of the sexual sciences, or what Foucault has called '*scientia sexualis*'.[89] By the end of the nineteenth century, sex had become scientised as a natural fact, rather than a problem of religious moralism. Yet, as Foucault has argued, the sciences began to elaborate a 'world of perversion' that threatened the harmony of the matrimonial unit.[90] The course of nature appeared inevitably to flow toward the 'legitimate couple, with its regular sexuality', and which 'tended to function as a norm'.[91] Dickinson invested heterosexual reproductive marital sex with the power of the norm because it was the end-point towards which the sexual instinct and its expression in sex practices, even homosexual ones, were thought to lead.

What is interesting about Dickinson's work is that he saw opportunities for perversion to arise from *within* normality. Sexual perverts were not necessarily an entirely different breed to sexually normal people: any couple could become perverted if they lacked the knowledge that could help them build and maintain a 'normal' sexual relationship. Because he saw heterosexual intercourse as natural and necessary, Dickinson argued, quite controversially, that the Christian model of abstinence was perverse. Consequently, women were seen to be more vulnerable to perversion because they were more repressed. In fact, Dickinson saw 'good women' as so profoundly ignorant that they possessed 'no language and no terminology, either for their feelings or their anatomy'.[92] As women did not understand their own sexual impulses, it was up to male physicians like Dickinson to explain it to them and provide proper advice about self-control. For Dickinson, female sexual freedom stopped at marriage, or, perhaps more precisely, *began* in marriage: women's sexual liberation was achieved when they took pleasure in the husband. This was why he advocated sex education. Hence, the overwhelming message of *A Thousand Marriages* was that the greatest impediment to female sexual freedom was not male sexual entitlement to female bodies, but women's own sexual repression and fear. His solution was for women to find pleasure from the very institution (marriage) that secured their sexual and financial oppression. In the 1930s, Dickinson was advising couples on how to improve their sex lives a good three decades before William H. Masters and Virginia E. Johnson instigated the sex-therapy industry in the 1960s and 1970s. Yet the limitations that plagued Masters and Johnson were the same ones that underlay Dickinson's work with married women. As historian Stephen Garton explains, 'sex therapy might have been a radical critique of women's experience of heterosexuality, but in trying to fix this experience therapy made sexual dissatisfaction an individual failing rather than a symptom of the wider power relationships that shaped relationships between men and women'.[93]

MASTURBATORS AND LESBIANS

In Dickinson's work, hidden female perversion became a target for exposure because of its potential to disrupt normal marital sexual relations. The most common form of perversion among his female patients was masturbation, and its most visible sign was hypertrophy of the labia minora. While Dickinson believed that masturbation was an average practice among women, and that 'moderate usage may be called a normal sex experience',[94] masturbation became a problem of perversity when it was frequent and substituted for (hetero)sexual intercourse.[95] Following Ellis, Dickinson regarded auto-erotism as a natural sex instinct, though it was not precisely 'normal' because, as Ellis had put it, 'the natural aim of the sexual impulse is sexual conjunction'.[96] In describing auto-erotism as an 'elaborate simulation of sexual union',[97] Dickinson inferred that it was an inauthentic or inferior version of heterosexual pleasure. Again, this was due to the influence of Ellis, who had referred to the opinion of a doctor called Smith Baker that female aversion to marital sex could be blamed upon the 'substitution of mechanical and iniquitous excitations' that offer 'more thorough satisfaction than the mutual legitimate ones do'.[98] The basic assumption underlying Dickinson's concerns about marital happiness was that heterosexual penetrative sex was designed by nature to be the one and only legitimate outlet for the expression of human sexual pleasure. Although Dickinson claimed to be largely ignorant of Freud, his sexological philosophy reproduced the Freudian split between infantile clitoral and adult vaginal sexuality, whereupon a woman achieved 'normal femininity' upon relinquishing clitoral, or 'phallic', pleasure for the vaginal orgasm, or 'passive aim'; in Freudian terms, a girl became a normal woman when she swapped the wish for a penis (located in the clitoris) for that of a baby (located in the vagina and womb).[99] This did not necessarily mean that Dickinson thought that non-penetrative sexual pleasures should never be permitted. On the contrary, he was eager to break down religious prohibitions associating sex with shame. Nevertheless, he did suggest that the vaginal orgasm was the most appropriate kind, given his concerns that in many newly married women who had masturbated regularly, 'vaginal orgasm was hard to obtain after the habit of vulvar orgasm had been strongly set'.[100]

Using Ellis's hydraulic model of sexual energy as the concentration and release of pressure, Dickinson likened auto-erotic feelings and practice to 'the charge and discharge of a battery of electric energy' and reassured his patients that as menstruation was the physical preparation for a baby, erotic feeling was 'a preparation for response to the husband'.[101] It was, he summarised, a 'normal provision of nature, as a stage preparatory for heterosexual response'.[102] Dickinson held that auto-erotic excitement was harmless when it was a preparatory instinct; but prolonged auto-erotism caused congestion in the genitals and 'might permanently side-track the perfect response after marriage. It could help develop the lascivious mind'.[103] He worried that in unmarried women, masturbation could become so pleasurably addictive that they would desensitise themselves to vaginal orgasm.[104] Dickinson felt that auto-erotism could certainly play a positive role in the tutelage of husbands in how to please their wives,[105] but he cautioned that it ought never to serve as a replacement for heterosexual penetrative sex. This was likely based on Ellis's opinion that auto-erotism may be practised judiciously for relief of 'physical oppression and mental obsession', but if it 'is practiced in preference to sexual relationships, it at once becomes abnormal and may possibly lead to a variety of harmful results, mental and physical'.[106] Following Richard von Krafft-Ebing, Ellis thought that masturbation could awaken latent homosexual feeling and unlock perverse inclinations, explaining that the aversion for coitus helped to 'furnish a soil on which the inverted impulse may develop unimpeded'.[107]

Krafft-Ebing had proposed that there were two kinds of homosexuality: congenital and acquired. The congenital kind referred to a 'contrary sex instinct' that indicated a degree of natural or inherent bisexuality or homosexuality. The acquired kind was the result of a transformation of an innate 'normal' sex instinct through sex practices that ran counter to the 'natural' procreative sex instinct. Krafft-Ebing's theory of 'congenital' homosexuality was essentially eugenic because he saw it as a product of hereditary degeneration. He thought that the ancestral lines of such people showed physical and mental peculiarities, neuroses, psychoses, and other degenerative signs, and he adopted the Lamarckian position that a person may acquire an inclination for the same sex and then pass this down genetically to their descendants. His suggestion for the 'cure' of congenital and inveterate homosexuality was the 'prohibition of reproduction of such unfortunates'.[108] (As I will go on to show, this theory carried important implications for the sexological research on homosexuals or 'sex variants' that Dickinson would become involved with towards the end of his life.)

Importantly, in Krafft-Ebing's account, masturbation was the deciding factor in determining whether homosexuality was congenital or acquired. If the homosexual instinct existed before indulgence in solitary or mutual onanism, there was no cure except sterility; but if homosexual feeling arose after the beginning of masturbation, then it was acquired and therefore potentially treatable—that is, if the psychiatrist intervened before it became permanent. Masturbation, far more than any other influence, was the main catalyst for perversity. It reduced the 'noble and ideal sentiments' of heterosexual love to a 'coarse, animal desire for sexual satisfaction', constituting a disturbance of 'normal sexual satisfaction'.[109] Masturbation could leech all desire for the opposite sex, especially if practised in preference to the 'natural mode of satisfaction', whence it could cause physical neurosis in 'defective pleasurable feeling in coitus'.[110] Women of a bisexual disposition could be pulled away from the opposite sex both by masturbation and by unsatisfying heterosexual experiences (for example, by inattentive or impotent male lovers and venereal disease infection). Historian Jennifer Terry explains that around the turn of the century, lesbianism was attributed by many in the medical community to the sexual cruelty, indifference or incompetence of husbands, which drove women to seek the comfort of other women. Indeed, Krafft-Ebing believed that congenital lesbians were relatively rare and that most lesbianism was of the acquired kind and therefore more amenable to psychiatric treatment.[111] The implication, writes Terry, was that 'most lesbianism would disappear if men were more sensitive to women'.[112] If lesbianism could be acquired, then it was all the more important for men to understand how to pleasure their wives.

Much of Dickinson's work on female masturbation did not address homosexuality directly because his research was directed toward the 'average' middle-class, heterosexual American woman.[113] While Dickinson thought masturbation was common among 'women of high grade mentality and socially normal',[114] his interest in masturbation as a sign of sexual maladjustment inevitably led him to the question of lesbianism. By 1933, at the age of seventy-two, he proposed a blend of biomedical, anthropological and psychiatric research into intersex and homosexual people so that science could better understand 'normal' sex and heterosexuality. The new scientific study of sex hormones had begun in the 1920s and influenced the psychiatric discourse of sexual abnormality and perversion. In light of such developments, Dickinson wanted to investigate the possible links between 'physical defect' and perversions of the sex instinct in homosexuals, calling for the study of body build, genital anatomy and sex hormones in conjunction with heredity and environmental influences in 'individuals with homosexual tendencies'.[115]

By 1935, Dickinson had been contacted by a lesbian journalist and gay rights advocate called Jan Gay, who had amassed her own research on lesbians, including 300 case histories compiled over a period of ten years, with a view to publishing her findings. But in order to publish her work, she first needed to obtain legitimacy from the medical community, which brought her to Dickinson.[116] Gay had the social connections by which she could recruit lesbian participants to a collaborative research project, while Dickinson provided the scientific authority and funding Gay needed to publish her research. This would be the beginning of Dickinson's new pet project to study the biographies and biologies of homosexual people. But as historian Henry L. Minton argues, Gay's agenda for social change could never be realised in such a project, which would reduce gay experience to a medical model of abnormality and cure.[117] Dickinson's attention was always drawn first and foremost to marital harmony; he was far less interested in reframing lesbian sexuality as socially normal than he was in understanding the physical and psycho-sexual conditions that might turn women away from heterosexual sex. Indeed, it is not difficult to see that Dickinson's obsession with female masturbation would inevitably lead him toward lesbian sexuality, given his conviction that masturbation became perverse if it did not culminate in regular and satisfying marital heterosexual intercourse.

THE SEX VARIANT STUDY

Dickinson's interest in sexual perversion led him to found the Committee for the Study of Sex Variants (CSSV), which conducted a 'sex variant' study from 1935 to 1941. The resulting publication, titled *Sex Variants: A Study of Homosexual Patterns*, was published as two volumes in 1941, and as a single volume in 1948.[118] The study, headed by psychiatrist George W. Henry, sought to present an objective, scientific account, with the twofold aim of the decriminalisation of homosexuality and social assimilation of homosexuals. The immediate aim was to better understand the 'sex variant' so that physicians would be equipped with the information that would assist them to intervene in marital and parenting relationships to encourage heterosexual and gender conformity via therapy, rather than penal incarceration. For Henry, the sex variant study's chief value was its interrogation of the 'factors in sexual maladjustment' with a view to preventing family breakdown and promoting 'mental hygiene', or psychological adjustment to social norms. It was envisaged as a public health project, to be of use primarily to physicians, who, Henry asserted, 'should be the mental hygiene leaders in the community'.[119] Henry described the sex variant in terms of social and sexual failure as a person who is unable to meet the demands of heterosexual marriage and reproduction, or unable to take on the responsibilities of parenthood, due to immature sexual development.[120]

The sex variant study was broadly assimilationist in its suggestion that incidence of sex variance could either be prevented in the first place by appropriate sex education, or be rechannelled into marital heterosexuality through psychiatric treatment. An aim of the study was therefore to break down religious sexual taboo in order to teach people, especially children, how to become happily heterosexual.[121] Because homosexuality was thought to be a product of both constitutional and environmental 'deficiencies', *Sex Variants* provided psychoanalytic case studies of men and women divided into bisexual, homosexual and narcissistic classes, appended with a variety of data on participants' biological and psychological characteristics, as well as family trees, to be read alongside their case histories.[122] These paratextual elements included charts of family lines showing evidence of inherited mental illness, as well as the degree of masculinity (aggressiveness) and femininity (submissiveness) in male and female ancestors; psychometric tests of masculinity and femininity of the sex-variant participants; charts showing the degree of masculinity and femininity in physical characteristics; and pelvic and genital measurements. The body measurements confirmed that 'the sex variant is intermediate between male and female' and possessed an 'immature form of skeletal development'.[123] As an intermediary, the sex variant was considered to be sexually underdeveloped, much like the foetal gonad before it undergoes hormonal change.

According to Henry, family patterns of gender maladjustment—masculinity in women and femininity in men—were extremely important factors in the continuance of homosexuality:

> If masculine females and feminine males reproduce, their children, even though they should be endowed with potentialities in keeping with their sex, grow up with a distorted conception of and an impaired emotional adaptability to masculinity and femininity. Such children are prone to psychosexual maladjustment which may become manifest in the form of sex variance, a neurosis or a psychosis.[124]

Although Henry stated that sex variants did not ordinarily reproduce for the obvious reason that they were generally not having procreative heterosexual sex, he did concede that 'as long as sex mating continues to be irrational, constitutionally predisposed sex variants are to be expected'.[125] Because Henry believed there was not a lot doctors could do about sex variants having children from their 'irrational' unions, he proposed sex education as the best way to enforce normative psychosexual development in children. In his view, children needed to be trained to become masculine men and feminine women so that they could participate fully in adult heterosexual life.[126] The theory was that if people understood their own sex urges, they could then make 'rational' mating decisions. Henry suggested that for adults, the best approach was institutional treatment to encourage heterosexual 'adjustment' through psychotherapy—particularly for middle-class patients who could afford to do so.

But what of those who failed to become heterosexual? What was to be done about these troublesome subjects of 'irrational' decision-making who would turn out to be bad marriage partners? Henry provided no clear answer to this question aside from the opinion that 'to the extent that a person of either sex has engaged in sex variant activity he or she is less likely to make a satisfactory heterosexual adjustment'.[127] If 'the most harmonious unions' were between people who were 'primarily heterosexual', where did that leave the maladjusted others—the bisexuals, homosexuals and narcissists? The unspoken alternative option was abstinence and segregation from the heterosexual community. This would have been the case for those socio-economically disadvantaged homosexual men and women who populated public homes, hospitals and asylums. As Terry has shown, American doctors had already been sterilising homosexual asylum patients since the late nineteenth century. She argues that the introduction of eugenics-based laws in a number of states from 1907 provided powerful support for widespread state-sponsored sterilisation of 'sexual perverts' and 'moral degenerates', categories that included homosexuals, prostitutes, drug addicts and syphilitics.[128]

Because Dickinson and Henry's sex variant study was essentially oriented toward creating the best conditions for heterosexual happiness, homosexuality was an object of scientific curiosity largely because it interfered with the happy marriage and social stability. When homosexuality wasn't represented as a threat, it served a pedagogical purpose to teach heterosexual men how to pleasure women. Dickinson wanted to understand the minute details of lesbian sex not because he wished to show that heterosexual and homosexual pleasures overlapped, though this was certainly one positive, if unintended, outcome of his sex research. Rather, he wanted to understand the procedure for female sexual satisfaction so that husbands could please their wives. As Henry wrote: 'Much can be learned from the study of the affectionate relations of sex variants which might contribute to the success of heterosexual unions'.[129] To this end, Dickinson provided comparative illustrations of man-on-woman and woman-on-woman sex to show how bodies could best be positioned for clitoral stimulation.

Dickinson also contributed educative illustrations of 'sex variant' vulvas, breasts and pelvic bones as well as gynaecological descriptions matched to the female case studies. Of the forty female volunteers selected for the *Sex Variants* publication, thirty-one submitted to gynaecological examination by Dr. L. Mary Moench, who measured their genitals and made tracings of them by placing a glass plate on the vulva, drawing an outline in crayon, and tracing it into paper; but these pictures were not detailed enough, so Dickinson reproduced drawings of his own that he felt matched Moench's descriptions and dimensions.[130] Terry notes that he was so meticulous in his sketches of the female genitals that he had been hailed as 'a cross between Havelock Ellis and Leonardo da Vinci'.[131]

In the sex variant study, Dickinson noticed 'certain striking *likenesses in genital anatomical morphology in autoeroticism and homosexual practice*'[132] and concluded that there were a number of signs that could be taken as evidence of masturbation and homosexuality: flush, wetness and erectility of the clitoris; a prepuce that is large and wrinkled or folded; a large glans clitoris; and long, protuberant labia minora that are also wrinkled, thickened or brawny.[133] Autoeroticism coupled with lesbian sexual experience strongly suggested present or future female maladjustment to marital heterosexuality. There is only one conceivable reason that Dickinson would have thought it necessary to identify masturbation and lesbian sex practices from the appearance of the labia minora, and that was because he thought that any sexual practice that did not involve a penis was automatically suspect.

The premarital exam (where engaged couples submitted themselves for medical examination and received sexual counselling) was an important first step in identifying female frigidity and lesbian desire in order to avert sexual trouble in marriage. It gave the doctor the opportunity to look for vulval or vaginal conditions that might be the cause of painful heterosexual intercourse, with a view to heading off acquired lesbianism at the pass, for Dickinson held that sexual distress upon coitus tended to drive a woman's newly awakened desire toward a woman.[134] The frigid woman could be taught to embrace the penis, thus extinguishing the opportunity for lesbian tendencies to overcome heterosexual ones, while the 'congenital' lesbian could be dissuaded from marriage altogether.

THE KINSEY REVOLUTION

In 1946, five years after the first volume of *Sex Variants* was published, Dickinson looked to colleague and friend Alfred Kinsey for advice on a research project he wanted to undertake on the signs of masturbation and homosexuality in the male genitals.[135] At this time, Kinsey was working on the book that would revolutionise the sexual mores of American society, *Sexual Behavior in the Human Male*.[136] Kinsey's work was groundbreaking, even for sexology, because it was an empirical study that flatly refused to interpret non-coital sex as perverse, preferring instead to emphasise sexual diversity. For Kinsey, consensual non-coital sex practices were natural and normal because they were statistically frequent. Terry relates that Kinsey 'politely criticised' Dickinson's project on methodological grounds,[137] but it is clear that he would not have supported Dickinson's investment in the psychiatric language of adjustment and maladjustment, his eugenic leanings, or his insistence on heterosexual normativity in centralising the sexual needs of the married couple. Had it got off the ground, the proposed project, 'Masturbation, Physical Signs in Males', would simply have been a re-hash of Dickinson's work correlating labial hypertrophy with lesbianism. Dickinson's proposed project not only revealed his intellectual and imaginative limitations, but it also illustrated the vast chasm between himself and Kinsey, who had left Dickinson's interpretive framework of perversity well and truly behind. Kinsey published *Sexual Behavior in Human Male* in 1948, with his follow-up volume on the female published in 1953.[138]

Dickinson wrote excitedly to Kinsey upon receipt of the first volume, 'I have my copy at last of SBHM! … Glory to God!'[139] Sadly, Dickinson did not live to see publication of *Sexual Behavior in the Human Female*, but in his acknowledgements Kinsey thanked Dickinson for his clinical data collected over many years and made frequent references to the Dickinson-Beam studies throughout the book. Dickinson was one of Kinsey's earliest influences, and he had used Dickinson's illustrations in *Human Sex Anatomy* in the short-lived marriage course that he taught at Indiana University from 1938 to 1940.[140] By the publication of *Sexual Behavior in the Human Male*, the two men had cultivated professional respect and fondness for one another through their shared desire to educate the public about sex, but although Kinsey had won Dickinson's admiration, he went further than Dickinson could have done to normalise deviant sex acts because he wanted to do away with the nor-mal-heterosexual/abnormal-homosexual dichotomy altogether.[141]

Most important for this chapter, however, is that unlike Dickinson, Kinsey saw no need to look for physical evidence of masturbation in the labia minora. This was because Kinsey did not see a reason to invent diagnostic criteria for the purpose of correcting female frigidity and les-bianism, which Dickinson saw as 'maladjustments' to heterosexuality. Moreover, Kinsey overtly rejected the psychoanalytic approach to female sexuality that had so ensnared Dickinson in his conviction that clitoral pleasure was merely preparatory for the vaginal orgasm. Controversially, Kinsey argued instead that female orgasm was essentially of the clit-oris and labia minora, not the vagina, which was actually 'of minimum importance in contributing to the erotic responses of the female'.[142] Kinsey was not at all interested in diagnosing 'abnormal' labia minora; rather, he wanted to know what role they played in sexual arousal. His gynaecological examinations were designed to demonstrate the sexual sensitivity of the labia minora as evidence that 'there are no structures in the female which are more sensitive than the clitoris, the labia minora, and the extension of the labia into the vestibule of the vagina'.[143]

Kinsey noted that both the inner and outer surfaces of the labia minora were 'supplied with more nerves than most other skin-covered parts of the body' and 'highly sensitive'. He concluded that 'as sources of erotic arousal, the labia minora seem to be fully as important as the clitoris. Consequently, masturbation in the female usually involves some sort of stimulation of the inner surfaces of these labia'.[144] Kinsey argued that male assumptions about the sensitivity of the vagina served selfish pur-poses and that as women knew how to please themselves better than men did, men could learn sex technique from female masturbation. Kinsey also suggested that both heterosexual men and women could learn much from lesbians because 'the partners in such [homosexual] contacts often know more about female genital function than either of the partners in a heter-osexual relation'.[145] While there are certainly resonances with Dickinson's work, Kinsey actively resisted going down the route of individual pathol-ogy, in large part because he did not position heterosexual marriage as the primary location of sexual normalcy as Dickinson had done. Kinsey did much to demystify and normalise the clitoral orgasm, female mastur-bation and lesbianism, providing empirical ammunition for second-wave feminist rebellion against Freudian doctrine, as exemplified in Anne Koedt's rousing essay, 'The Myth of the Vaginal Orgasm' (1970).[146]

But this extraordinary legacy has apparently been forgotten in contemporary medical efforts to pathologise the 'hypertrophied' labia minora. This is because, as with Dickinson, a medical approach generally implies a distinction between normal and abnormal. That is, you cannot have a diagnosis of a condition such as labial 'hypertrophy' without the suggestion of abnormality. The current problem for women, then, is figuring out what exactly constitutes genital normality, and to what extent this is defined by medical specialists to the detriment of female sexual autonomy. Are there things that a feminist sexology can teach us that masculinist medicine has forgotten or ignored?

CONCLUSION

Over the past ten years there has been growing concern about female genital cosmetic surgery among medical professionals and psychologists spearheaded by the feminist criticism that labiaplasty is an expression of sexism, rather than disease. It should come as no surprise that it is women who are leading critical discussion on the need for and efficacy of labiaplasty surgery, particularly in relation to claims of improved sexual response.[147] For instance, urologist Justine Schober of Rockefeller University published a paper in 2010 detailing the nerve sensitivity and vascularity of the labia minora, using waste-tissue samples from '10 normal girls ... who underwent surgery for labial fusion'.[148] She concluded that due to the high innervation all along the edge of the labial tissue and the vascular process of engorgement during sexual arousal, labiaplasty 'has the potential and risk for removal of tissue with an important contribution to sensory sexual arousal'.[149] In 2015, she narrowed her focus to the 'cutaneous sensory receptors', while also being careful to emphasise that 'sexual arousal in humans depends on neural, hormonal and genetic factors, and on cultural and contextual influences'.[150] In 2004, she had conducted a study of sexual sensitivity in sexually active women (with no history of genital feminising surgery or genital/vaginal excision surgery), who were asked to self-report on their sexual anatomy and feeling.[151] The study produced the same findings as Kinsey: namely, that labial sensation was more important to orgasmic intensity than the introitus of the vagina. In this paper, Schober emphasised the importance of 'a woman's judgement of her sensation' for scientific understanding of areas of erotic sensitivity.[152]

Yet despite these studies, in 2016, a research team comprising six men and one woman (Kelishadi et al.) published a paper in the *Aesthetic Surgery Journal* titled 'The Safe Labiaplasty: A Study of Nerve Density in Labia Minora and Its Implications'.[153] Its purpose was to respond to criticisms, coming largely from female gynaecologists and psychologists, about the lack of data on the possible negative impacts of labiaplasty surgery on female sexual function. The study aimed to understand the extent of nerve density distribution in the labia minora by analysing tissue samples from two female cadavers. As in Schober's study of waste-tissue samples, Kelishadi et al. used similar staining techniques to show up the presence of nerve bundles in the labia minora tissue. The authors found that the labia minora have heterogeneous nerve distribution, which means that the nerves are spread out and not concentrated in any particular part. Therefore, they argued, when labiaplasty is performed correctly and the labia minora are not entirely amputated, the post-operative tissue that remains is fully sensate. They thus concluded that most labiaplasty techniques can be performed safely and are unlikely to cause loss of sensation.

Kelishadi and his research team may well have used sophisticated modern technologies to test for nerve sensitivity in dead tissue, but the belief that unnecessary surgery on the female genitals is harmless is by no means new. We would do well to remember the recommendations by Isaac Baker Brown and others that excision of the clitoris and labia minora in girls and women could cure hysteria, nymphomania and masturbation. It is also salutary to take stock of the professional opinion of nineteenth-century physician Dr. Charles Henry Felix Routh that 'clitoridectomy did not remove sexual sensations'. As proof, he cited cases where 'women who had never before experienced any pleasurable sensations before the operation, did so during the subsequent natural intercourse with their husbands'.[154] From a historian's point of view, the medical mistakes of the past can be seen clearly in a phenomenon that may otherwise appear to us to be entirely novel. In the present day, medical men, and some women, are eager to amputate the genitals as a quick, and profitable, solution to a problem of female desire that they themselves are perpetuating. Cosmetic labiaplasty is merely another proposed solution, in the long history of gynaecological medicine, to female sexual deficit thought to spring from a woman's own defective body. The 'hysterisation' of the female body in the medical sciences that began in the nineteenth century is ongoing. In the nineteenth and early twentieth centuries, women were being treated with clitoral and labia minora excision for the dubious female-specific illnesses of 'frigidity' and 'hysteria', which have now disappeared from the clinical vocabulary, and for good reason. Why, then, is 'hypertrophy of the labia minora' considered by many present-day specialists to be a legitimate diagnosis when it appears to be a mere iteration of the *cultural* narrative of female frigidity?

Ironic as it sounds, Dickinson's advocacy for sex education could prove more empowering for women today than plastic surgery. There are a growing number of scholarly voices critical of cosmetic labiaplasty calling for better educational resources for women about labial diversity and what constitutes normality. Özer et al., for instance, provide the following advice: 'Experience suggests that a large number of women seeking labiaplasty want to be assured that they are normal; they want to hear that nothing is wrong with their genitals. Counselling and education could make a difference in these circumstances and prevent this group of women from undergoing medically unnecessary surgery.'[155] In his most radical moments, Dickinson sought to release masturbation from shame in his belief that some experience of masturbation augured well for enjoyable heterosexual sex. In his time period, doctors had begun to be outspoken about sexual taboos and to encourage 'frank speech' about distasteful or deeply embarrassing subjects of masturbation, venereal disease and sexual intercourse. But many decades on from Dickinson's visionary project of educating heterosexual men and women about sexual pleasure, women are still bearing the burden of heterosexual anxiety.

In the current era, the vulval lips still speak of sexual abnormality, though the moral landscape has changed. Dickinson, for instance, was more obsessed than his female patients were about the size and shape of their labia minora. The married women he surveyed did not come to him because they felt that their labia were literally getting in the way of their sex lives. Their feelings of sexual dissatisfaction were not stored in the labia but in the heterosexual relationships that supported male sexual selfishness and female submission. This is why Dickinson made it a priority to educate men on how to please women, even though he also regarded unhappy women as sexually frigid. I offer this comparison between the language of marital 'maladjustment' and labial 'hypertrophy' to suggest that female sexual shame is profoundly historical and social and felt in the body in myriad ways, but usually misdiagnosed as a problem of female sexual physiology. In exploring the historical link between sexual perversion and genital hypertrophy, this chapter has sought to show how the medical discourse of 'labial hypertrophy' is invested in cultural narratives that define 'normal' female sexuality as passive, receptive and entirely dependent on penetrative heterosexuality. It is only by scrutinising the cultural values with which 'normal' femininity is imbued that we can begin to understand female genital dissatisfaction and the rationale behind cosmetic labiaplasty.

NOTES

1. Robert L. Dickinson, 'Hypertrophies of the Labia Minora and Their Significance', *American Gynecology* 1, no. 3 (1902): 225–54. I would like to acknowledge my debt in this chapter to historian Jennifer Terry's excellent work on Robert Latou Dickinson. Terry provides a much more comprehensive analysis than I am able to do in this book. See Jennifer Terry, *An American Obsession: Science, Medicine, and Homosexuality in Modern Society* (Chicago and London: University of Chicago Press, 1999), esp. chaps 4 and 6; Jennifer Terry, 'Anxious Slippages between "Us" and "Them": A Brief History of the Scientific Search for Homosexual Bodies', in *Deviant Bodies: Critical Perspectives on Difference in Science and Popular Culture*, ed. Jennifer Terry and Jacqueline Urla (Bloomington and Indianapolis: Indiana University Press, 1995), 129–69.
2. Dickinson, 'Hypertrophies of the Labia Minora and Their Significance', 231.
3. Dickinson, 'Hypertrophies of the Labia Minora and Their Significance', 235n*c*.
4. Robert L. Dickinson, 'Masturbation in Women', in Howard A. Kelly, *Medical Gynecology* (New York and London: D. Appleton and Company, 1912), 309. Kelly states in the preface that the section on masturbation is by Dr. R. L. Dickinson.
5. Michel Foucault, *The History of Sexuality*, vol. 1, trans. Robert Hurley (London and New York: Penguin, 1978), 104–5.
6. Sigmund Freud, 'Femininity', in *The Standard Edition of the Complete Psychological Works of Sigmund Freud, Volume 22. New Introductory Lectures on Psycho-Analysis and Other Works*, trans. James Strachey (London: Vintage, 1933), 113.
7. Foucault, *The History of Sexuality*, 68.
8. Foucault, *The History of Sexuality*, 68.
9. Dickinson, 'Masturbation in Women', 315.
10. Dickinson, 'Hypertrophies of the Labia Minora and Their Significance', 247.

11. Havelock Ellis, 'Auto-Erotism', in *The Evolution of Modesty; The Phenomena of Sexual Periodicity; Auto-Erotism* (Philadelphia: F. A. Davis Company, 1901), 136–7.
12. Dickinson, 'Masturbation in Women', 309.
13. Carol Groneman, 'Nymphomania: The Historical Construction of Female Sexuality', in *Deviant Bodies*, ed. Jennifer Terry and Jacqueline Urla (Bloomington and Indianapolis: Indiana University Press, 1995), 233.
14. A. J. Bloch, 'Sexual Perversion in the Female', *New Orleans Medical Surgical Journal* 22, no. 1 (1894): 3–4.
15. Robert L. Dickinson and Lura Beam, *A Thousand Marriages: A Medical Study of Sex Adjustment* (Baltimore: Williams and Wilkins Company, 1931), 50.
16. Dickinson, 'Hypertrophies of the Labia Minora and Their Significance', 228.
17. Dickinson, 'Hypertrophies of the Labia Minora and Their Significance', 226.
18. Dickinson, 'Hypertrophies of the Labia Minora and Their Significance', 228–9.
19. Dickinson, 'Hypertrophies of the Labia Minora and Their Significance', 228.
20. Robert L. Dickinson, *Human Sex Anatomy: A Topographical Hand Atlas* (Baltimore: Williams and Wilkins Company, 1933), 40.
21. Dickinson, *Human Sex Anatomy*, 40.
22. Dickinson, 'Hypertrophies of the Labia Minora and Their Significance', 225.
23. Dickinson, *Human Sex Anatomy*, 42, emphasis in original.
24. Dickinson, 'Hypertrophies of the Labia Minora and Their Significance', 252. Also see Dickinson, 'Masturbation in Women', 314.
25. Dickinson and Beam, *A Thousand Marriages*, 354.
26. Ellis, cited in Dickinson, 'Hypertrophies of the Labia Minora and Their Significance', 251, 251np. See also Dickinson, *Human Sex Anatomy*, 55.
27. Dickinson, 'Hypertrophies of the Labia Minora and Their Significance', 251. Also see Ellis, 'Auro-Erotism', 185–8.
28. Dickinson, 'Hypertrophies of the Labia Minora and Their Significance', 251.
29. Dickinson, 'Hypertrophies of the Labia Minora and Their Significance', 247.
30. Dickinson, 'Hypertrophies of the Labia Minora and Their Significance', 250.
31. Dickinson, 'Hypertrophies of the Labia Minora and Their Significance', 252.
32. Dickinson, 'Hypertrophies of the Labia Minora and Their Significance', 253.

33. Ellis, cited in Dickinson, 'Hypertrophies of the Labia Minora and Their Significance', 253n*q*.
34. Thomas Laqueur, *Solitary Sex: A Cultural History of Masturbation* (New York: Zone Books, 2003).
35. M. Tissot, *Onanism: or, A Treatise upon the Disorders Produced by Masturbation: or, The Dangerous Effects of Secret and Excessive Venery*, trans. A. Hume (London: Printed for the translator, [c. 1712] 1766).
36. Tissot, *Onanism*, 41–2.
37. Tissot, *Onanism*, 43.
38. Leonard Sowerby, *The Ladies Dispensatory: or Every Woman Her Own Physician* (London: Printed for James Hodges and John James, [1652] 1739), 6–7.
39. Sowerby, *The Ladies Dispensatory*, 13.
40. Laqueur, *Solitary Sex*, 192.
41. Tissot, *Onanism*, 42.
42. Johann Dolaüs, *Systema Medicinale, A Compleat System of Physick, Theorical and Practical*, trans. William Salmon (London: Printed for T. Passinger, T. Sawbridge and T. Flesher, 1686), 309; Jean (John) Astruc, *A Treatise on All the Diseases Incident to Women*, trans. J. R___n (London: Printed for T. Cooper, 1743); William Cullen, *Synopsis Nosologiae Methodicae* (Edinburgh, 1769), 67.
43. M. D. T. Bienville, *Nymphomania, or, a Dissertation concerning the Furor Uterinus*, trans. Edward Sloane Wilmot (London: Printed for J. Bew, 1775), 90–1.
44. Bienville, *Nymphomania*, 31.
45. See for example Léopold Deslandes, *A Treatise on the Diseases Produced by Onanism, Masturbation, Self-Pollution, and Other Excesses* (Boston: Otis, Broaders, and Company, 1839); C. W. Hufeland, *The Practice of Medicine*, 2nd ed., trans. Caspar Bruchhausen (New York: William Radde, 1844); James Ashton, *The Book of Nature* (New York: Wallis & Ashton, 1861), 27–8.
46. Tissot, *Onanism*, 42.
47. One woman had swollen 'Testicles [ovaries] full of a seminal Matter', while another had a 'tumify'd' ovary, 'black as Soot, stinking extremely'. Marten, *A Treatise of the Venereal Disease*, 233–4. With the hindsight of current medical knowledge, it is likely that such women were probably suffering from such gynaecological conditions as endometriosis, ovarian cysts, Polycystic Ovary Syndrome, ovarian torsion, or ovarian cancer.
48. Sowerby, *The Ladies Dispensatory*, 10.
49. Marten, *A Treatise of the Venereal Disease*, 233; Bienville, *Nymphomania*, 74.
50. Lockhart, cited in *American Journal of Insanity*, vol. 22 (New York: State Lunatic Asylum, 1865–6), 556.

51. Colombat de L'Isère, *A Treatise on the Diseases and Special Hygiene of Females*, trans. Charles D. Meigs (Philadelphia: Lea and Blanchard, [1838] 1845), 514.

52. Samuel Ashwell, *A Practical Treatise on the Diseases Peculiar to Women* (Philadelphia: Lea and Blanchard, 1848), 500.

53. David D. Davis, *Elements of Obstetric Medicine; with the Description and Treatment of Some of the Principal Diseases of Children*, 2nd ed. (London: Printed for Taylor and Walton, 1841), 347. Also see for example John Harvey Kellogg, *Ladies' Guide in Health and Disease: Girlhood, Maidenhood, Wifehood, Motherhood* (Des Moines: W. D. Condit and Co., 1883), 546; Paul Moreau (de Tours), *Des Aberrations du Sens Génésique* (Paris: Asselin et Cie, 1880), 202.

54. Hufeland, *The Practice of Medicine*, 251–2.

55. Kellogg, *Ladies' Guide in Health and Disease*, 546; Heywood Smith, *Practical Gynaecology: A Handbook of the Diseases of Women* (London: Henry J. Glaisher, 1900), 176.

56. For a detailed account of Baker Brown's surgical practice and expulsion, see Elizabeth Sheehan, 'Victorian Clitoridectomy: Isaac Baker Brown and His Harmless Operative Procedure', in *The Gender/Sexuality Reader: Culture, History, Political Economy*, ed. Roger N. Lancaster and Micaela di Leonardo (New York and London: Routledge, 1997), 325–34.

57. See the discussion between C. H. F. Routh, Bedford Fenwick, Fenton Jones and Heywood Smith in *The British Gynaecological Journal*, vol. 2, ed. Fancourt Barnes (London: Smith, Elder, & Co., 1887), 485–506.

58. Franz Winckel, *Diseases of Women: A Handbook for Physicians and Students*, trans. J. H. Williamson and Theophilus Parvin (Philadelphia: P. Blakiston, Son & Co., [1886] 1887), 33.

59. Morton Monroe Eaton, *A Treatise on the Medical and Surgical Diseases of Women, with Their Homeopathic Treatment* (New York, Philadelphia and London: Boericke & Tafel, 1880), 724.

60. Eaton, *A Treatise on the Medical and Surgical Diseases of Women*, 725.

61. Eaton, *A Treatise on the Medical and Surgical Diseases of Women*, 725.

62. Joseph W. Howe, *Excessive Venery, Masturbation and Continence: The Etiology, Pathology and Treatment of the Diseases Resulting from Venereal Excesses, Masturbation and Continence* (New York and London: Bermingham and Co., 1883).

63. Review of *Excessive Venery, Masturbation and Continence: The Etiology, Pathology and Treatment of the Diseases Resulting from Venereal Excesses, Masturbation and Continence*, by Joseph W. Howe, *The American Lancet* 12 (1888): 386.

64. Howe, *Excessive Venery, Masturbation and Continence*, 41–2.

65. Howe, *Excessive Venery, Masturbation and Continence*, 17.
66. Dickinson and Beam, *A Thousand Marriages*.
67. Dickinson and Beam, *A Thousand Marriages*, 4, 11.
68. Dickinson and Beam, *A Thousand Marriages*, 10.
69. George W. Kosmak, Robert T. Frank and Ransom S. Hooker, 'Introduction', in Dickinson and Beam, *A Thousand Marriages*, xix.
70. Kosmak, Frank and Hooker, 'Introduction', xix.
71. Robert L. Dickinson and Henry H. Pierson, 'The Average Sex Life of American Women', *JAMA* 85, no. 15 (1925), 1117. See also Wendy Kline, *Building a Better Race: Gender, Sexuality, and Eugenics from the Turn of the Century to the Baby Boom* (Berkeley and Los Angeles: University of California Press, 2001), 62.
72. Dickinson and Beam, *A Thousand Marriages*, 254.
73. Dickinson and Beam, *A Thousand Marriages*, 269.
74. Jane Carey, 'The Racial Imperatives of Sex: Birth Control and Eugenics in Britain, the United States and Australia in the Interwar Years', *Women's History Review* 21, no. 5 (2012): 740.
75. Terry, *An American Obsession*, 143.
76. Sanger, cited in Carey, 'The Racial Imperatives of Sex', 740.
77. Robert L. Dickinson, 'Simple Sterilization of Women by Cautery Stricture at the Intra-Uterine Tubal Openings compared with Other Methods', *Surgery, Gynecology and Obstetrics* 23 (1916): 205.
78. Dickinson, *Human Sex Anatomy*, 1.
79. Dickinson and Beam, *A Thousand Marriages*, 10. In this regard, historian James Reed is quite correct in surmising from this confession that Dickinson 'ignored Freud'. James Reed, *The Birth Control Movement and American Society: From Private Vice to Public Virtue* (Princeton: Princeton University Press, 1978), 192. This is probably because Dickinson's main psychoanalytic influence was Havelock Ellis, who is known to have influenced Freud. However, Dickinson's 1902 paper shows that he was clearly familiar with literature on neurasthenia and other nervous disorders (to which he, like Freud, attributed a sexual aetiology), such as neurosis, melancholia, hysteria and nymphomania. These were existing categories of nervous illness that Dickinson, Ellis and Freud would have encountered as medical students and practitioners. And while Freud is only mentioned twice in *A Thousand Marriages*, Dickinson nonetheless articulated a psychoanalytic theory of the libido that could explain the various sufferings of maladjusted, unhappy women. Indeed, some of his analysis of maladjustment appears to be an obvious reproduction of Freud's work on the sexual foundations of anxiety neurosis. See Sigmund Freud, 'On the Grounds for Detaching a Particular Syndrome from Neurasthenia under the Description "Anxiety

Neurosis"' in *The Standard Edition of the Complete Psychological Works of Sigmund Freud*, vol. 3, ed. and trans. James Strachey (London: Vintage, 1962), 90–115; Sigmund Freud, 'Sexuality in the Aetiology of the Neuroses', in Strachey, *The Standard Edition of the Complete Psychological Works of Sigmund Freud*, vol. 3, 263–85. Because Freud's theories of sexual repression and satisfaction were so pervasive and revolutionary in their influence, it is likely that they were refracted back into Dickinson's own more prosaic and descriptive accounts of female sexual unhappiness.

80. Dickinson and Pierson, 'The Average Sex Life of American Women', 1113.
81. Dickinson and Beam, *A Thousand Marriages*, 15.
82. Dickinson and Beam, *A Thousand Marriages*, 364.
83. Dickinson and Beam, *A Thousand Marriages*, 364.
84. Dickinson and Beam, *A Thousand Marriages*, 364.
85. Havelock Ellis, 'Foreword', in Dickinson and Beam, *A Thousand Marriages*, xi.
86. Ellis, 'Foreword', xii.
87. Ellis, 'Foreword', xii.
88. Dickinson and Beam, *A Thousand Marriages*, 107.
89. Foucault, *The History of Sexuality*.
90. Foucault, *The History of Sexuality*, 40.
91. Foucault, *The History of Sexuality*, 38.
92. Dickinson, 'Masturbation in Women', 314.
93. Stephen Garton, *Histories of Sexuality* (London: Equinox, 2004), 208.
94. Dickinson, 'The Average Sex Life of American Women', 1114.
95. Dickinson and Beam, *A Thousand Marriages*, 346–68.
96. Ellis, 'Auto-Erotism', 202.
97. Dickinson and Beam, *A Thousand Marriages*, 346.
98. Baker, cited in Ellis, 'Auto-Erotism', 188.
99. Freud, 'Femininity'.
100. Dickinson and Beam, *A Thousand Marriages*, 356.
101. Dickinson and Beam, *A Thousand Marriages*, 348.
102. Dickinson, *Human Sex Anatomy*.
103. Dickinson and Beam, *A Thousand Marriages*, 348.
104. Dickinson and Beam, *A Thousand Marriages*, 356.
105. Dickinson and Beam, *A Thousand Marriages*, 355.
106. Ellis, 'Auto-Erotism', 191.
107. Ellis, 'Auto-Erotism', 188. Ellis followed Richard von Krafft-Ebing in this belief. See Richard von Krafft-Ebing, *Psychopathia Sexualis, with reference to Contrary Sexual Instinct: A Medico-Legal Study*, trans. Charles Gilbert Chaddock (Philadelphia and London: F. A. Davis Co., 1892), 187–191, 231.

108. Krafft-Ebing, *Psychopathia Sexualis*, 320.
109. Krafft-Ebing, *Psychopathia Sexualis*, 188, 319.
110. Krafft-Ebing, *Psychopathia Sexualis*, 188–9.
111. Krafft-Ebing, *Psychopathia Sexualis*, 428.
112. Terry, *An American Obsession*, 63.
113. In his 1902 paper, Dickinson reproduced an entire paragraph from Ellis on female masturbation causing aversion for coitus, but stopped short at Ellis's final sentence suggesting it may lead to inversion. It seems reasonable to assume that this is because his research was initially focused on married heterosexuals.
114. Dickinson, *Human Sex Anatomy*, 69.
115. Dickinson, *Human Sex Anatomy*, 83.
116. Henry L. Minton, *Departing from Deviance: A History of Homosexual Rights and Emancipatory Science in America* (Chicago: University of Chicago Press, 2002), 35.
117. Minton, *Departing from Deviance*, 35–6.
118. George W. Henry, *Sex Variants: A Study of Homosexual Patterns* (New York and London: Paul B. Hoeber, 1948).
119. Henry, *Sex Variants*, xi.
120. Henry, *Sex Variants*, 1023.
121. Henry, *Sex Variants*, 1026.
122. Henry, *Sex Variants*.
123. Henry, *Sex Variants*, 1045–6.
124. Henry, *Sex Variants*, 1024.
125. Henry, *Sex Variants*, 1026.
126. Henry, *Sex Variants*, 1026–7.
127. Henry, *Sex Variants*, 1027.
128. Terry, *An American Obsession*, 81–2.
129. Henry, *Sex Variants*, 1027.
130. Dickinson, 'The Gynecology of Homosexuality', in Henry, *Sex Variants*, 1099.
131. Terry, *An American Obsession*, 148.
132. Dickinson, 'The Gynecology of Homosexuality', in Henry, *Sex Variants*, 1072, emphasis in original.
133. Dickinson, 'The Gynecology of Homosexuality', in Henry, *Sex Variants*, 1080–2.
134. Dickinson, 'The Gynecology of Homosexuality', in Henry, *Sex Variants*, 1082.
135. Terry, *An American Obsession*, 434n63.
136. Alfred C. Kinsey, Wardell B. Pomeroy and Clyde E. Martin, *Sexual Behavior in the Human Male* (Bloomington and Indianapolis: Indiana University Press, 1948).

137. Terry, *An American Obsession*, 434n63.
138. Alfred C. Kinsey, Wardell B. Pomeroy and Clyde E. Martin and Paul H. Gebhard, *Sexual Behavior in the Human Female* (Bloomington and Indianapolis: Indiana University Press, 1953).
139. Dickinson, cited in Regina Markell Morantz, 'The Scientist as Sex Crusader: Alfred C. Kinsey and American Culture', *American Quarterly* 29, no. 5 (1977): 563.
140. See Donna J. Drucker, '"A Noble Experiment": The Marriage Course at Indiana University, 1938–1940', *Indiana Magazine of History* 103, no. 3 (2007): 231–64.
141. In *Sexual Behavior in the Human Female* Kinsey wrote: 'It is a characteristic of the human mind that it tries to dichotomize in its classification of phenomena. Things either are so, or they are not so. Sexual behaviour is either normal or abnormal, socially acceptable or unacceptable, heterosexual or homosexual; and many persons do not want to believe that there are gradations in these matters from one to the other extreme'. Kinsey et al., *Sexual Behavior in the Human Female*, 469.
142. Kinsey et al., *Sexual Behavior in the Human Female*, 592.
143. Kinsey et al., *Sexual Behavior in the Human Female*, 575.
144. Kinsey et al., *Sexual Behavior in the Human Female*, 576–7.
145. Kinsey et al., *Sexual Behavior in the Human Female*, 575.
146. Anne Koedt, 'The Myth of the Vaginal Orgasm', in *Feminism and Sexuality: A Reader*, ed. Stevi Jackson and Sue Scott (New York: Columbia University Press, 1996), 111–116.
147. See for example R. Bramwell, C. Morland and A. S. Garden, 'Expectations and Experience of Labial Reduction: A Qualitative Study', *BJOG* 114, no. 12 (2007): 1493–9; Virginia Braun, 'In Search of (Better) Sexual Pleasure: Female Genital "Cosmetic" Surgery', *Sexualities* 8, no. 4 (2005): 407–24; Virginia Braun, 'Female Genital Cosmetic Surgery: A Critical Review of Current Knowledge and Contemporary Debates', *Journal of Women's Health* 19, no. 7 (2010): 1393–1407; Naomi S. Crouch, Rebecca Deans, Lina Michala, Lih-Mei Liao and Sarah M. Creighton, 'Clinical Characteristics of Well Women Seeking Labial Reduction Surgery: A Prospective Study', *BJOG* 118, no. 12 (2011): 1507–10; Lih-Mei Liao and Sarah M. Creighton, 'Requests for Cosmetic Genitoplasty: How Should Healthcare Providers Respond?', *BMJ* 334 (2007): 1090–2; Lih-Mei Liao, Lina Michala and Sarah M. Creighton, 'Labial Surgery for Well Women: A Review of the Literature', *BJOG* 117 (2010): 20–5; Jillian Lloyd, Naomi S. Crouch, Catherine L. Minto, Lih-Mei Liao and Sarah M. Creighton, 'Female Genital Appearance: "Normality" Unfolds', *BJOG* 112, no. 5 (2005):

643–6; Justine M. Schober, Heino F. L. Meyer-Bahlburg and Philip G. Ransley, 'Self-Assessment of Genital Anatomy, Sexual Sensitivity and Function in Women: Implications for Genitoplasty', *BJU International* 94, no. 4 (2004): 589–94; Justine Schober, Timothy Cooney, Donald Pfaff, Lazarus Mayoglou and Nieves Martin-Alguacil, 'Innervation of the Labia Minora of Prepubertal Girls', *Journal of Paediatric and Adolescent Gynecology* 23, no. 6 (2010): 352–7; Justine Schober, Nathan Aardsma, Lazarus Mayoglou, Donald Pfaff and Nieves Martin-Alguacil, 'Terminal Innervation of Female Genitalia, Cutaneous Sensory Receptors of the Epithelium of the Labia Minora', *Clinical Anatomy* 28, no. 3 (2015): 392–8; Gemma Sharp and Marika Tiggemann, 'Educating Women about Normal Female Genital Appearance Variation', *Body Image* 16 (2016): 70–8.

148. Schober et al., 'Innervation of the Labia Minora of Prepubertal Girls', 352.

149. Schober et al., 'Innervation of the Labia Minora of Prepubertal Girls, 357.

150. Schober et al., 'Terminal Innervation of Female Genitalia', 395.

151. Schober, Meyer-Bahlburg and Ransley, 'Self-Assessment of Genital Anatomy', 589–94.

152. Schober, Meyer-Bahlburg and Ransley, 'Self-Assessment of Genital Anatomy', 593.

153. Shahrooz Sean Kelishadi, Rawhi Omar, Nicole Herring, John Paul Tutela, Saeed Chowdhry, Ron Brooks and Bradon J. Wilhelmi, 'The Safe Labiaplasty: A Study of Nerve Density in Labia Minora and Its Implications', *Aesthetic Surgery Journal* 36, no. 6 (2016): 705–9.

154. C. H. F. Routh, 'On the Etiology and Diagnosis, Considered Specially from a Medico-Legal Point of View, of Those Cases of Nymphomania Which Lead Women to Make False Charges against Their Medical Attendants', *The British Gynaecological Journal* 2 (1887): 510–11.

155. Müjde Özer, Indiana Mortimore, Elise P. Jansma and Margriet G. Mullender, 'Labiaplasty: Motivation, Techniques, and Ethics', *Nature Reviews. Urology* 13, no. 3 (2018): 179.

CHAPTER 7

Desiring Normality

Over the last few years, in Australia at least, cosmetic surgery advertising is no longer making explicit claims that the normal or average vulva is characterised by non-protuberant labia minora. For instance, the *Australian Cosmetic Surgery Magazine* claimed in 2007 that 'in the majority of women, the labia minora are covered by the labia majora (outer lips) and are only seen with the legs separated'.[1] The advertising language is now changing to reflect an acknowledgement of genital diversity due to demands from feminist gynaecologists, urologists and psychologists for evidence-based claims. As this book has also made clear, there is not a shred of valid evidence for the assertion that the 'average' labia minora, or that which is common to most women, are hidden behind or flush with the labia majora. In 2015 the Royal Australian College of General Practitioners (RACGP) issued a set of guidelines for GPs and other health professionals on how to deal with female genital cosmetic surgery, in which it was unambiguously stated that 'exactly what constitutes "normal" female genitalia is an area of medicine in which very few studies have been published … There are currently no criteria that measure and describe normal female genital anatomy and medical textbooks also lack detail regarding range of diversity and measurements'.[2]

Cosmetic surgeons presumably know that protuberant labia minora does not constitute a disease or abnormality. It is classed as a medical problem for the simple reason that it is making women unhappy. In cosmetic surgery advertising and in the surgical literature, labiaplasty

© The Author(s) 2019
C. Nurka, *Female Genital Cosmetic Surgery*,
https://doi.org/10.1007/978-3-319-96490-4_7

is framed as an empowering choice for women who have struggled for many years with the crippling psychosocial effects of labial disgust and have an avenue available to them to do something about it. Both cosmetic surgeons and some feminists have found an unlikely comradeship in the argument that women are not 'cultural dupes' and are making rational choices according to the resources they have available to them. This argument holds that we need to recognise women as agents who are making sensible choices from a limited range of options, rather than people who make choices against their own self-interest because they have unconsciously internalised sexist belief systems.[3]

One thing I find problematic about the 'rational decision-making' argument is the lack of attention paid to how individual feelings articulate with cultural fantasies of belonging. As queer feminist theorist Sara Ahmed has argued, normality promises happiness through belonging, in particular heterosexual belonging. There are many ways that the feeling of happiness, thought of as intrinsically good, is used 'to redescribe social norms as social goods'.[4] When a social norm directs happiness toward heterosexual love, marriage and family, those who do not fit that picture—such as single women, childless women and lesbians—are classed as unhappy and in need of fixing. As we saw in Chapter 6, George W. Henry's solution for unhappy homosexuals was to treat them into becoming heterosexual; Robert Latou Dickinson's solution for unhappy women was to teach them to enjoy heterosexual sex and men to pleasure them. In both cases, female infertility and sexual desires that were not ultimately directed toward men were the subjects of great anxiety because they disrupted a very deeply entrenched idea of happiness located in heterosexual coupling. This amounts to a kind of misrecognition, in which the source of unhappiness is misconceived as stemming from the unhappy subject rather than a symbolic structure that sorts us into socially desirable and undesirable, where we are made to feel unhappy by virtue of being in the wrong place. As Ahmed argues, the promise of happiness is dependent on obtaining social legitimacy, or on finding happiness 'in the right place'.[5]

In my view, a consideration of the interdependency of normality and happiness is quite essential to an analysis of female genital cosmetic surgery (hereafter FGCS), where the primary reason for its existence is to alleviate the unhappy feelings of abnormality, shame and deficiency. Psychoanalytic thought from Sigmund Freud to Melanie Klein has demonstrated convincingly that the deepest recesses of our emotional lives are developed and continually recalibrated in relation to others within a social world. That is, the inner imaginative world is built and remade from the emotional and linguistic materials of the external social world into which we are born and through which we accomplish, or reject, a sexual identity. A sociological qualitative analysis can describe the sensible rationales that female cosmetic surgery patients have for desiring normality, but it has trouble articulating answers to the question of what kind of normality is being desired, and what cultural fantasies are attached to a concept of normality that may preclude or cut off other ways of being and desiring. While I agree that a feminist enquiry into cosmetic surgery must respect women's decision-making processes so as not to be patronising, I also think that we need to investigate the realm of feeling and fantasy that produces bodies of desire. When plastic surgeon Scott Turner promises that labiaplasty surgery can 'restore your confidence and femininity',[6] he is speaking of feelings and desire. The achievement or restoration of a lost 'femininity' is the fantasied end product. How is it that femininity makes us feel lovable? What extraordinary or magical qualities must femininity possess in order that our bodies might be transformed into signs of social and personal value?

WHAT IS FANTASY?

In psychoanalytic thought there are different ways of defining and interpreting fantasy, but at its most basic level, fantasy is the mental projection of a desire for a thing or state of being that is currently inaccessible to us. This is Sigmund Freud's pleasure-unpleasure principle, which describes the internal struggles, which all of us experience, between satisfaction and frustration. For Freud, psychical processes tend towards the narcissistic (self-centred) 'pleasure principle', or satisfaction from things that make us feel good. Unfortunately for us, our projected satisfactions, or wishes, are often frustrated by the real conditions of our existence. Fantasies of gratification are therefore mediated by the 'reality principle', which presents the boundary line against which we 'test' and adjust our expectations. The 'reality principle' is how we learn that the world imposes limitations on us and how to live with that fact. Fantasy, as Freud describes it, is a thought process that becomes split off from reality-testing to remain 'subordinate to the pleasure principle alone'.[7] Freud saw neurosis and psychosis as forms of psychic alienation from reality. But, as is usual with Freud, he explained that these more extreme states of mental struggle could tell us something about the general process of psychic development for all of us—and that is that everybody needs some kind of fantasy life to get by. As he put it: 'The life imposed on us is too hard to bear: it brings too much pain, too many disappointments, too many insoluble problems. If we are to endure it, we cannot do without palliative measures'.[8] For Freud, life is pain, and fantasy is a substitutive satisfaction that enables us to bear a cruel, indifferent and unfathomable world.

I am inclined to agree with Freud's insights that all human individuals, cultures and societies are self-delusional at least some of the time to make life bearable. A feminist psychoanalytic approach to cosmetic surgery recognises the importance of the body as a critical site of fantasy production. Freud's thinking is useful insofar as he understood fantasies to be deeply and fundamentally embodied, particularly in his astute observation that the biological body itself can be a source of pain, frustration and limitation: 'Suffering threatens us from three sides: from our own body, which, being doomed to decay and dissolution, cannot dispense with pain and anxiety as warning signals; from the external world, which can unleash overwhelming, implacable, destructive forces against us; and finally from our relations with others'.[9] Freud argues that science and religion are sublimations of these primal organic anxieties. Medical science, for instance, strives to intervene in nature to relieve the burdens of suffering caused by disease. Freud noted that 'the most interesting methods of preventing suffering are those that seek to influence one's own constitution'.[10] I do not wish to instate a nature/culture binary here; rather, I draw on Freud to show how scientific techniques for managing life and mediating suffering intervene in the world to change the existing limits of what is biologically possible and desirable.

While Freud pointed to the body as a frustrating object that interferes with our attempts at gratification, it is also the locus of cultural fantasies of normal and abnormal sex and sexuality. The work of anthropologist Mary Douglas on pollution and taboo demonstrates how the human body itself serves as a template for the symbolic divisions we make in the social world between desirable and undesirable. Douglas explains that social beliefs about disgusting or taboo objects can usually be traced back to the way we compartmentalise the fluids and orifices of the body as clean and proper or dirty and improper. Religious prohibitions on menstruating women or types of non-procreative sexual gratification, for example, rely on a basal distinction between purity and pollution.

If, as Douglas suggests, the function of taboo is to establish social order and eliminate ambiguity, then the human body and its fluids and excretions are the first targets of this impulse to order. After all, it is toilet training that teaches us that shit is bad and undesirable. Psychoanalyst Julia Kristeva calls this a 'primal mapping' of the body that marks out the territories of 'proper-clean' and 'improper-dirty'.[11] Kristeva calls that which we expel or prohibit 'abject'. It is what threatens the boundaries of what she terms the 'clean and proper body'.[12] Kristeva writes: 'It is ... not lack of cleanliness or health that causes abjection but what disturbs identity, system, order. What does not respect borders, positions, rules. The in-between, the ambiguous, the composite'.[13] Bodies are always both organic and cultural, and they are key sites of abjection.

For Douglas, bodily order is the mirror image of social order. This means, as feminist philosopher Elizabeth Grosz explains, that the body functions 'to represent, to symbolize, social and collective fantasies and obsessions: its orifices and surfaces can represent the sites of cultural marginality, places of social entry and exit, regions of confrontation or compromise. Rituals and practices designed to cleanse or purify the body may serve as metaphors for processes of cultural homogeneity'.[14] In other words, we impose order on the body as we impose order on our social relations, and operations on the former are often requisite for entry into the latter. That is, the body is *mapped onto* a social order and we become social subjects through processes that socialise the body. Bodily taboos and ordering processes thus support and reflect social systems of order: bodies that are culturally marked as unclean, polluting or wrong indicate a breakdown in the coherence of a given system.

Feminist philosopher Judith Butler has famously argued that 'compulsory heterosexuality' is the social system in and through which we become culturally recognisable as 'men' and 'women', which, she argues, are phantasmic identity categories. Butler draws on Douglas to show how compulsory heterosexuality imposes order according to a binary logic that opposes male to female (sex) and masculine to feminine (gender). There is no empirical basis for the belief that there are only two distinct sexes among humans when we know that many people are sexual intermediaries, or for the belief that girls are constitutionally unable to throw a ball with power and precision. Thus, what Butler calls the 'heterosexual matrix' is in fact a complex fantasy structure that works to uphold rigid distinctions between types of bodies and behaviours. What this means is that 'masculinity' and 'femininity' are recognisable qualities of gender identity that only acquire social meaning and legitimacy in their oppositional relationship and in their attachment to bodies coded 'male' or 'female'. Further, the idea that men desire women and masculinity desires femininity is what gives this binary its heterosexual coherence. Hence, Butler argues, the categories of man and woman, masculine and feminine, configure desire as always already 'heterosexual' because there is no way of thinking about desire and identity beyond the boundaries of mutually exclusive opposites.

Gender, Butler argues, is nothing but an elaborate fantasy that *feels* real because we do so much to ensure that it *becomes* real through all the ways we continually make ourselves readable as one sex or another, even to ourselves. This is essentially her argument about gender performativity, which is that sex is actually determined by gender and not the other way around: that is, that we look to the biological category of 'sex' to be the foundational bedrock of the rigid cultural binaries that regulate gender and sexuality. For Butler, gender is an illusion, or fantasy, that we make real through repeatedly calling it into being by stylising ourselves as men or women, masculine or feminine. The problem with the gender binary is that it presumes that 'there is some kind of *sex* that exists in hazy biological form that is somehow *expressed* in the gait, the posture, the gesture; and that some sexuality then expresses both that apparent gender or that more or less magical sex'.[15] Butler calls 'sex' magical because it transforms gender into something that appears substantial. In Butler's account, 'sex' appears as the origin of gender, even though it is actually the product.

For the sake of providing conceptual clarity for what follows, I should explain that my own view, contra Butler, is that sex is biologically real, that there is an extracultural quality to sex as a material facticity, and that it is more than two. I define sex as any combination of material characteristics indicative of dimorphic human reproductive capacity or physiology—such as breasts, uterus, clitoris, labia, vagina, penis, testicles, menstrual blood, eggs, semen and sex hormones—regardless of whether such organs are functionally reproductive (i.e., whether an individual reproduces), or of how closely they conform to a statistically typical sexually dimorphic body. While human sex dimorphism is a product of the deep history of human evolution, I view sex as malleable and therefore open-ended, and see no reason why any individual ought to be defined as normal or abnormal, superior or inferior, on the basis of their sexual constitution or their sexual pleasures, and especially not on the basis of whether their sexual constitution agrees with their gender identity. It became clear to me that I could not write a book about the labia minora without acknowledging that they are a sex characteristic, which is why I see 'sex' as an important and meaningful definitional category. I do agree with Butler, however, that obtaining a socially legitimate gender identity as a man or woman, or even as a gender-neutral person, is a cultural process that is both material and ideational.

A Dream Come True

Like other forms of cosmetic surgery, labiaplasty realises a fantasy. As Australian plastic surgeon Scott Turner puts it, 'a labiaplasty can be a dream come true'.[16] I want to suggest here that female genital surgery appeals to a cultural fantasy of 'normality'. I consider the 'normal vulva' to be a fantasy because it is an imaginary projection of sex that is intolerant of actual, pluralistic, non-binary variation. That is, the genital norm that excludes 'hypertrophy' effectively eliminates genital diversity. It protects an unambiguous distinction between masculine men and feminine women and preserves active/passive heterosexual roles in intercourse. For instance, the aim of FGCS—inclusive of labiaplasty, hymenoplasty and vaginal tightening—is to feminise women in a part of the body that matters most to female classification and identification based on appearance: the vulva and vagina. In the words of Melbourne surgeon Jane Paterson: 'A labiaplasty will reconstruct and enhance your feminine form to help you feel more comfortable and confident ... Many [women] report they feel more feminine and are no longer embarrassed, and as a result [labiaplasty] can help improve intercourse'.[17] It is no coincidence that labiaplasty advertising swings inexorably back to fantasies of acceptable sex organs and pleasurable (hetero)sexual acts. Across the cosmetic surgery advertising and the medical literature, the feminine vulva is implicitly heterosexual; the only stories we see of sexual dysfunction are by women who say the labia interfere with heterosexual intercourse (penetration).[18] The perfect vulva is far more than an object of beauty. As an object of desire, the beautified vulva promises femininity and heterosexual functionality: that is, it offers an alluring fantasy of the 'normal woman'.

In Paterson's fairly representative account of the benefits of labiaplasty, the genital cut is made meaningful in its relation to heterosexuality in promising better sex with men and the binary gender system in promising femininity. This interlocking relationship between gender and sexual desire is an effect of compulsory heterosexuality, or what Butler calls 'the heterosexual matrix'.[19] I propose that the desire for labiaplasty on the part of both surgeons and their female patients is shaped through the heterosexual matrix, which sustains the fantasy of 'normal femininity'. In making such an argument, this chapter conceives labiaplasty as just one knot in an interlocking web of practices of genital cutting that contribute in some way to the production of desire for a heterosexual norm. The phenomenon of non-medically necessary labiaplasty shares some structural similarities with surgery on intersex infants for the purpose of creating a coherent sex, as well as with practices like ritual female genital cutting (hereafter ritual FGC) among some ethnic groups in Africa, Asia and the Middle East. In this chapter, I prefer to use the term 'ritual genital cutting' or 'female genital cutting' rather than 'female genital mutilation' (FGM) for reasons of cultural sensitivity. Likewise, I do not use the term 'mutilated women' because it implies that a woman's identity can be reduced to her cut genitals, a view to which I do not subscribe. I use the term FGM where it refers to activist discourse and World Health Organization (WHO) definitions. I am aware of the ethical difficulties of introducing cross-cultural comparisons,[20] but as we shall see, there are good reasons for a consideration of how operations on undiseased genitals literally inscribe cultural fantasies of 'normal sex' upon the body. One compelling reason is that the feminist literature on genital cutting reveals political alliances between intersex and anti-FGC activists. My contribution here is to suggest that feminist criticism of FGCS surgery also intersects with these diverse political projects.

There is one other form of genital surgery, and that is transsexual surgery, which I do not have the space to address properly in this chapter. It would be disingenuous of me not to acknowledge that the surgically reconstructed bodies of transsexual men and women, too, are the literalisation of a dream come true. And yet elective labiaplasty and elective gender affirmation surgery are not at all symmetrical insofar as the changes to which they aspire carry vastly different cultural tolerances: there are qualitative differences in relation to the kinds of bodies that undergo surgery that must be taken into account. For instance, a cisgender woman is more likely to reap social benefit and recognition for her adherence to a culturally defined 'feminine' ideal than is a transwoman or transman, because she is not seen to be reconstructing an 'unnatural' body in her quest for authenticity; rather, her wish for 'feminine' genitals merely affirms the normalcy of the female desire to become feminine. There is nothing especially unusual about the female desire to correct perceived bodily imperfection in a culture which places a high premium on female beauty, and the cosmetic surgery industry sustains the continuation of this form of valuation. It is this system of aesthetic value—which dictates the cultural laws of male and female attractiveness—that is responsible, in part, for transphobia. There is a sense in which culturally normative standards of beauty function to safeguard the taboos against transcrossings, and this is precisely why 'passing' successfully can be so important, especially given that trans people are vulnerable to the violent policing of gender norms; if you look too trans (for example, not female or male enough), you may find it hard to find work and be vulnerable to physical attacks in public spaces.[21]

A yearning for 'normality' does not have the same symbolic weight for everyone. Transwomen may experience a similar desire for recognition of feminine belonging on the basis of appearance, but their experience is doubly freighted with the pressure to 'pass'. Ciswomen may be uncomfortable with their genitals, but they are not required to prove that they have a right to call themselves women because they have already accepted their female embodiment as aligned with their gendered identity as female-feminine. For ciswomen seeking genital cosmetic surgery, to be abnormal is to have 'ugly' or 'abnormal' genitals that must be improved in the achievement of desirable and appropriate femininity; yet for transwomen and transmen, the desire to transfigure the genitals to become the 'other' sex is complicated by social taboos that insist that the body determines gender identity—and that attempts to change what is considered to be the natural bedrock of gender are entirely unnatural and perverse.

This chapter does not seek to invalidate transsexual experience or to suggest that transsexual people are perpetuating sex normativity, which is one implication that could be drawn (erroneously) from the argument I am making. Rather, I want to challenge cultural constructions of sex and gender that classify certain types of biological female genital embodiment as shameful, improper and abject. I do not mean to give the impression of the sanctity of the natural body or that bodily integrity might be considered to be important because it indicates naturalness. If I am critical of FGCS, it is not because I think that it is a violation of nature, but because the fantasy of proper sex is offered to women as the cure for their suffering when it is in fact the cause.

CORRECTING AMBIGUITY

In 1984, American plastic surgeons Darryl J. Hodgkinson and Glen Hait published the first paper to describe female demand for labiaplasty for aesthetic reasons.[22] In this paper, Hodgkinson and Hait drew a clear distinction between genital surgery on intersex bodies; female circumcision as a ritual practice in Islamic/Arabic countries; and consumer-driven elective cosmetic surgery in the United States. They paid particular attention to the reputed sexual health benefits of elective consumer-driven cosmetic genital surgery:

> Aesthetic external genital surgery may be requested by females who feel that their sexual enjoyment will be enhanced by exposing the clitoris or that a shorter labia minora or a reduction in the size of the clitoris may be aesthetically more appealing. Other patients may feel more feminine by defining the external genitalia with a 'partial circumcision'. Still others may want a reduction in size of the labia minora purely for hygienic reasons or to relieve chafing and irritation.[23]

Hodgkinson and Hait also stated that while genital surgery on girls and women (in the United States) had usually been reserved for patients with adrenogenital syndrome or ambiguous genitalia, women without intersex 'conditions' had begun to approach plastic surgeons for surgery on aesthetic grounds.[24] In addition, the authors situated modern elective cosmetic surgery in cross-cultural context, citing Islamic/Arabic practices of female circumcision conducted under the rationale that 'uncircumcised women retain male characteristics that render them unfit for marriage'.[25] Egyptian anthropologist Fadwa El Guindi has made a similar observation about the relationship between circumcision and gender identity in a two-sex/gender system:

> The prevalent view in Africa is that male circumcision defeminizes men and female circumcision demasculinizes women. Female circumcision is seen as removing maleness through the cutting of the phallic clitoris and thus enhancing femaleness ... Removal or reduction of this masculine appearance is the way to feminize women. From this perspective, female circumcision is about altering the female body to confirm its femininity.[26]

It is therefore unsurprising that, as intersex activist Cheryl Chase has pointed out, immigrant African anti-FGC activists in the United States have formed political alliances with intersex opponents of normalising surgery performed on infants.[27] What distinguishes intersex surgeries and ritual FGC from elective FGCS is the issue of consent. I do not have the space to explore these differences here because this chapter focuses on the commonalities, but it must be acknowledged that ritual FGC and intersex surgery are usually conducted on children, and therefore take place under conditions in which consent cannot be given.

In locating elective genitoplasty on a continuum with both ritual FGC and the medical management of intersex bodies, Hodgkinson and Hait draw our attention to the desire for gender identity that medically non-essential genital surgery generates and sustains. Both ritual FGC and cosmetic operations on the vulva are *feminising*: they aim to alter the female body to confirm its femininity. A similar gendering process is at work in Western medical approaches to intersex bodies. In fact, the large majority of surgeries on infant intersex genitalia are feminising: 90 per cent of children diagnosed with Disorders of Sex Development (DSD) are surgically remade as girls because it is easier to reduce the size of a clitoris/penis and to create a functional (penetrable) vagina than it is to create a functional (penetrating) penis.[28] Feminising surgery reduces the size of the clitoris/penis and creates a vagina or enlarges an existing one.[29] Thus, when Hodgkinson and Hait suggest that a 'reduction in the size of the clitoris may be aesthetically more appealing', they refer to a procedure that has been perfected, in Western medicine, through surgical experimentation on intersex genitalia.

While staged vaginal reconstructions began in the nineteenth century, it was Hugh Hampton Young, Professor of Urology at Johns Hopkins University, who introduced the standard methods of diagnosis and surgical treatment laid out in his influential textbook *Genital Abnormalities, Hermaphroditism and Related Adrenal Diseases* (1937).[30] The protocols and techniques for the surgical management of intersex were later revolutionised in the 1950s by John Money and the Psychosocial Research Unit of the Johns Hopkins Medical Center, who took the approach that sex determination from infancy would direct the course of social gender identity if parents were to raise their children according to their surgically confirmed sex.[31]

In the world of intersex case management, functionality has everything to do with aesthetic appearance and very little to do with sensation; pleasure and freedom from pain is less important than the capacity of the constructed organ to perform heterosexuality.[32]

This may well be the exemplary case for Butler's theory of gender performativity, where the 'sex' only obtains its reality through the iterative performance of gender. American urologist Justine Schober, who advocates non-surgical intervention on intersex infants, explains that the surgical techniques used in feminising surgery cannot yet create a perfectly functional, sensate vagina. In addition, she adds that the biomaterials derived from other sites on the body, such as bowel lining or skin, do not always integrate well with the genital tissue.[33] Some of the many problems Schober lists that can occur with introduced tissue are infection, erosion, mineral deposits and calcifications, migration of tissues, scarring and lack of resilience when subjected to stresses they would not have originally been subject to in a different part of the body. While the biosciences are currently experimenting with tissue engineering for the surgical replacement of absent, lost, traumatised or infected bodily tissue, 'optimal outcomes cannot be guaranteed'.[34] This means that people who have had feminising surgery on their genitals as infants are likely to have recurrent medical problems, such as introital stenosis (narrowing of the vagina due to build-up of scar tissue), and multiple follow-up surgeries.[35] The accumulation of scar tissue is a common problem, which, when it occurs in the urethra, leads to painful and recurrent urinary tract infections.[36]

As intersex activists and medical specialists such as Schober have shown, surgery to confirm sex in intersex infants where there is no existing functional problem is self-perpetuating and likely to cause more problems than it purports to solve. Let's take clitoral surgery, for instance, and the reduction and recession techniques for the enlarged clitoris developed by Hugh Hampton Young. There are three methods: clitorectomy, or the removal of the corpora (or clitoral body) and the glans, which was commonly practised until around the early 1980s; clitoral recession, which involves tucking the clitoral shaft under the pubic bone without removing any erectile tissue; and clitoral reduction, which is currently the most commonly used technique. This last technique removes most of the erectile clitoral tissue while preserving the glans clitoris and neurovascular bundle running along the dorsal aspect of the clitoral shaft.[37]

It is noteworthy that clitorectomy and clitoral recession are no longer practised. Clitorectomies cause scarring and numbness, while clitoral recession causes pain upon arousal of the clitoral erectile tissue. Clitoral reduction is currently routine in feminising surgeries and generally assumed to have very little impact on sexual feeling.

However, intersex activists have long argued that irreversible surgery on infant bodies causes physical and psychological harm. Intersex Human Rights Australia, for example, cites a 2004 report by the San Francisco Human Rights Commission, which found that clitoral surgery risks a reduction or loss of sensation in the genital region, and that there is no evidence that the reconstructed genitals are structurally and functionally 'normal', or that quality of life has been improved.[38] According to a 2017 Human Rights Watch report on 'Medically Unnecessary Surgeries on Intersex Children in the US', any form of clitoral surgery 'carries the risk of pain, nerve damage, and scarring, and yields no medical benefit'.[39]

Intersex activist groups who protest non-consensual surgery have traditionally been silenced by the medical community's insistence that infant genital surgeries do not interfere with, but enhance, a person's sexual autonomy or feeling. In fact, in the course of my research, I have found a surprising lack of medical studies that express concern about the effect that surgery on the clitoris might have to sexual response. It is only relatively recently that feminist medical professionals have questioned the poor quality of evidence in the surgical literature of satisfactory outcomes in sexual function.[40] British gynaecologist Sarah M. Creighton is one prominent researcher who is questioning the evidence of medical benefit of feminising surgery on intersex infants and also of female genital cosmetic surgery. Creighton specialises in paediatric and adolescent gynaecology and is based at the University College London Hospital and the Great Ormond Street Hospital. In her extensive work with intersex patients, she found that nearly a third had had two or more clitoral procedures, and that intersex women who had undergone clitoral surgery were significantly less likely to achieve orgasm than those who had not had surgery.[41] She also cited studies that had reported poor outcomes in satisfaction with cosmetic appearance following clitoral surgery.[42] Complications of feminising vaginal and clitoral surgery include urinary infection, vaginal fistula (an abnormal opening that connects the vagina to another organ, such as the bladder, colon or rectum), vaginal stenosis, and clitoral pain.[43] Both intersex experiences and Creighton's studies demonstrate that feminising surgery is usually not a single-stage solution and tends to cause health complications related to the *surgery* and not to the anatomical arrangement of the original genital structure. Clitoral reduction surgery, more specifically, is conducted on a particularly sensitive part of the body that has until very recently been poorly understood. We now know, thanks to Australian urologist Helen O'Connell, that the clitoris is actually a complex structure with multiple parts: the external glans clitoris is coextensive with the internal erectile clitoral body and the crura, which are continuous with the paired bulbs and paired corpora.[44] The clitoral complex also provides extensive supporting tissue to the mons and labia.[45] Given the reach, depth and continuity of the clitoral nervous system, Creighton concludes that 'any incision to the clitoral glans, corpora, or hood may damage the innervation'.[46]

And yet, as Alice Dreger observes, it is not uncommon for surgeons to see themselves as restoring the intersex infant to normality through 'reconstructive' surgery.[47] Through this restitution narrative, surgical intervention is cast as compassionate, even though it is medically unnecessary and often traumatic and ongoing, with no solid evidence that the reconstructed genital apparatus provides adequate sexual sensitivity. Cosmetic surgeons are apt to represent themselves as heroically bestowing the gift of a much wished-for normal life. For instance, Hodgkinson and Hait had claimed that they stepped in to help women who had been refused surgery by gynaecologists on the grounds that their 'hypertrophied' labia minora were a 'normal variant' and didn't need surgical alteration.[48] American surgeon Gary Alter claims on his website that women with an enlarged clitoris 'are routinely told that nothing can or should be done because of fear of injury to the sensation and nerves of the clitoris. In reality, this is NOT true'. He explains that 'the large clitoris can look like a small penis and can get large and unsightly at rest or when sexually aroused ... These women are usually very embarrassed, both in and out of clothing and when sexually aroused'.[49] Alter is well-known among cosmetic surgeons for inventing the 'wedge resection' technique for labiaplasty, which he offers in conjunction with clitoral reduction surgery. Plastic surgeons such Alter, who pride themselves on being good at what they do, will normally not stop at one part of the genitalia, but will need to 'correct' adjacent structures in order to create a symmetrically consistent look. From a feminist perspective, however, cosmetic surgeons are part of the problem because they perpetuate fantasies of normality that exclude and shame those who do not conform, or do not perceive themselves as conforming, to the desired body-image. What they are doing is not heroic; it is contributing to stigma by confirming for women that their bodies are not female enough.

This panic over sexual ambiguity extends to the cosmetic correction of 'hypertrophied' labia minora. In 1987, Costas H. Pappis and Philip S. Hadzihamberas stated that labial hypertrophy was worrisome for its sex deviance: 'Hypertrophy of the labia minora is a rare abnormality which appears in girls in late childhood and early adolescence. The unexpected protrusion of the previously normal labia minora and the disfigured appearance of the vulva, which sometimes resembles a scrotum, cause anxiety and fear in the parents, who may initially regard it as a mani-festation of hermaphroditism'.[50] Anthropologist Lindy Joan McDougall has argued that contemporary cosmetic surgeons associate long labia with 'deficient femininity', citing one who said, upon brandishing a pho-tographic example, 'It looks like a penis, doesn't it?' Another explained that 'they [women] see it as a problem, too bulky; you know it looks like they have got testicles'.[51] Cosmetic genital surgery is offered as the best solution to sexual shame, even though the language surgeons use is *shaming*. I would suggest instead that the best way to reduce sexual stigma, anxiety and shame is sex education, first and foremost for medical professionals.

GOOD MEDICINE AND BAD MUTILATION

It is puzzling that while Western medical professionals continue to justify unnecessary cosmetic surgery on the healthy clitoris and labia minora—as well as the clitoral hood, labia majora and vagina—on the basis that it does no harm to sexual sensitivity, there is no such argument being made in support of ritual FGC, which comprises many of the same sorts of procedures. Ritual FGC is a traditional practice of cutting the genitals to mark a girl's entry into womanhood and is practiced by some ethnic groups in Africa, Asia and the Middle East. The WHO lists four types:

Type 1 Often referred to as clitoridectomy, this is the partial or total removal of the clitoris (a small, sensitive and erectile part of the female genitals), and in very rare cases, only the prepuce (the fold of skin sur-rounding the clitoris).

Type 2 Often referred to as excision, this is the partial or total removal of the clitoris and the labia minora (the inner folds of the vulva), with or without excision of the labia majora (the outer folds of skin of the vulva).

Type 3 Often referred to as infibulation, this is the narrowing of the vaginal opening through the creation of a covering seal. The seal is formed by cutting and repositioning the labia minora, or labia majora, sometimes through stitching, with or without removal of the clitoris (clitoridectomy).

Type 4 This includes all other harmful procedures to the female genitalia for non-medical purposes, e.g. pricking, piercing, incising, scraping and cauterizing the genital area.[52]

The medical evidence is that ritual FGC, particularly the first three types, can cause chronic pain, iatrogenic complications and psychological trauma, though complications are not universally experienced. Studies have documented the various long-term complications of chronic clitoral pain, obstetric fistula, pain during sexual intercourse, vulvar cysts, genitourinary tract infections, postpartum haemorrhage, painful scarring and keloids, anaemia, and maternal and foetal deaths. Ritual FGC has also been associated with anxiety, post-traumatic stress disorder and psycho-sexual problems leading to bodily identity problems.[53]

And yet despite evidence coming from intersex and anti-FGM activists that medically unnecessary clitoral cutting causes nerve damage that may lead to chronic pain and complications, American surgeon Gary Alter offers clitoral-reduction surgeries as part of his service, while French surgeon Pierre Foldès has made it his mission to give women their clitorises back. Foldès developed the surgical technique known as 'clitoral reconstruction', which aims to 'restore' the glans clitoris removed in ritual FGC. I question why is there so much importance attached to the preservation of the clitoris in 'mutilated' African, Asian and Middle Eastern women when no such concern exists for intersex women, or those with, as Alter put it, an 'unsightly' organ? Further, why is it that all four types of non-medically necessary FGC are outlawed in Western countries, but non-medically necessary cosmetic surgery such as clitoral, clitoral hood and labia minora reduction are legal? The reason for this contradiction, as Shakira Hussein and I have argued elsewhere,[54] is Orientalism: that is the idea that Eastern cultures are barbaric and backward, and that Western medical science is modern, advanced and benevolent. Plastic surgery, then, is cast as heroically rescuing the violated sexuality of African, Asian and Middle Eastern women through clitoral restoration, while also heroically rescuing intersex infants and unhappy women from the problem of their own bodies. The aim is to help women to feel *normal*; but what 'normality' is changes according to the cultural location of the body that is being surgically altered.

Depending upon a woman's racial or ethnic identity, normal femininity is restored by the surgeon either by recreating the missing clitoris or
excising the genital tissue that stands in for an intolerable blurring of
boundaries between masculine and feminine. The common goal of these
procedures is to make a fantasy of femininity align with the real, material
body.

In a piece titled 'The Pleasure Doctor Fighting to Restore Clitorises
after Female Genital Mutilation', published in online media outlet for
academic research *The Conversation*, Dr. Annemarie Middelburg approv-
ingly describes the work of Californian gynaecologist Marci Bowers, who
performs clitoral reconstructions for women who have undergone ritual
FGC.[55] Bowers was the world's first transsexual doctor to perform gender affirmation surgery, which is her main specialty. In 2007, and again
in 2009, she received funding from an organisation called 'Clitoraid' to
travel to Paris for training in clitoral reconstruction from Foldès himself. She describes herself as 'one of several surgeons in the world who
perform a functional reversal of FGM'.[56] Clitoraid is a private, not-for-
profit organisation run by a cult called the Raëlian movement founded
by Frenchman Claude Vorilhon, who calls himself Raël. Raëlians believe
that life on Earth was scientifically created by aliens, which they call the
Elohim, and claim to have produced successful experiments in human
cloning.[57] Clitoraid is a charity that was established in the mid-2000s by
wealthy Raëlians living in California and Canada. In a major fundrais-
ing campaign, Clitoraid invited donors to 'sponsor a clitoris' and raised
US$400,000, which funded the building of a hospital for clitoral recon-
structions in Burkina Faso. The building of the 'Pleasure Hospital' began
in 2006 and it was due to open in March 2014.[58] Bowers was to perform the first operation in the new hospital, but before it was due to
open in March 2014, the government withdrew its support. A local doctor in Bobo offered Bowers and colleagues the use of his clinic, where
they performed twenty-nine surgeries in three days, before the Burkina
Faso government revoked their medical licences.[59] Bowers is not herself
a Raëlian but sees Clitoraid as providing the opportunity for her to provide a humanitarian service to women affected by ritual FGC. She is still
affiliated with Clitoraid and, according to its website, will be going to
Nairobi this year (2018) as a volunteer.[60]

In 2010, renowned American sexologist Betty Dodson encouraged the San Francisco-based sex shop chain Good Vibrations to
give its support to the 'adopt a clitoris' campaign. At that time, the

Assistant Professor of Politics at the University of San Francisco Wanjiru Kamau-Rutenberg protested Good Vibrations's involvement with Clitoraid on two grounds: first that such clitoral reconstructive surgeries ought to be, and in fact were, provided by responsible state-funded programs, and second, that Clitoraid's campaign to 'adopt a clitoris' was demeaning to African women. She wrote in her blog:

> Nobody's genitalia should be talked about in the way that Clitoraid is talking about African women's genitalia. In fact, no part of anyone's body should be up for adoption in this way that reminds us too much of the slave trade ... As an African woman I'm sick and tired of my entire experience reduced to what is between my legs ... Why is it o.k. for Western feminist [*sic*] to argue that they should not be reduced only to what is between their legs while an allegedly feminist organization like Good Vibrations engages in such a practice? Where is the sisterhood there?[61]

When Clitoraid was due to open its hospital in 2014, BBC journalist Sue Lloyd-Roberts reported anticipation among some local women, quoting one as having said, 'We can be like other women!' and 'We can be made whole again!'[62] Surgeon Marci Bowers drew on her own trans experience to explain her humanitarian reasons for volunteering: 'I empathise with women who have to have surgery to achieve and regain their womanhood. They are struggling to regain their identity, just like I had to do once upon a time myself'.[63]

What is interesting about this frankly weird story about the alien-worshipping cult and Bowers the trans surgeon from California is the importance placed on the restoration of a feminine identity through what is essentially a cosmetic operation to bring some of the internal clitoral body to the surface to become a pseudo-glans. What is counted as a 'feminine' body depends, as I have shown, on its difference from the male body; but it also depends on its resemblance to an imaginary 'normal' woman who serves as a point of comparison. In the case of the 'Pleasure Hospital', it is the intact, natural genitals that serve as the restorative image, while American surgeons like Alter build an imaginary—and homogenising—template of what they think the natural genitals ought to look like.

In 2012, Pierre Foldés, Béatrice Cuzin and Armelle Andro published a one-year follow-up study of a cohort of 2,938 women who had received clitoral reconstructive surgery between 1998 and 2009 at

Poissy-St Germain Hospital in France. The stated aim of the surgery was 'to restore both clitoral anatomy and clitoral function',[64] which the authors claimed to have successfully produced in finding that most of the patients who returned for the follow-up study reported reduced pain and restored clitoral pleasure. They described the procedure as recreating the (glans) clitoris from the preserved 'dorsal-region neuro-vascular bundle' they found buried underneath the scarring from the original ritual excision.[65] Three months after the Foldés study was published in *The Lancet*, Sarah Creighton, Susan Bewley and Lih-Mei Liao published a critical response arguing that Foldés et al. did not have the evidence to claim that they could restore the clitoral sensation that had been lost with the cutting of the glans clitoris.[66] Creighton et al. make the point that because the dorsal nerve is actually cut in clitoral excisions, one cannot possibly say that the sensory apparatus has been 'preserved'. Furthermore, they argue, follow-up studies of intersex surgery show that even when the neurovascular bundle *has* been preserved in clitoral reduction surgery, it still carries unacceptable risk of loss of sensation. This is because such procedures have been positively associated with poorer sexual function. The reason they make this comparison is to demonstrate that when a clitoris is cut, there is a loss of sensation that you can never get back. As they write: 'Formation of a "neoglans" … cannot restore the lost or damaged innervation'.[67] A major methodological problem with the Foldés study was that they only had a 30 per cent response rate, which is incredibly poor, given that a 75 per cent response rate or more is considered the standard measure of reliability.[68] In statistics, a low response rate constitutes what is known as a 'self-selected sample', which means that the findings are not generalisable to the whole population, simply because we don't actually know what that other 45–70 per cent have experienced.

In their reply to criticism, Foldés et al. made the counter-claim that Creighton, an eminent professor in gynaecology, and her team 'show a lack of knowledge about FGM'.[69] In her interview with Middelburg, Bowers claimed that 'You see the [buried] clitoris every single time. You can't deny it's there' and that the response of Creighton's team reflected 'antiquated but persistent notions of female sexuality',[70] while another student of Foldés, Dr. Pere Barri Soldevila claimed: 'It's a matter of knowing what you're talking about … I've never seen any mutilated woman without remaining clitoris … Normally the patients, at least the ones that survive the FGM, will always have a remaining clitoris.

So they can always benefit from replacing it in the right place.'[71] When confronted with well-founded criticism from women gynaecologists, these (male and female) medical practitioners fall back on the claim that the women don't know what they are talking about, which is the predictable product of institutional sexism, particularly in the cosmetic plastic surgery context, where the majority of operations are performed on female bodies, often by men. There is an unequal power structure at work here. But I also think that these opponents are talking past each other. As I see it, Creighton et al. are talking specifically about the glans clitoris and the external part of the clitoral body, which they shorten to 'the clitoris' as defined by the WHO in its FGM Types, while Foldés et al. understand 'the clitoris' as the entire external and internal complex.

The problem for me, and I suspect also for Sarah Creighton, is that offering more surgery to fix the original surgery makes cosmetic operations self-perpetuating. There is also the question of risk versus harm, which is the principle that guides medical ethics. As Creighton et al. have suggested, even if only 4 per cent of Foldés's female participants in the study required readmission to hospital with surgical complications, this is an unacceptable risk, given that the surgery is essentially cosmetic. Moreover, in a 2017 literature review, Nigerian gynaecologist Ifeanyichukwu Ezebialu stated that he found no evidence in support of clitoral reconstruction as a viable treatment for clitoral pain, and that 'the procedure may sometimes result in worsening of the painful symptoms'.[72] It is not therefore ethical to subject women to more pain if there is no need to. This is why evidence-based medicine is absolutely crucial. Without the support of reliable evidence, cosmetic surgeries like clitoral reconstruction are unable to deliver on their promises of restored sexual function, if, indeed, that were even possible, given that glans sensation is removed when the glans is removed. Certainly, claims that cosmetic labiaplasty surgery increases sexual pleasure are dubious at best, given that the labia minora are innervated structures that, like the clitoris, also respond to tactile stimulation. What cosmetic genital surgeries do perform, however, is psychological work. As Spanish surgeon Dr. Barri Soldevila said of his clitoral reconstructions: 'There's a physical outcome from the procedure, but there's also a psychological one. And that's about not being different any more.' His patient Rosa confirmed, 'I want to feel like other women'.[73] It is the medical delivery of this alluring promise of normality that is considered 'healthful' in Western cosmetic surgery discourse.

Clitoral reconstruction surgery for African women in particular has been promoted in online media outlets as unquestionably good because in normalising the 'mutilated' genitals, it restores African women to the womanly body that was taken from them. It is this kind of rationale that supports Western enthusiasm for the psychological health benefits of cosmetic genital surgery against the 'mutilating' violence of ritual FGC. As feminist theorist Nikki Sullivan has argued, laws in Western countries that criminalise ritual FGC are inconsistent because similar cutting operations on the genitals are routinely and legally performed by plastic surgeons on intersex infants as well as girls and women who undergo FGCS.[74] Virginia Braun has similarly pointed out that while FGCS is viewed as a choice made by rational and autonomous agents, FGM is represented as violently oppressive, when in fact cultural pressures that victimise women are brought to bear in both contexts.[75] Shakira Hussein and I have also argued that anti-FGM law is hypocritical because it relies on an Orientalist discourse that positions non-Western FGM as barbaric and Western FGCS as medically legitimate.[76] Here, we follow Sullivan's argument that the demonisation of Muslim women's 'mutilated' bodies is symptomatic of what she calls a 'white optics', which '(re)affirms and naturalises western norms and ideals regarding subjectivity, gender, sexuality, the body, pleasure, orgasm, the common good, and at the same time constructs the "other" woman as an unenlightened and passive victim in need of rescue'.[77]

Kenyan theorist Wairimũ Ngaruiya Njambi explains that white representations of African practices of genital cutting as violating women's sexuality are problematically imperialist because when white Westerners do the same thing, they are perceived as agents making a choice. Thus, she asks: How do we discuss genital cutting 'without creating an imperialistic impression that only those with some social, political, and economic power and who live in the west have rights to take risks with their bodies?'[78] Juliet Rogers has taken a similar position in arguing that white feminist campaigns to end ritual FGC are crafted from a monolithic and persistent image of the African girl held down against her will and brutally violated with a knife. This image, she suggests, cannot account for women's real, diverse, plural and complex experiences of ritual cutting and strips them of agency.[79]

In Western medicine and in legal and feminist discourse, female genital integrity gains special importance when it serves as the symbol of female oppression in non-Western cultures. And yet no such overriding concern for female genital integrity exists among cosmetic surgeons, and some gynaecologists, in nations like Australia, the US and the UK. Fantasies of femininity, then, change their shape according to the cultural work that they do to differentiate and homogenise. Femininity can produce racialised differences between women, in which some are 'free' while others are 'unfree', some are 'normal' while others are 'abnormal', as we saw in earlier chapters, where the genitals served as proof of the evolutionary difference between black and white women. As Kenyan theorist Naomi Onsongo writes, by describing African women who have undergone ritual cutting as mutilated, 'Westerners considered them less than feminine even though their own cultures saw them as feminine'.[80]

But femininity is also a mechanism of sexual and gender conformity as that which appears as the ideal, 'normal' female body. Across cultures and ethnicities, fantasies of femininity make certain demands on female bodies, and this is reflected in genital-cutting practices. There are strikingly similar rationales for genital cutting among ethnic groups that practice FGC and those that practice FGCS. Western cosmetic surgeons promise (hetero) sexual desirability and a normal, feminine appearance. The achievement of normal femininity is also the goal of ritual FGC. According to Professor of Obstetrics and Gynaecology Gamal Serour, ritual cutting on the female genitals not only marks a girl's entry into womanhood, but 'is also performed to identify a gender identity'. He continues:

> For a girl to be considered a complete woman FGM is often deemed necessary. FGM marks the divergence of the sexes concerning their roles in life and marriage. FGM is supported by the widespread belief that the human body is androgynous at birth. To ensure adulthood, girls must be relieved of their male part, the clitoris and or/labia. Excision of such parts of a woman's body is thought to enhance the girl's femininity.[81]

Feminist scholars such as Fiona J. Green have noted such similarities between FGCS and FGC in conceiving them as contiguous practices supporting hetero-patriarchal gender and sexual inequality. Both practices control or manage female (hetero)sexuality and associate the cut vulva with desirability, beauty and cleanliness.[82] Others such as Cheryl Chase, Alice Dreger and J. Steven Svoboda have explored the connections between surgical interventions on intersex bodies, ritual FGC and FGCS.[83] We also know that in Australia, for example, there is a not insignificant population of mothers bringing their daughters to see medical professionals for labiaplasty surgery. A recent news article reported that an audit of referral letters for labiaplasty surgery at the Royal Children's Hospital in Melbourne revealed that about 25 per cent of requests came from mothers.[84] By way of comparison, it is well documented that in societies that practice ritual FGC, it is the mothers who arrange for their daughters to undergo the procedure.

There are, of course, obvious differences between ritual FGC and FGCS. Ritual cutting is prevalent in African societies with their own histories of medicine and approaches to health, illness and the body. The central difference lies in the ritual nature of the operation. Ritual FGC is considered necessary for entrance into womanhood and is usually performed on girls. FGCS in Western nations, on the other hand, is a comparatively arbitrary practice because it doesn't carry the same weight as an expression of a deeply felt and communal cultural or religious identity. That is, ritual FGC binds a woman to her community and ancestry, while FGCS comprises isolated cases, where patients are treated individually. This individualised and individualising approach is a product of the way in which white Western societies have historically organised their social relationships through enlightenment rationalism, capitalism and colonialism, including the enslavement of African people to enable the accumulation of wealth for white nations.

Carolyn Pedwell argues that if we treat African ritual FGC and Western genital cosmetic surgery as analogous or continuous with one another, we may unwittingly be erasing the differences between race, culture and nation by which white privilege and power are sustained and reproduced. That is, in conceiving genital cutting as a mechanism that supports a universal two-sex/gender system, blurring national and racial distinctions, white feminists risk 'privileging gender above and beyond (or through the erasure of) other axes', like race.[85] She also argues that when intersex activists such as Cheryl Chase connect intersex surgery to ritual genital cutting, they may in fact be re-fetishising the African 'victim' of genital 'mutilation'. The upshot of Pedwell's argument, which is very similar to Rogers's critique of the white imperialist fantasy of the 'mutilated woman', is that all we are seeing in theories that locate ritual FGC on a continuum with Western FGCS and intersex surgery are white representations of African women victimised by 'bad' practices endemic to their cultures.[86]

I certainly take Pedwell's point, and hope that this book does some of the work she calls for in locating the diagnosis of 'hypertrophy of the labia minora' in historical context, with its undeniable colonial association with inferior, degenerate black animality vis-à-vis superior, perfectible white humanity. I also hope to have made visible the racial power differential that we see in Raëlian attempts to 'rescue' African women by offering to restore their clitorises. This example also muddies the distinction between white 'agents' and black 'victims' by showing African women to be consumers of clitoral reconstruction surgery.

But I am not entirely convinced of Pedwell's criticisms that placing ritual FGC, FGCS and intersex surgery on a continuum inevitably leads us back to the binary identities of 'oppressed' African women and 'liberated' white women. In Pedwell's view, the logic of comparison is dualistic, where sameness and difference reduce to an opposition between white and black, with its attendant power inequalities, thereby keeping that structure of inequality intact. But such comparisons are necessary to make because they *already exist* in white legal structures that criminalise ritual FGC but not FGCS or genital surgeries on intersex infants. Any activist or theorist who wants to criticise, defend, or simply consider these practices is going to confront the problem of the law and the WHO definition of FGM. Feminist arguments against FGCS, such as the one in this book, would not be complete without some reference to ritual FGC because the two practices are evidently proximate and women activists around the globe treat this proximity as significant.

Not all feminist critics who compare ritual FGC with FGCS are white Westerners, and this is evident in the debates that surround African practices of ritual FGC in particular. Sierra Leonean activist Fuambai Ahmadu is well-known for her support for ritual FGC, as she views it as an important and meaningful tradition in the communities where it occurs, and an important expression of African female identity and autonomy that poses a powerful challenge to white (feminist) imperialist attempts to eradicate it. In 2016, Ahmadu's *SiA Magazine* publicised her new campaign called 'Imitated Not Mutilated', which proudly proclaimed 'Labiaplasty=BONDO'.[87] 'Bondo' is an all-female society in Sierra Leone, which practices ritual FGC to initiate girls into womanhood and to Bondo. Ahmadu is part of the African diaspora. She is a cosmopolitan African woman who grew up in a Western nation, the United States, that profited from the slave trade and brutal exploitation of her people. Ahmadu was born in the United States in 1967 but returned to

Sierra Leone with her mother and brother when she was a year old. They moved back to the States in 1973, when her father received his Master's degree. Ahmadu was raised in a middle-class home in Washington, DC, where she attended a private school and later won a scholarship to the prestigious Washington International School. In 1991, at the age of twenty-one, Ahmadu went back to the Kono district in Sierra Leone, where her parents were raised, to take part in the genital-cutting ritual that would make her Bondo.[88] In her campaign 'Imitated Not Mutilated', Ahmadu argues that labiaplasty 'is an imitation of a common procedure performed during Bondo initiation'.[89]

On the other side of the debate is anti-FGM activist Nimko Ali. Ali was born in Somalia in 1982 to a middle-class family. They migrated to the UK when she was four, and three years later, her mother flew her to Djibouti to undergo Type 3 FGM. Ali is now a high-profile anti-FGM activist. She argues that white feminist anxieties about cultural imperialism are misplaced and prefers to use the term 'mutilation' over 'modification' or 'cutting' because she views the practice as 'a violation of a girl's basic right to her integrity and her body'.[90] Ali also sees a problematic connection between ritual FGC and consumer-driven FGCS. As she put it, 'Both involve oppression … Both are about women being abused.'[91] She is a strong supporter of the 'Muff March' organised by UK Feminista, which began in 2011 as a protest against female genital cosmetic surgery. UK Feminista member Rosie Mockett wrote at the time that the Muff March was to be 'a creative protest against the pornified culture driving women under the knife to get a "designer vagina". We'll also be protesting against the cosmetic surgeries ruthlessly profiting from this practice … Activists will be wearing fake "muffs" and demanding that pornography and cosmetic surgery industries "Keep their mitts off our bits"'.[92]

Similarly, South African organisation Transgender Intersex Africa (TIA), which was founded in 2010 by African transgender people, has invoked ritual FGC in order to argue for intersex rights to bodily integrity. On Intersex Awareness Day on 26 October 2015, TIA released a press statement, in which intersex activist Nthabiseng Mokoena was quoted as saying: 'It is troubling that society is able to see that Female Genitals Mutilation (FGM) as a human right violation but struggle to make the same connection when it comes to Intersex Genital Mutilation, simply because the latter often happens in medical settings … Bodily integrity and anatomy should be everyone's right'.[93]

The political aims of African intersex and anti-FGM activists intersect. They both argue for the right to bodily autonomy and freedom from ritual or medically authorised bodily violence. Black activists such as Nimko Ali see value in comparing ritual FGC with FGCS because they *do not see gender as exclusionary of race*, where race must disappear for gender to come into view, as Pedwell suggests happens when we make such comparisons. I would like to think that there can be fruitful transnational alliances between women, even though they are complicated by racialised power differences. Feminist criticism of contiguous forms of genital cutting is important because these practices demonstrate that women are unfairly judged according to aesthetic conceptions of genital normality which produce the female genitals as shameful and female pleasure as subordinate to male pleasure.

BECOMING BETTER, BECOMING POSTHUMAN

While white French cosmetic surgeon Foldés offers African women the opportunity to recover their humanity by restoring the lost clitoris, consumers of FGCS in white nations are invited to become more perfect. In a way, this striving toward the more-than-human reprises deeply entrenched colonial narratives that represent black women as less evolved, less-than-human. The contemporary expression of this racially and culturally specific drive to perfection is arguably 'makeover culture'. According to feminist theorist Meredith Jones, cosmetic surgery epitomises makeover culture, which, she argues, is less about achieving a static point of completion than about 'becoming something better'.[94] It is difficult not to see the vestiges of European eugenics in contemporary makeover culture, with its emphasis on making better bodies, and, as a consequence, happier citizens.

But it is even more intriguing that the morally condemnatory language of 'mutilation' has shifted into the cosmetic surgical lexicon to denote unskilled surgery. In the United States, prominent gynaecologist Michael Goodman has labelled poorly performed aesthetic labiaplasties '*avoidable unintentional genital mutilations* (aka "botched labiaplasties")'.[95] Although he is himself a member of the American College of Obstetricians and Gynecologists (ACOG), Goodman blames gynaecologists for the majority of botched procedures.[96] He is highly critical of the college for failing to train its fellows in plastic and reconstructive technique and aesthetic genital surgery, which has led, he says, to poor aesthetic outcomes, unhappy women and malpractice suits.[97] ACOG's position is that gynaecologists have no business doing cosmetic genital surgery because that is not their field of expertise.[98]

In Australia and the UK, the question of who is, or should be, authorised to perform plastic surgery is more likely to revolve around the rivalry between 'plastic surgeons' and 'cosmetic surgeons'. As Jones notes, in these countries, any General Practitioner can legally call themselves a 'cosmetic surgeon' and perform procedures such as labiaplasty, which explains why plastic surgeons are at pains to distinguish their work as specialised, skilled and legitimate. In Australia, for instance, the Australian Society of Plastic Surgeons will only certify a doctor as a plastic surgeon if they have had at least eight years of specialist plastic surgery training.[99] In the United States, however, there is palpable hostility among plastic surgeons toward gynaecologists. In this regard, Goodman is unusual as a gynaecologist who also specialises in aesthetic plastic surgery. Part of this animosity is because modern-day gynaecologist associations such as ACOG or RANZCOG (Royal Australian and New Zealand College of Obstetricians and Gynaecologists) don't consider aesthetic surgery to be medically indicated. They are also quite rightly sceptical of diagnostic nomenclature and surgical procedures that have been developed in an unregulated, marketised private health context, which prioritises profit over the best interests of the patient. This professional animosity has been accentuated in recent years by ACOG's official position that it does not support non-medically indicated cosmetic vaginal procedures because there is no evidence that they are safe or effective.[100] More recently, in 2017, ACOG released a statement on breast and labial cosmetic surgery in adolescents (females under the age of eighteen) urging counselling and education, and strongly discouraging surgery. It also stated very clearly that performing non-medically necessary labiaplasty on adolescents is illegal under the federal law banning FGM.[101] Notably, in its 2007 committee opinion on labiaplasty, ACOG relied heavily on the feminist clinical research by Jillian Lloyd et al., which found a wide range and variability of labial normality.[102]

Goodman's response is predictably dismissive. His website states that 'the fact that something is in the range of normality doesn't mean that you as an individual are comfortable with the size and appearance'.[103] While Goodman also boasts expertise in labiaplasty revision, he reassures the reader that if their anatomy is 'especially challenging', he may refer them to Gary Alter, whom he describes as 'the most experienced "reviser" in the world'.[104] Labiaplasty expert Gary Alter is now capitalising on the incidence of 'botched' surgery in promoting himself as a specialist in 'Revision or Restoration Labiaplasty'.[105] As he melodramatically laments on his website:

> Many unfortunate women are left with outer vaginal deformities due to a botched labiaplasty surgery. These women are so devastated with their failed labia reduction procedure that they feel *mutilated* and often have resulting pain and tenderness of the genital region. They often feel that they have been robbed of their femininity and 'womanhood'. These women may then avoid sexual relationships due to feelings of shame and embarrassment. These are the women that seek labiaplasty revision to correct their botched labiaplasty.[106]

As with clitoral reconstructions, labial reconstruction promises to restore a woman's femininity following 'mutilating' surgery. This rhetoric enables plastic surgeons to claim legitimacy for procedures that are not considered legitimate by established professional gynaecological associations. Comparisons between cosmetic labiaplasty and female genital 'mutilation' can be conveniently displaced in the new boundary erected between good cosmetic surgery performed by skilled artists and bad surgery conducted by amateurs. In this revised rendering, uncivilised, 'barbaric' ritual FGC reappears in the form of the ignorant, fumbling doctor while aesthetic surgeons become the entrusted guardians of the modernised, perfectible body. Similarly, the hypertrophied labia is becoming grudgingly acknowledged as normal (but ugly), rather than a deformity, which is attributed instead to intersex genitals and other 'birth defects', as well as the effects of botched labiaplasty, cancer surgery, ritual cutting, and other kinds of trauma.[107]

German plastic surgeon Stefan Gress claims that 'labial deformities are most often iatrogenic in nature' (which gives us reason to wonder how it is that the aesthetic surgery literature boasts such high satisfaction and low complication rates). The most common problem, according to Gress, is when the physician cuts the labia but leaves the clitoral hood intact for fear of damaging the clitoris, 'giving the appearance of a microphallus'. Other problems include frayed edges, scarring, distortion, asymmetry, and 'contour defects'.[108] According to Goodman, the more difficult cases are those where the labia minora has been overresected, or where too much has been cut off, because it is 'impossible to "put some back" or build new labia from nothing'.[109] Goodman and Gress both advise that the best option is to use Alter's technique of using tissue from the clitoral hood, which can be stretched downward and stitched to the sides of the vaginal opening to form new labia.[110] Fashioning labia from vag inal skin is viewed by Gress as a 'last resort' option due to the difficulty of achieving sufficient labial height (Fig. 7.1).[111]

When I look at images of Gress's work, it is difficult not to be impressed by his artistry in recreating non-existent labia minora from the clitoral hood and resculpting the jagged, uneven and strangely puckered 'botched' vulvas, some with masses of droplet-shaped nodules giving the appearance of melted wax. It *is* enticing and marvellous to see the steps of the surgery, the careful and delicate incisions, the plasticity of membrane and the final result, with the clitoris sitting snugly under its newly smooth and stretched covering. If they weren't so humanly fleshy, they could almost approximate Gress's clinical digital representations of the labia minora, devoid of detail and smooth as plastic (Fig. 7.2).

In his textbook *Aesthetic and Functional Labiaplasty* (2017), Gress provides digital images of the vulva, all in a clinical shade of blue, to show the anatomy and explain surgical procedures. For Gress, the 'ideal appearance' of the labia minora is variable: 'Some patients want their inner vaginal lips to be as short as possible, while others prefer a longer version, usually gently curved. In most cases, however, the prepuce should lie tightly over the clitoral shaft and the clitoral hood fit firmly over the glans, covering some two-thirds to all of it.'[112] The skill is in making the skin conform to the image on the screen.

Gress's flat and lifeless digital images of labial anatomy are perfect examples of Meredith Jones's concept of 'media-bodies', in which she argues that 'contemporary citizens inhabit worlds *made up of images* such that images, bodies, and senses are intertwined'. We are, Jones argues, living in an intensely digital-image-saturated historical moment 'in which bodies and media are formed *together* and continually re-form each other in an ongoing and under-examined tension between two- and three-dimensional ways of being'.[113] Similarly, Barbara Maria Stafford has used the term 'biomedia' to describe the mutual incorporation or 'fundamental equivalency' of the 'biological and digital domains' rendering the two interchangeable.[114] These digital information technologies, argues Stafford, are 'transforming us into a culture of self-perfection

Patient 4
Labia reconstruction with lateral perpuce-flaps

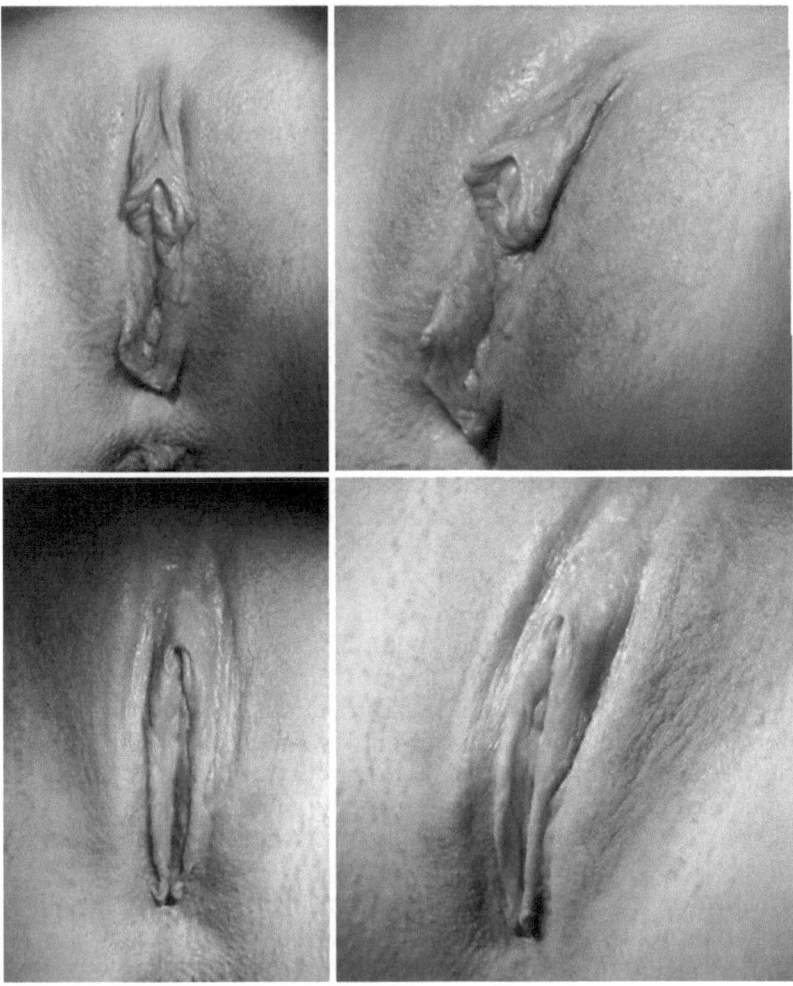

Fig. 7.1 An example of a 'botched' labiaplasty and surgical correction. Before and after photos. Stefan Gress, *Aesthetic and Functional Labiaplasty* (Munich: Springer, 2017), 93. Permission Springer Nature

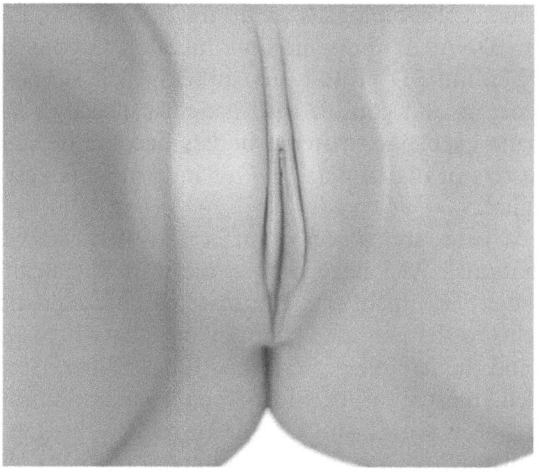

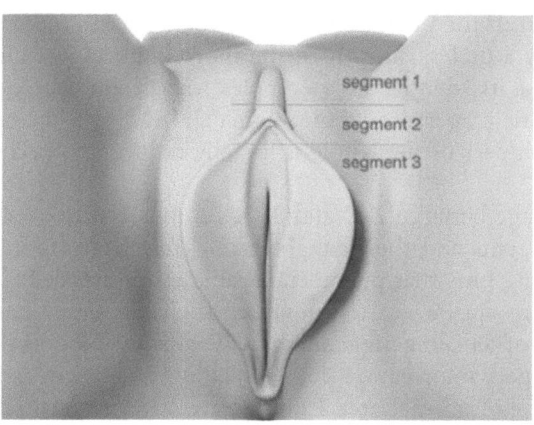

Fig. 7.2 Digital image of the 'ideal' vulva and diagram of the subdivisions of the hypertrophied labia minora. Stefan Gress, *Aesthetic and Functional Labiaplasty* (Munich: Springer, 2017), 26. Permission Springer Nature

from the cellular to the gross anatomical level',[115] and they express 'an obsession with beyondness',[116] with becoming more-than-human. In the age of bioinformatics, scientists are storing digital information in

DNA, while molecular biologists are using DNA sourced from bacteria to edit human DNA. At the same time, plastic surgeons are using digital technologies and 3D printing to improve their surgical techniques, train other doctors and consult with patients. Through such processes of bioinformatic exchange, material bodies become depersonalised and treated as clusters of digital data.[117] Our innermost fantasy worlds have now gone digital.

Skins, like screens, are projective surfaces at the nexus of the real and the representational. As I have been arguing in this chapter, the vulva is a fantasy object as much as it is a material characteristic of sex, and labiaplasty helps to sharpen the imaginary boundary between the masculine exterior and the feminine interior. As Jones argues, labiaplasty cleans up the 'folded, pleated, frilly, in-between area' to remove ambiguity and clearly delineate inside and outside to reduce the gap between the two-dimensional image and the three-dimensional body.[118] The female sexual parts of heterosexual fantasy are internal because the primary value of the vagina in coitus is its capacity to give and receive pleasure to and from the penis. Thus, when the labia minora are reduced to being merely a useless adjunct of the more important vagina, the vulva is 'robbed of its identity as a complex visual and tactile structure to become a simple aperture to the vagina'.[119] Or, as I like to think of it, the vulva as a part of the whole is literally reduced to become a part of the hole.

This slippage between 2-D and 3-D, combined with a lack of sex education for parents and their daughters, is likely contributing to the perception among girls that protuberant labia is abnormal. It is concerning that some girls appear not to know that the labia have a name and are a normal part of female genital anatomy. Seli from London posted on the cosmetic-surgery information site RealSelf: 'my vagina doesn't look good I have loose skin on that area I don't have any idea what should I need to do?? I'm confused please healp me'.[120] Similarly, annoymoussss345 from Virginia (US), wrote: 'I have something hanging from my vagina, what is it? Is there anyway to get rid of it?'[121] The authority of the material body itself to determine the limits of *natural diversity* is dwindling in an intensely mediatised world where fact and fantasy are increasingly difficult to tell apart, and where it may be easier to find cosmetic surgery websites online than practical information about basic biological anatomy.

Conclusion

I began this chapter with a meditation on the nature of fantasy because I believe that what we might like to call 'normal femininity', or just plain old 'femininity', is a social idea or construct of language, rather than an empirically observable fact. By contrast, what we know to be indisputably true is that there is a very wide natural variety of labial shapes, sizes and colours that is only just beginning to be documented by researchers such as Jillian Lloyd, though as we saw in Chapter 5, Frenchman Félix Jayle had, at the beginning of the twentieth century, posited four types. In his estimation, the membraniform type, which he compared to a lily, was the one he most frequently encountered and therefore the typical type. That exact same shape is now considered 'hypertrophic' by today's cosmetic surgeons. This history shows us that discourses of normality and femininity are as insubstantial as air and temporally contingent. Organic diversity is materially observable and measurable; femininity is not. This is why, as flawed as medical science can be in its propositions about sex and sexed behaviours, we need evidence-based approaches to medicine and sex education that support a queer feminist commitment to sexual diversity. Hence, the bioethical feminist position underpinning in this chapter would be that loss of sensation in a highly innervated part of the body essential to sexual pleasure is a more important consideration than the social gains awarded to women by the phantasm of femininity.

But I also wanted to interrogate fantasy as the psychic mechanism by which feelings of desire become affixed to cultural processes of normalisation. Cosmetic surgeries and cutting rituals produce magical transformations that provide a social identity by robbing the material body and its sensory apparatus of its capacity to feel. I have tried to bring together non-medically necessary female genital cosmetic surgery, intersex surgery and ritual female genital cutting because I see them as interconnected practices that in their various ways seek to affirm some notion of femininity through operations on the genitals. The fantasy of femininity differentiates and classifies, codifying absolute oppositional difference between men and women, and between white women and women of colour. As technologies of gender, ritual FGC, FGCS and intersex surgeries produce genital conformity within the logic of an assumed heterosexual desire, where the receptive hole is more important than the autonomous whole. The imagined pleasures of femininity are granted on the condition that the very site of pleasure—the genitals—are deprived of their sexual sensitivity. As a technology of race, genital cutting is implicated in what feminist theorist Patricia Hill Collins calls 'sexualised racism',[122] which renders black bodies without clitorises hypervisible as sexually deviant. While white Western cosmetic surgery procedures like labiaplasty commoditise the vulva as a purchasable luxury item, black women are reminded of their dependence on white benevolence, in which a charity organisation like Clitoraid claims the honour of bestowing the white gift of pleasure when black women themselves ought to be the agents and authors of their own sexuality. As Kamau-Rutenberg pointed out, Clitoraid's 'sponsor a clitoris' campaign recalls white paternal ownership of black female bodies. By taking an intersectional approach, we can see how labiaplasty and clitoral reconstructive surgery mobilise 'agency' in racially specific ways.

I think it necessary to question the attachment of 'agency' to economies of consumption because they are inevitably entwined with economies of exploitation. Cosmetic genital surgery may award social agency, but in doing so, it treats the body as an exploitable resource for the perpetuation of a certain model of 'normal' female heterosexuality. Cosmetic surgeons emphasise the psychological benefit that genital surgery brings in transforming unhappy women into sexual agents; but this promise is only fulfilled on the contradictory condition that they remove the material sensory apparatus that makes sexual agency possible to begin with. I want to gesture, then, toward a materialist conception of bodily agency that locates sexual autonomy in biodiversity. What we need now is a return to Kinsey: how we become sexual ought to be no more limited by cultural conceptions of normal and abnormal genitals than by normal and abnormal sexual practices.

NOTES

1. Lauren Alexander, 'Labioplasty Explained', *Australian Cosmetic Surgery Magazine* 35 (February–April 2007), 190.
2. Royal Australian College of General Practitioners (RACPG), *Female Genital Cosmetic Surgery: A Resource for General Practitioners and Other Health Professionals* (Melbourne: RACGP, 2015), 2.
3. See for example Kathy Davis, *Reshaping the Female Body: The Dilemma of Cosmetic Surgery* (New York: Routledge, 1995).
4. Sara Ahmed, *The Promise of Happiness* (Durham and London: Duke University Press, 2010), 2.

5. Ahmed, *The Promise of Happiness*, 58.
6. Scott Turner, 'Labiaplasty Surgery', Labiaplasty Specialist by Dr Turner, 2017, https://labiaplastyspecialist.com.au/procedure/labiaplasty/.
7. Sigmund Freud, 'Formulations on the Two Principles of Mental Functioning', in *On Freud's 'Formulations on the Two Principles of Mental Functioning'*, ed. Lawrence J. Brown and Gabriela Legorreta (London and New York: Routledge, 2016), 222.
8. Sigmund Freud, *Civilization and Its Discontents*, trans. David McClintock (Camberwell: Penguin Group, 2010), 13.
9. Freud, *Civilization and Its Discontents*, 15.
10. Freud, *Civilization and Its Discontents*, 16.
11. Julia Kristeva, *Powers of Horror: An Essay on Abjection*, trans. Leon S. Roudiez (New York: Columbia University Press, 1982), 72.
12. Kristeva, *Powers of Horror*, 72.
13. Kristeva, *Powers of Horror*, 4.
14. Elizabeth Grosz, *Volatile Bodies: Toward a Corporeal Feminism* (St Leonards: Allen and Unwin, 1994), 193.
15. Judith Butler, 'Imitation and Gender Insubordination', in *The Lesbian and Gay Studies Reader*, ed. Henry Abelove, Michèle Aina Barale and David M. Halperin (New York and London: Routledge, 1993), 317, emphasis in original.
16. Turner, 'Labiaplasty Surgery'.
17. Jane Paterson, 'Labiaplasty Melbourne', Plastic Surgery Melbourne, 2018, https://www.drjanepaterson.com.au/plastic-surgery/labiaplasty/.
18. For instance, all the participants in recent Australian qualitative studies investigating motivations and predictors for labiaplasty identified as exclusively or predominantly heterosexual. See Gemma Sharp, Marika Tiggemann and Julie Mattiske, 'Factors That Influence the Decision to Undergo Labiaplasty: Media, Relationships, and Psychological Well-Being', *Aesthetic Surgery Journal* 36, no. 4 (2016): 469–78; Gemma Sharp, Julie Mattiske and Kirsten I. Vale, 'Motivations, Expectations, and Experiences of Labiaplasty: A Qualitative Study', *Aesthetic Surgery Journal* 36, no. 8 (2016): 920–28; Gemma Sharp, Marike Tiggemann and Julie Mattiske, 'Predictors of Consideration of Labiaplasty: An Extension of the Tripartite Influence Model of Beauty Ideals', *Psychology of Women Quarterly* 39, no. 2 (2015): 182–93. I am not aware of any studies that include lesbian participants apart from the quantitative paper that Bethany Jones and I published on the influence of pornography on genital satisfaction and openness to labiaplasty. Our study found that women who identified as primarily homosexual had higher levels of genital satisfaction. We provided the hypothesis that this was because a lesbian population was likely to have higher exposure to

vulvar variation than a heterosexual one. See Bethany Jones and Camille Nurka, 'Labiaplasty and Pornography: A Preliminary Investigation', *Porn Studies* 2, no. 1 (2015): 62–75.

19. Judith Butler, *Gender Trouble: Feminism and the Subversion of Identity* (New York and London: Routledge, 1990).

20. See for example Carolyn Pedwell, 'Theorizing "African" Female Genital Cutting and "Western" Body Modifications: A Critique of the Continuum and Analogue Approaches', *Feminist Review* 86, no. 1 (2007): 45–66.

21. See Paris Lees, 'We're in the Midst of an Epidemic of Violence against Trans People', *Guardian*, 23 January 2018, https://www.the-guardian.com/commentisfree/2018/jan/22/epidemic-violence-transgender-people-experienced-stonewall.

22. Darryl J. Hodgkinson and Glen Hait, 'Aesthetic Vaginal Labioplasty', *Plastic and Reconstructive Surgery* 74, no. 3 (1984): 414–16. See also Michael P. Goodman, 'Genital Plastics: The History and Development', in *Female Genital and Plastic Cosmetic Surgery*, ed. Michael P. Goodman (West Sussex: Wiley, 2016), 3.

23. Hodgkinson and Hait, 'Aesthetic Vaginal Labioplasty', 414.

24. Hodgkinson and Hait, 'Aesthetic Vaginal Labioplasty', 414.

25. Hodgkinson and Hait, 'Aesthetic Vaginal Labioplasty', 414.

26. Fadwa El Guindi, '"Had This Been Your Face, Would You Leave It as Is?" Female Circumcision among the Nubians of Egypt', in *Female Circumcision: Multicultural Perspectives*, ed. Rogaia Mustafa Abusharaf (Philadelphia: University of Pennsylvania Press, 2006), 36.

27. Cheryl Chase, 'Hermaphrodites with Attitude: Mapping the Emergence of Intersex Political Activism', *GLQ* 4, no. 2 (1998): 205.

28. Chase, 'Hermaphrodites with Attitude'; Sarah M. Creighton, Lina Michala, Imran Mushtaq and Michal Yaron, 'Childhood Surgery for Ambiguous Genitalia: Glimpses of Practice Changes or More of the Same?', *Psychology & Sexuality* 5, no. 1 (2014): 34–43.

29. Creighton et al., 'Childhood Surgery for Ambiguous Genitalia', 35.

30. Hugh Hampton Young, *Genital Abnormalities, Hermaphroditism and Related Adrenal Diseases* (Baltimore: Williams and Wilkins Company, 1937). See also Chase, 'Hermaphrodites with Attitude', 190; Justine Schober, 'Ethics and Futuristic Scientific Developments Concerning Genitoplasty', in *Ethics and Intersex*, ed. Sharon E. Sytsma (Dordrecht: Springer, 2006), 314. Reviews for Young's groundbreaking publication *Genital Abnormalities, Hermaphroditism and Related Adrenal Diseases* were glowing and acknowledged its importance as a textbook that would be certain to become a standard resource for medical practitioners for many years to come. See for example H. P. W-W, review of

Genital Abnormalities, Hermaphroditism and Related Adrenal Diseases,
by Hugh Hampton Young, *British Journal of Urology* 10, no. 2 (1938):
213–16; Unsigned review of *Genital Abnormalities, Hermaphroditism
and Related Adrenal Diseases,* by Hugh Hampton Young, *British
Journal of Surgery* 26, no. 101 (1938): 212.

31. Sarah M. Creighton and Lih-Mei Liao, 'Changing Attitudes to Sex
Assignment in Intersex', *BJU* 93, no. 5 (2004): 659–64; J. David
Hester, 'Intersex(es) and Informed Consent: How Physicians' Rhetoric
Constrains Choice', *Theoretical Medicine and Bioethics* 25, no. 1 (2004):
21–49.

32. Alice Domurat Dreger, *Hermaphrodites and the Medical Invention of Sex*
(Cambridge: Harvard University Press, 1998), 184; Justine Schober,
'Feminizing Genitoplasty: A Synopsis of Issues Relating to genital
Surgery in Intersex Individuals', *Journal of Pediatric Endocrinology and
Metabolism* 17, no. 5 (2004), 697.

33. Schober, 'Feminizing Genitoplasty', 697.

34. Schober, 'Ethics and Futuristic Scientific Developments Concerning
Genitoplasty', 314.

35. Naomi S. Crouch and Sarah M. Creighton, 'Long-Term Functional
Outcomes of Female Genital Reconstruction in Childhood', *BJU* 100,
no. 2 (2007): 403–6.

36. Dreger, *Hermaphrodites and the Medical Invention of Sex*, 174.

37. Sarah M. Creighton, 'Adult Outcomes of Feminizing Surgery', in
Sytsma, *Ethics and Intersex*, 209.

38. Intersex Human Rights Australia, 'A Human Rights Investigation
into the Medical "Normalization" of Intersex People', Intersex
Human Rights Australia, 19 March 2009, https://ihra.org.au/348/
sanfrancisco-hrc-intersex-report/.

39. Human Rights Watch, *'I Want to Be Like Nature Made Me': Medically
Unnecessary Surgeries on Intersex Children in the US*, 25 July 2017,
https://www.hrw.org/report/2017/07/25/i-want-be-nature-
made-me/medically-unnecessary-surgeries-intersex-children-us.

40. Catherine L. Minto, Lih-Mei Liao, Christopher R. J. Woodhouse, Phillip
G. Ransley and Sarah M. Creighton, 'The Effect of Clitoral Surgery on
Sexual Outcome in Individuals Who Have Intersex Conditions with
Ambiguous Genitalia: A Cross-Sectional Study', *Lancet* 361 (2003):
1252.

41. Sarah M. Creighton, 'Long-Term Outcome of Feminization Surgery:
The London Experience', *BJU* 3, no. s3 (2004), 45; Crouch and
Creighton, 'Long-Term Functional Outcomes of Female Genital
Reconstruction in Childhood'; Minto et al., 'The Effect of Clitoral
Surgery on Sexual Outcome'.

42. Creighton, 'Long-Term Outcome of Feminization Surgery', 44.
43. Creighton, 'Long-Term Outcome of Feminization Surgery', 45.
44. Helen E. O'Connell, Kalavampara V. Sanjeevan and John M. Hutson, 'Anatomy of the Clitoris', *Journal of Urology* 174, no. 4 (2005): 1189–95; Helen E. O'Connell, Norm Eizenberg, Marzia Rahman and Joan Cleeve, 'The Anatomy of the Distal Vagina: Towards Unity', *Journal of Sexual Medicine* 5, no. 8 (2008): 1883–91.
45. Rachel N. Pauls, 'Anatomy of the Clitoris and the Female Sexual Response', *Clinical Anatomy* 28, no. 3 (2015): 376–84.
46. Creighton, 'Adult Outcomes of Feminizing Surgery', 209.
47. Dreger, *Hermaphrodites and the Medical Invention of Sex*, 78.
48. Hodgkinson and Hait, 'Aesthetic Vaginal Labioplasty', 416.
49. Gary J. Alter, 'Clitoral Reduction', Gary J. Alter Plastic and Reconstructive Surgeon, 2018, https://www.garyalterplasticsurgeon.com/female-genital-surgery/clitoral-reduction/.
50. Costas H. Pappis and Philip S. Hadzihamberas, 'Hypertrophy of the Labia Minora', *Pediatric Surgery International* 2 (1987): 50.
51. Lindy Joan McDougall, 'Towards a Clean Slit: How Medicine and Notions of Normality are Shaping Female Genital Aesthetics', *Culture, Health & Sexuality* 15, no. 7 (2013): 777.
52. World Health Organization, 'Female Genital Mutilation' (fact sheet), 31 January 2018, http://www.who.int/news-room/fact-sheets/detail/female-genital-mutilation.
53. See for example Jasmine Abdulcadir, Jean-Christophe Tille and Patrick Petignat, 'Management of Painful Clitoral Neuroma after Female Genital Mutilation/Cutting', *Reproductive Health* 14, no. 22 (2017): https://doi.org/10.1186/s12978-017-0288-3; Ifeanyichukwu Ezebialu, Obiamaka Okafo, Chukwudi Oringanje, Udoezuo Ogbonna, Ekong Udoh, Friday Odey and Martin M. Meremikwu, 'Surgical and Nonsurgical Interventions for Vulvar and Clitoral Pain in Girls and Women Living with Female Genital Mutilation: A Systematic Review', *International Journal of Gynaecology and Obstetrics* 136, suppl. 1 (2017): 34–7; Lillian Mwanri and Glory Joy Gatwiri, 'Injured Bodies, Damaged Lives: Experiences and Narratives of Kenyan Women with Obstetric Fistula and Female Genital Mutilation/Cutting', *Reproductive Health* 14, no. 38 (2017): https://doi.org/10.1186/s12978-017-0300-y.
54. Shakira Hussein and Camille Nurka, 'Entitled to Be Free: Exposing the Limits of Choice', in *Freedom Fallacy: The Limits of Liberal Feminism*, ed. Miranda Kiraly and Meagan Tyler (Ballarat: Connor Court, 2015), 81–94.
55. Annemarie Middelburg, 'The Pleasure Doctor Fighting to Restore Clitorises After Female Genital Mutilation', *The Conversation*, 16 June 2014, http://theconversation.com/the-pleasure-doctor-fighting-to-restore-clitorises-after-female-genital-mutilation-25880.

56. Marci L. Bowers, 'Senator Harry Reid Announces First Ever US Summit to End FGM', *Marci L. Bowers, MD Gynecology Surgery* (blog), 2018, https://marcibowers.com/blog/senator-harry-reid-announces-first-ever-us-summit-to-end-fgm/.
57. 'Raëlism', Wikipedia, last updated 27 May 2018, https://en.wikipedia.org/wiki/Ra%C3%ABlism.
58. Sue Lloyd-Roberts, 'The Unopened "Pleasure Hospital" of Bobo', *BBC News Magazine*, 17 March 2014, http://www.bbc.com/news/magazine-26577358.
59. Saira Khan, 'Trying to Rebuild Women's Bodies after Female "Circumcision"', SBS, 18 December 2017, https://www.sbs.com.au/guide/article/2017/12/14/trying-rebuild-womens-bodies-after-female-circumcision; Lloyd-Roberts, 'The Unopened "Pleasure Hospital" of Bobo'.
60. Clitoraid, '"Restore My Clitoris!" Kenyan FGM Survivors Claim Their Womanhood on Woman's Day and Everyday!', Clitoraid, 6 March 2018, http://www.clitoraid.org/news.php.
61. Wanjiru Kamau-Rutenberg, 'R-E-S-P-E-C-T: Find Out What It Means to Me (Still Ranting about Clitoraid)', *Can? We? Save? Africa?* (blog), 8 April 2010, https://savingafrica.wordpress.com/2010/04/08/r-e-s-p-e-c-t-find-out-what-it-means-to-me-still-ranting-about-clitoraid/.
62. Sue Lloyd-Roberts, 'FGM, Clitoraid and the Pleasure Hospital: US Sect the Raëlians' Quest to "Restore" Women Scarred by Female Genital Mutilation in Burkina Faso', *Independent*, 16 March 2014, https://www.independent.co.uk/news/world/africa/fgm-clitoraid-and-the-pleasure-hospital-us-sect-the-ra-lians-quest-to-restore-women-scarred-by-9195795.html; Lloyd-Roberts, 'The Unopened "Pleasure Hospital" of Bobo'.
63. Middelburg, 'The Pleasure Doctor'.
64. Pierre Foldés, Béatrice Cuzin and Armelle Andro, 'Reconstructive Surgery after Female Genital Mutilation: A Prospective Cohort Study', *Lancet* 380 (2012): 135.
65. Foldés, 'Reconstructive Surgery after Female Genital Mutilation', 135.
66. Sarah Creighton, Susan Bewley and Lih-Mei Liao, Correspondence, *Lancet* 380 (2012): 1469.
67. Creighton et al., Correspondence, 1469.
68. Kenneth D. Bailey, *Methods of Social Research*, 4th ed. (New York: Free Press, 1994); Floyd J. Fowler, Jr, *Survey Research Methods*, 4th ed. (Thousand Oaks: Sage Publications, 2009).
69. Pierre Foldés, Béatrice Cuzin and Armelle Andro, Correspondence, *Lancet* 380 (2012): 1469.
70. Middelburg, 'The Pleasure Doctor'.

71. Linda Pressly, 'The Surgeon Helping Women after Genital Mutilation', *BBC News Magazine*, 25 July 2013, http://www.bbc.com/news/magazine-23287032.

72. Ezebialu et al., 'Surgical and Nonsurgical Interventions', 36.

73. Pressly, 'The Surgeon Helping Women after Genital Mutilation'.

74. Nikki Sullivan, '"The Price to Pay for Our Common Good": Genital Modification and the Somatechnologies of Cultural (In)Difference', *Social Semiotics* 17, no. 3 (2007): 395–409.

75. Virginia Braun, '"The Women Are Doing It for Themselves": The Rhetoric of Choice and Agency around Female Genital "Cosmetic Surgery"', *Australian Feminist Studies* 24, no. 60 (2009): 233–49.

76. Hussein and Nurka, 'Entitled to Be Free'.

77. Sullivan, 'The Price to Pay for Our Common Good', 406.

78. Wairimü Ngaruiya Njambi, 'Dualisms and Female Bodies in Representations of African Female Circumcision: A Feminist Critique', *Feminist Theory* 5, no. 3 (2004): 299.

79. Juliet Rogers, 'A Child Is Being Mutilated', *Australian Feminist Studies* 24, no. 60 (2009): 181–94.

80. Naomi Onsongo, 'Female Genital Cutting (FGC): Who Defines Whose Culture as Unethical?', *International Journal of Feminist Approaches to Bioethics* 10, no. 2 (2017): 113.

81. G. I. Serour, 'Medicalization of Female Genital Mutilation/Cutting', *African Journal of Urology* 19, no. 3 (2013): 147.

82. Fiona J. Green, 'From Clitoridectomies to "Designer Vaginas": The Medical Construction of Heteronormative Female Bodies and Sexuality through Female Genital Cutting', *Sexualities, Evolution and Gender* 7, no. 2 (2005): 153–87.

83. Chase, 'Hermaphrodites with Attitude'; Dreger, *Hermaphrodites and the Medical Invention of Sex*; J. Steven Svoboda, 'Promoting Genital Autonomy by Exploring Commonalities between Male, Female, Intersex, and Cosmetic Female Genital Cutting', *Global Discourse* 3, no. 2 (2013): 237–55.

84. Olivia Lambert, 'Mother Takes 15-year-old Daughter to GP to Discuss Labiaplasty Surgery', news.com.au, 12 September 2016, http://www.news.com.au/lifestyle/health/health-problems/mother-takes-15yearold-daughter-to-gp-to-discuss-labiaplasty-surgery/news-story/87efa0881003dc150c58e0fd7572efc0.

85. Carolyn Pedwell, 'Theorizing "African" Female Genital Cutting and "Western" Body Modifications: A Critique of the Continuum and Analogue Approaches', *Feminist Review* 86 (2007): 56. For a similar argument, see Sara Johnsdotter, 'Projected Cultural Histories of the Cutting of Female Genitalia: A Poor Reflection as in a Mirror', *History and Anthropology* 23, no. 1 (2012): 91–114.

86. Pedwell, 'Theorizing "African" Female Genital Cutting; Rogers, 'A Child Is Being Mutilated'.
87. Fuambai Ahmadu, '"Imitated Not Mutilated": SiA Magazine comes to Freetown!', *SiA Inc.* (blog), 20 September 2016, http://www.fuambaisiaahmadu.com/blogs/imitated-not-mutilated-sia-magazine-comes-to-freetown.
88. Carlos David Londoño Sulkin, 'Fuambai's Strength', *HAU: Journal of Ethnographic Theory* 6, no. 3: 107–33.
89. Ahmadu, 'Imitated Not Mutilated'.
90. Nimko Ali, 'Mitts Off My Muff', interview with Hazel Healy, *New Internationalist*, 2 July 2014, https://newint.org/features/2014/07/01/female-genital-mutilation. Also see Nimko Ali, interview with Anne Summers, 'Anne Summers in Conversation with Nimco Ali', Anne Summers, 28 September 2015, http://www.annesummers.com.au/conversations/nimco-ali-melbourne/.
91. Paola Totaro, 'The Fanny Defender', *Anne Summers Reports*, August 2015, http://www.annesummers.com.au/wp-content/uploads/2015/08/NimcoAliv5.pdf.
92. Rosie Mockett, 'Our Muff March Is a Stand Against Pornified Culture', *Guardian*, 10 December 2011, https://www.theguardian.com/commentisfree/2011/dec/09/muff-march-against-pornified-culture.
93. Transgender and Intersex Africa, 'Intersex Invincibility with the Work of Intersex Human Right', 26 October 2015, http://transgenderintersex-africa.org.za/?p=313.
94. Meredith Jones, *Skintight: An Anatomy of Cosmetic Surgery* (Oxford and New York: Berg, 2008), 1.
95. Michael P. Goodman, 'Commentary on: A Retrospective Study of the Psychological Outcomes of Labiaplasty', *Aesthetic Surgery Journal* 37, no. 3 (2017): 332–6, emphasis in original.
96. Michael Goodman, 'Revisions, Redos and Botched Genital Plastic Surgery', Michael Goodman MD, 2018, http://www.drmichaelgoodman.com/revisions-redos-and-botched-genital-plastic-surgery/.
97. Michael Goodman, 'FAQ. Who should you STAY AWAY FROM?', Michael Goodman MD, 2018, http://www.drmichaelgoodman.com/labiaplasty-california/.
98. ACOG Committee Opinion Number 253, March 2001 (reaffirmed 2017), https://www.acog.org/Clinical-Guidance-and-Publications/Committee-Opinions/Committee-on-Gynecologic-Practice/Nongynecologic-Procedures.
99. Jones, *Skintight*, 60.
100. ACOG Committee Opinion Number 378, September 2007 (reaffirmed 2017), https://www.acog.org/Clinical-Guidance-and-Publications/

Committee-Opinions/Committee-on-Gynecologic-Practice/Vaginal-Rejuvenation-and-Cosmetic-Vaginal-Procedures.

101. ACOG Committee Opinion Number 686, January 2017, https://www.acog.org/-/media/Committee-Opinions/Committee-on-Adolescent-Health-Care/co686.pdf?dmc=1&ts=20170217T0416002970.

102. See reference to Lloyd et al. in ACOG Committee Opinion Number 387; Jillian Lloyd, Naomi S. Crouch, Catherine L. Minto, Lih-Mei Liao and Sarah M. Creighton, 'Female Genital Appearance: "Normality" Unfolds', *BJOG* 112, no. 5 (2005): 643–6.

103. Michael Goodman, 'Labiaplasty – "Labial Reduction/Beautification" for Large Labia', Michael Goodman MD, 2018, http://www.drmichael-goodman.com/labiaplasty-california/.

104. Michael Goodman, 'Revisions, Redos and Botched Genital Plastic Surgery'.

105. Gary J. Alter, 'Botched Labiaplasty Revision Surgery: About the Procedure', Gary J. Alter MD Plastic and Reconstructive Surgeon, 2018, https://www.labiaplastyrevisionsurgeon.com/botched-labiaplasty/.

106. Gary Alter, 'Labiaplasty Revision Surgery', Gary J. Alter MD Plastic and Reconstructive Surgeon, 2018, https://www.labiaplastyrevisionsur-geon.com/, emphasis added.

107. Gary Alter, 'Reconstruction of the Vagina and External Genitalia Deformities', Gary Alter MD, 2018, https://www.altermd.com/reconstruction-vagina-external-genitalia/.

108. Stefan Gress, *Aesthetic and Functional Labiaplasty* (Munich: Springer, 2017), 77–8.

109. Goodman, 'Revisions, Redos and Botched Genital Plastic Surgery'.

110. Goodman, 'Revisions, Redos and Botched Genital Plastic Surgery'; Gress, *Aesthetic and Functional Labiaplasty*, 79.

111. Gress, *Aesthetic and Functional Labiaplasty*, 79.

112. Gress, *Aesthetic and Functional Labiaplasty*, 25.

113. Meredith Jones, 'Expressive Surfaces: The Case of the Designer Vagina', *Theory, Culture & Society* 34, nos 7–8 (2017): 30.

114. Barbara Maria Stafford, 'Self-Eugenics: The Creeping Illusionising of Identity from Neurobiology to Newgenics', *New Formations* 60 (2007): 110.

115. Stafford, 'Self-Eugenics', 102.

116. Stafford, 'Self-Eugenics', 111.

117. Stafford, 'Self-Eugenics', 108.

118. Jones, 'Expressive Surfaces', 34.

119. Jones, 'Expressive Surfaces', 42.

120. Seli, 'I want to cut loose skin on my vagina area. What treatment would you recommend?', RealSelf, 2018, https://www.realself.com/question/london-gb-i-want-cut-loose-skin-my-vagena-area.

121. annoymoussss345, 'I have something hanging from my vagina, what is it? Is there anyway to get rid of it?', RealSelf, 2018, https://www.real-self.com/question/bent-mountain-va-i-hanging-vagina%23.
122. Patricia Hill Collins, *Black Feminist Thought* (New York and London: Routledge, 2000), 140.

CHAPTER 8

Conclusion: DIY Sex

In this book I hope to have shown how men of science have been active participants in the social (re)production of the ideology of female perfectibility, which is the guiding principle of modern cosmetic surgery. After all, it was the ancient Greek Aristotle who proposed that women were simply imperfect men, which explained why their genitals were the wrong way around. The development of medical knowledge is an objective process to the extent that it requires empirical observation, experimentation and testing for validity; but it is also imaginative work. This situation is fraught with political implications for how the female body has come to be pictured and envisioned as an object of scientific enquiry. Medical texts serve as a significant source of authority on the functions and morphology of the body, and if they have mostly been authored by men, this presents us with the problem of cultural bias, which is at work in scientific processes of naming and classifying body parts. The words used to describe the female genitals refer back to social arrangements of marriage and heterosexual ownership. Feminists have pointed out that the word 'vagina' literally means 'sheath' or 'scabbard', by which it has acquired an identity as a passive receptacle for the penis.[1] The Greek *nymphe* summoned the veiled bride, while the Latin word *tentigo* conjured the interchangeable figures of the despised and perverted tribade and the monstrous hermaphrodite. In scientific discourse, names are also pivotal in clarifying body parts and functions. A name indicates that something matters enough to be given a label. Inadequate description of vulval structures produced hundreds of years of confusion about

© The Author(s) 2019
C. Nurka, *Female Genital Cosmetic Surgery*,
https://doi.org/10.1007/978-3-319-96490-4_8

whether physicians were talking about the labia minora or the clitoris and has contributed to the longstanding cultural myth that the site of female pleasure is too difficult or complex to understand and therefore doesn't *matter*. As we have seen from Galen to Vesalius, descriptive confusion often arose in relation to the question of precisely which fleshy part it was necessary to cut off in cases of enlargement because the offending part was seen to interfere with penetrative heterosexual intercourse: it was the principle of male pleasure that determined the need for surgical excision.

The gender disparity in knowledge production has governed how scientists throughout Western history have made sense not only of the differences they perceived between men and women, but also of differences between women in demarcating biological boundaries between normal and abnormal femininity. The medical discourse of hypertrophy of the labia minora has its modern roots in European colonisation of Africa and anthropological study of the genital differences between white and black women. The story of the abnormally enlarged labia minora originated with the Hottentot apron and was popularised in the denigrating and dehumanising display of Sarah Baartman both to circus audiences and to medical men like Georges Cuvier. The French naturalists François Péron and Charles Alexandre Lesueur, who had visited the Cape of Good Hope in 1804, insisted that the apron was an appendage belonging exclusively to Bushwomen, which served as proof that they were of an entirely different, sub-human, species. Lesueur's sketches of the apron reappeared in medical publications into the twentieth century. The art of illustration would be supplanted by anthropological photography of the kind that graced the pages of Hermann Heinrich Ploss, Max Bartels and Paul Bartels's salacious volume *Woman: An Historical Gynaecological and Anthropological Compendium*.[2]

From its colonial beginnings, the Hottentot apron came to mark the boundary between human and animal, civilised and savage, evolved and less evolved. As we saw from Félix Jayle's classification of vulval types, African women's 'hypertrophic' genitalia became synonymous with racial degeneration. In early-twentieth-century medicine, which was dominated by eugenic philosophy, the cultivation of beauty and health via reproduction was thought to lead to a perfect bodily ideal. This ideal was envisaged as an aspirational norm which would serve as a guide for white racial progress; the right combination of heredity and environment would produce a vigorous and strong national population.

Today, the protuberant labia are perceived as evolutionarily redundant, with cosmetic surgery on the genitals taking us to new frontiers of civilisation through technologies of the body. Unlike traditional eugenics, which targets human sexual reproduction as the key to reproducing the perfect population, the new eugenics activates evolutionary progression through recrafting the body surgically. According to the site LabiaplastySurgeon.com, for instance, 'Aesthetic and self-esteem indications/reasons for labiaplasty are largely being driven by societal evolution regarding sexual habits, wants, and expectations. There is a societal evolution currently occurring about how men and women perceive each other in areas of sexual expectation ... when it comes to sexual performance and appearance'.[3]

Plastic surgeons have also become the new sexologists and self-appointed arbiters of what is sexually normal or abnormal and trusted advisers on how to overcome sexual shame and achieve sexual gratification. They perform the educative role that early-twentieth-century Robert Latou Dickinson had done in his gynaecological practice. Fast-forward to the digital age, and we're seeing girls and women posting questions about whether they are sexually normal on a website called RealSelf, which provides information about cosmetic surgery procedures, and through which surgeons sell their services. On this site, women express fears that masturbation has caused their labia to become enlarged. One confesses that 'Im 18 years old and I believe I have damaged my inner labia by over masturbation', and another writes, 'I'm still a virgin but worried that maybe labia is too big? I used to masturbate lots and think it may be stretched out'.[4] While surgeons reassure such women that masturbation does not cause elongated labia, they do advise that if the woman feels her labia are a problem, she can fix it with surgery. Today's sexual sciences have dismissed the theory that masturbation causes ill health, yet women's concerns that they have wrecked their labia through masturbation clearly have historical parallels in the masturbation panics of earlier centuries.

In Dickinson's time, masturbation was a moral problem indicating lack of self-restraint and was thought to cause nervous illness. The 'condition' of elongated labia was also the physical manifestation of the *moral* problem of sexually deviant femininity in its association with masturbators, nymphomaniacs and lesbians. These figures variously connoted sexual aggression, rather than passivity; a love of sex for pleasure rather than procreation; and 'unnatural' desire for the self (onanism) or the same sex (lesbianism). In traditional Christian morality, which views sexual pleasure for its own sake as sinful, this amounted to a perversion of the course of 'natural' femininity, which ought to have been directed toward marriage and children. With the long sexual revolution, the Judeo-Christian foundations of modern sexual morality have been powerfully challenged by socially progressive sexologists and feminist and queer activists. And yet modern women are still worried that their own sexual behaviour is responsible for bringing them physical grief. As one woman wrote on RealSelf, 'I had labiaplasty about 5 weeks ago. I started masterbating again with my whirlpool bath tub jets. it doesn't cause any problems but I'm afraid it's going to make my labia's stretch and get gross again. Should i not do this?'[5] Even though feminists and sexologists have made great progress, since the beginning of the twentieth century, in destigmatising female sexual desire as an ordinary quality of a body capable of feeling sexual pleasure, women are still worried about whether they are entitled to it because their bodies are consistently represented—and experienced—as a sexual *problem*. This is hardly surprising in a sexist culture that encourages men to take and women to give. We can see this principle operating in Dickinson's sexological work in teaching men how to give pleasure and women how to receive it. And yet, in spite of his compassionate intentions, Dickinson only ended up reinforcing the notion that wives owed sex to their husbands: pleasurable sex was desirable not because it had anything to do with female sexual autonomy, but because it would aid social stability by keeping married people together. While Dickinson saw elongated labia as a symptom of sexual trouble and marital breakdown, today's women, and cosmetic surgeons, see the elongated labia as the *cause* of sexual dysfunction as something that stops them from having sexual relationships with others.

Female genital cosmetic surgery (FGCS) is part of a long scientific history of representing the female body as a site of perpetual biological trouble and technological improvement. Culturally, the female body is the exemplary aesthetic object, which is why 90 per cent of cosmetic surgery consumers are women, and it is beholden to a concept that we call 'femininity'. The concept of femininity makes no sense without reference to the opposite concept of masculinity: this is binary logic at work, and—as things currently are—it is an inescapable foundation of our internal sense of self and social identity. I have argued in this book that FGCS appeals to femininity as a normative aspiration that determines what is acceptable female embodiment and what is not. Femininity and masculinity are, I would argue, fundamentally socially normative concepts in that they are invoked—in the name of appropriate sex, sexual behaviour or appearance and so on—in order to enforce conformity to a type. Another way of saying this is to ask: who might we be if femininity and masculinity did not exist? Hence, the argument I end with in Chapter 7 is that FGCS, along with other forms of genital cutting, is a product of a binary logic that demands genital conformity in exchange for social and sexual citizenship. Many of the contemporary feminist criticisms of FGCS come from surgeons who are working with intersex and transgender people. Urologists and gynaecologists point to the damaging effects of intersex surgeries to sexual sensitivity, capacity for pleasure and quality of life and relationships. Like intersex surgery, labiaplasty is not usually performed because there is an issue with physiological function; it is performed for the purpose of enforcing sex conformity for no good reason other than adherence to cultural gender norms. Critics of FGCS have made similar comparisons to ritual female genital cutting (ritual FGC). It is not difficult to see the parallels between the two when they are viewed as operations on the body that legitimise or otherwise confer genitally appropriate womanhood. I have taken it as a given that the sex of a body is of unquestionable importance in most, if not all, human cultures, not just Western ones; sexed bodies are always culturally significant in some way as objects of inscription by ritual or other symbolic means. In the post-Enlightenment Western setting, where the sacred ritual element in genital cutting is absent, medical science becomes the inscriptive technology through which the sexed body is invented and reinvented within historical processes of medical knowledge formation. In the absence of a cosmological rationale, practitioners of cosmetic female genital cutting in the West come up with an *individual* one that is apparently tailored to the health needs of women who don't embody femininity the way they would desire to. The difference between ritual FGC and FGCS does not reside in black oppression versus white agency; rather, the first binds a woman to her community and establishes her place in the social and cosmic order, while the second intervenes in a woman's relationship to herself. That is, Western FGCS is enabled by capitalist economics and the profoundly individualist middle-class ideology of consumer entitlement. This does not mean, however, that it is any less normalising. On the contrary, the disciplinary purpose of FGCS is to produce genital conformity to an aesthetic ideal that conforms to a very narrow idea of 'normal' and 'healthy'. Labiaplasty provides women who can afford it access to a fantasy of normal and desirable femininity. I am not saying, however, that fantasy in and of itself is a bad thing. Fantasy is an important part of sexual life; but when that fantasy produces as an object of disgust the one part of the body intimately associated with sexuality (the genitals), then we must ask ourselves if it is worth it.

Through beauty regimes such as laser pubic hair removal and labiaplasty, we are busily erasing the signs of our biological dependence by attempting to manage and control the body as natural resource—to make it do what we want it to. Biomedical technologies intervene to help us resist disease and live longer, but they also impose new models of bodily conformity, from designer babies to designer vaginas. The cosmetic surgeon's job is to erase the signs of biological species belonging to create a posthuman *feminine* belonging that looks remarkably homogeneous. It is an attempt to leave the traces of animal belonging behind, which has a pernicious historical precedent; the present-day difference between labiaplasty and clitoral reconstruction reprises the colonial distinction between evolved white women and animal African women. The concept of biodiversity, developed within the environmental sciences, poses an important challenge to the eugenic racism inherent in biotechnologies aimed at creating the 'perfect' or 'normal' appearance (by whose standards?) and the sexist emphasis on female perfectability that are literally shaping matter into a single fetishised aesthetic ideal. To fight for biodiversity is to acknowledge bodily variation as naturally occurring and to resist political economic processes that seek to narrow the field of biological difference for profit.

Feminist Imaginaries

Over the past ten or so years feminist criticism of labiaplasty by medical professionals, scholars and public commentators has grown. The argument we are making is that 'hypertrophy of the labia minora' is not a medical problem, but a cultural one. Therefore, the solution should be cultural change, with female-centred strategies that support body-positivity for women, rather than surgery. To put it simply and clearly: the problem is not the length of a girl's or woman's labia but an oppressive culture of objectification that locates the primary social value of girls and women in their appearance. Cosmetic surgery is therefore making female dependence on appearance worse, not better.

In an intensely mediatised society, in which we experience ourselves as living images or, as Meredith Jones terms it, 'media-bodies',[6] cosmetic surgery can approximate the effect of digital airbrushing to make us look less disappointingly human and more like ageless plastic (unlike the human body, plastic takes at least 500 years to break down). In a society in which women unequally bear the burden of appearing for the other and also for themselves, the phenomenological demand to 'appear for' results in female self-objectification and body anxiety (let's keep in mind those cosmetic surgery statistics). Psychologists Barbara L. Fredrickson and Tomi-Ann Roberts developed 'objectification theory' to refer to 'the experience of being treated *as a body* (or collection of body parts) valued predominantly for its use to (or consumption by) others'.[7] In a digital world where, as Jones puts it, 'two- and three-dimensional ways of being' are increasingly 'conflated and culturally intertwined',[8] there are proliferating and innumerable modes of female self-objectification. Many of these provide a stage for agentic self-representation. As Amy Shields Dobson argues in her book *Postfeminist Digital Cultures*, girls and young women are too often treated as the passive victims of oppressive technologies rather than active users and producers of their own self-authored images.[9] My own feminist work on gender and social media, for instance, argues that when the capacity for female self-expression is reduced to the image, it reinforces the social expectation that female self-worth resides in appearance and provides others with the authority to judge our appearance, impoverishing the capacity for autonomous self-definition.[10] I admit that girls and women were already inhabiting images of themselves long before digital technology and social media came along; however, the difference is that now there is no escape from the image because our lives are thoroughly embedded, for better or worse, in the digital mediascape. Nevertheless, while my feminist analysis tends toward the 'glass half-empty' approach, I do take Dobson's point and recognise that this is only one side of a more complex story of female self-avowal and self-negation. I want to end the book on a positive note with stories of female self-avowal in the face of self-objectifying discourses that make us feel ashamed of ourselves and disgusted with our genitals. What do we do in a media-saturated society where the image reigns? We make our own.

Figure 8.1 is a photograph of graffiti in the female toilets at the Villa Neukölln bar in Berlin. It can be thought of as a spatial inscription that belongs to the order of what philosopher Michel de Certeau calls 'everyday practices'.[11] In his book *The Practice of Everyday Life*, de Certeau shifts our attention away from disciplinary techniques that produce order and conformity (such as those that I outline in this book) to consider how people respond to and enliven 'the mute processes that organize the establishment of socioeconomic order'.[12] De Certeau's concept of everyday practices refers to the ways in which everyday people—the consumerist 'we' of popular culture—bring life to the impersonal systems and institutions that impose a certain order on human relations. He looks at the various ways people creatively consume, manipulate or use dominant economic and representational systems not of their own making in their own ways and for their own ends.

While this book has centred on the disciplinary discourses of the Western sciences, including anthropology and medicine, I do want to

Fig. 8.1   Toilet graffiti at the Villa Neukölln bar, Berlin. Photographer: Tereza Hendl, 2017. Reproduced with permission from Tereza Hendl

give some space here to the everyday feminist discourses that resist these patriarchal voices of authority. In this case, the 'patriarchy' is no exaggeration: it is clear from the evidence presented in this book that our present state of knowledge about the female genitals comes mostly from scientific observations made by men. I do not wish to give the impression that there were never any women in the biological sciences, but I do want to impress upon the reader that it is only with very recent interventions by women gynaecologists that we have been able to understand such things as how deep into the body the clitoris actually extends and the wide variation of the labia minora size, shape, colour and texture.

The graffiti on a toilet wall in a bar in Berlin is a kind of quotidian political speech act that resists the pathologising medical and aesthetic discourse of labial 'hypertrophy'. This intimate and self-affirming speech scrawled on the tiled surface of a shared communal space reserved for women is an example of the fleeting, evasive and secret languages of sex that will not be found in any medical textbook. In time, this playful drawing in black texta will no doubt be written-over, scrubbed off and replaced by something else. I must acknowledge the important criticisms, from queertrans quarters, that the toilet space is itself a disciplinary mechanism that polices and enforces gender conformity (for example, if you are too butch or do not look 'female' enough, you may be subject to hostility and abuse from other women in a female toilet space). These critiques are important and valid; but I wish to emphasise the potential of such a space to be a potent political site of imaginative, self-affirming and inclusive togetherness. There is no reason why we might not imagine that the depictions of genitals on the toilet wall also include surgically constructed transsexual vaginas. The point I am making is that this is political speech that rejects the dominant sexually objectifying discourses of beauty and desire, the flipside of which is ugliness and disgust.

As I have shown in this book, a state of 'health' is not necessarily an appraisal based on objective empirical measures of physical disorder, because it is often affixed to an aesthetic concept of 'beauty'. The discourse of 'hypertrophy', from gynaecology to plastic surgery, is an authorised and authorising medical terminology that alienates women from their own bodies. But there is a counter-language that we find in public toilet walls, in the bedrooms of lovers, and in the online spaces of amateur porn.[13] De Certeau calls these 'natural languages' because they are a kind of living and evolving mode of speech developed from within social groups in contrast to the relatively static artificial languages of specialised fields such as medicine.[14] 'Artificial' languages are reserved for 'experts' and work to exclude outsider laypeople, who develop their own vocabularies, which may run counter to discourses of the body established by experts in positions of authority, such as plastic surgeons, gynaecologists and GPs. The vocabularies of sexual desire shared in both private and public community spaces do not come from authoritative institutions but from everyday social practices developed by people who are actively defining and redefining the terms of their engagement with one another. By contrast to the opulent waiting rooms of plastic surgeons whose furnishings attest to their position as authorities on body aesthetics, toilet graffiti is the vulgar sign of a common authority that pronounces its own judgements as to what is beautiful. These are speech acts that perform political resistance to the authority of those who have something to gain, symbolic or material, in judging women's bodies to be inadequate.

In pondering the graffiti in the toilets at the Villa Neukölln bar, I wonder if it belongs to an order of intimate knowledge of which the ancient Greek lyric poet Sappho might have sung. We know frustratingly little of the ancient vernacular upon which Sappho might have drawn, and which she herself may have composed, to pay tribute to the female pudenda. We do not know because there is nothing of her voice in the medical texts that survived from Hippocrates onward, and which have formed the foundation for millennia of male-dominated medical knowledge about the female body. Sappho is symbolic of a submerged language of female delight in the pleasures of the body that has been consistently overwritten by voices of authority that perpetually remind us that our bodies are imperfect, shameful and disgusting.

But such voices do not go unchallenged. We have resources of resistance made available to us through the vocabulary of sexual pride developed by queer feminist activists and thinkers—poets, artists, musicians, public commentators, storytellers, medical professionals and public servants, among many other cultural producers. Labia pride movements have emerged as distinctly modern forms of counter-cultural resistance that demand sexual and bodily diversity. The political force of labia pride is so visible that it even has its own Wikipedia entry.[15]

The Muff March first organised by UK Feminista in 2011 is a prominent example of feminist activism against female genital cosmetic surgery. The first Muff March took place on London's Harley Street and participants chanted slogans such as 'Keep your mitts off our muffs!',

'I love my vagina!' and 'You've put my chuff in a huff!'[16] UK Feminista organised the march to protest the culture of female body hatred they perceived to be instigated mainly by pornography and the cosmetic surgery industry.[17] In Australia, the state-government-funded organisation Women's Health Victoria recently developed the 'Labia Library', which is an online resource that provides a photo gallery of real women's genitals, with and without pubic hair, in order to illustrate genital diversity and 'bust a few common myths about how normal labia look'.[18] Melbourne plastic surgeon Jill Tomlinson refers the reader to this site on her own webpage providing information about the labiaplasty procedure. Tomlinson's page states:

> It is very important to realise that the appearance of the labia varies widely – there is no single 'normal' appearance of the female genitalia, just as there is no single 'normal' appearance of male genitalia. It is not abnormal for the labia minora (the 'inner lips') to protrude past the labia majora (the 'outer lips'). In fact, this is very common. If you're wondering if your labia are normal the Labia Library from Women's Health Victoria is a great resource.[19]

Similarly, in 2016, Amsterdam-based illustrator Hilde Atalanta created the *Vulva Gallery*, which is 'a series of illustrations of all kinds of vulvas—celebrating the vulva in all its diversity all over the world'.[20] Atalanta combines art and sex education as a feminist critique of labiaplasty and a celebration of natural genital diversity. Importantly, the gallery includes 'people of all kinds of genders … because having a vulva doesn't define your gender'.[21] Atalanta takes care to impress upon the reader that the Vulva gallery is 'body positive, gender inclusive and welcomes all'.[22]

In the UK, there are currently exciting plans afoot for a Vagina Museum, which aims to take 'a holistic view of vaginas, from science to history to their place in culture'. The website for the project states explicitly that 'the museum is dedicated to being gender inclusive and intersectional'.[23] In 2011, UK artist Jamie McCartney created a sculpture called *Great Wall of Vulva* made from plaster casts of the vulvas of 400 women, including mothers and daughters, identical twins, and transgender men and women. Described as 'art with a social conscience', McCartney's *Great Wall of Vulva* aims to make a positive change in female body image and reduce genital anxiety.[24] In Australia, artist Greg Taylor created a similar artwork called *Cunts … and Other Conversations,* which was exhibited at the MONA in Hobart, Tasmania. Taylor's artwork features 151 sculpted portraits of vulvas.[25] And in the pop culture scene, American singer Janelle Monáe recently released the song 'Pynk', which appears on her album *Dirty Computer*. Released in 2018, the song is described by Monáe as a 'celebration of creation, self-love, sexuality and pussy power'.[26] The music video features Monáe and her back-up dancers dressed in vagina pants.[27]

One of the things I find most heartening about these various forms of activism is that they do not seek to draw hard feminist lines between 'authentic' ciswomen and 'inauthentic' transwomen and men. On the contrary, they seek to forge productive intersectional alliances between women of all colours and embodiments in their political demands for genital diversity. These voices have contributed to the emergence of a public debate about the political causes of female body dissatisfaction that is broadly informed by second-wave feminist consciousness-raising techniques and critiques of mass culture. What they are telling us is that female genital cosmetic surgery is not a medical issue, but a feminist one. This book contributes to this feminist project by scrutinising the historical origins of contemporary ideas about the 'normal vulva' in order to strip this concept of its authority to speak for women and to make a space for a politically revised and inclusive concept of 'normality' that embraces bodily diversity.

NOTES

1. See for example Virginia Braun and Sue Wilkinson, 'Socio-Cultural Representations of the Vagina', *Journal of Reproductive and Infant Psychology* 19, no. 1 (2001): 17–32; Germaine Greer, 'Her Twist in the Knickers', *Sydney Morning Herald*, 15 September 2012, https://www.smh.com.au/entertainment/books/her-twist-in-the-knickers-20120914-25wyh.html; Emma L. E. Rees, *The Vagina: A Literary and Cultural History* (New York: Bloomsbury, 2013).
2. Hermann Heinrich Ploss, Max Bartels and Paul Bartels, ed. and trans. Eric John Dingwall, *Woman: An Historical Gynaelogical and Anthropological Compendium*, vol. 1 (London: William Heinemann, 1935).
3. 'Labiaplasty, Vaginoplasty, and Clitoral Unhooding – Feminine Cosmetic Genital Surgery (FCGS)', LabiaplastySurgeon, 2003–2018, http://www.labiaplastysurgeon.com/.

4. Sammy7520, 'Over masturbation has damaged my inner labia. What can do to get the color back? Have I damaged nerve endings?', RealSelf, 2018, https://www.realself.com/question/phoenix-az-masturbation-damaged-my-inner-labia; lisavirgin, 'I'm still a virgin but worried that maybe labia is too big? I used to masturbate lots and think it may be stretched out', RealSelf, 2018, https://www.realself.com/question/burlington-vt-labia-big.

5. Briannabacon, 'Labiaplasty: Masturbating. Will this make my labia go back to the way it was before Labiaplasty?', RealSelf, 2018, https://www.realself.com/question/colts-neck-nj-labiaplasty-masturbating-labia-back-before-labiaplasty.

6. Meredith Jones, 'Expressive Surfaces: The Case of the Designer Vagina', *Theory, Culture & Society* 34, nos 7–8 (2017): 29–50.

7. Barbara L. Fredrickson and Tomi-Ann Roberts, 'Objectification Theory: Toward Understanding Women's Lived Experiences and Mental Health Risks', *Psychology of Women Quarterly* 21, no. 2 (1997): 174.

8. Jones, 'Expressive Surfaces', 30.

9. Amy Shields Dobson, *Postfeminist Digital Cultures: Femininity, Social Media, and Self-Representation* (New York: Palgrave, 2015).

10. See for example Camille Nurka, 'Public Bodies', *Feminist Media Studies* 14, no. 3 (2014): 485–99.

11. Michel de Certeau, *The Practice of Everyday Life*, trans. Steven Rendall (Berkeley: University of Caloifornia Press, 1984), xv.

12. de Certeau, The Practice of Everyday Life, xiv.

13. See for example Pornhub, https://www.pornhub.com/video/search?search=amateur+teen+large+labia.

14. de Certeau, *The Practice of Everyday Life*, 4–8.

15. See 'Labia Pride', Wikipedia, last edited 15 June 2018, https://en.wikipedia.org/wiki/Labia_pride.

16. Viv Groskop, 'The Muff March Against "Designer Vagina" Surgery', *Guardian*, 9 December 2011, https://www.theguardian.com/life-andstyle/the-womens-blog-with-jane-martinson/2011/dec/08/muff-march-designer-vagina-surgery.

17. Rosie Mockett, 'Our Muff March Is a Stand Against Pornified Culture', *Guardian*, 10 December 2011, https://www.theguardian.com/commentisfree/2011/dec/09/muff-march-against-pornified-culture.

18. Women's Health Victoria, The Labia Library, 2011, http://www.labialibrary.org.au/.

19. Jill Tomlinson, 'Labiaplasty', Dr Jill Tomlinson Plastic and Reconstructive Surgeon, 11 December 2011, http://jilltomlinson.com/body/labiaplasty.

20. Hilde Atalanta, 'About', The Vulva Gallery, 2018, https://www.thevulvagallery.com/about/.

21. Hilde Atalanta, 'About', The Vulva Gallery, 2018, https://www.thevul-vagallery.com/about/.
22. Hilde Atalanta, 'The Vulva Gallery', The Vulva Gallery, 2018, https://www.thevulvagallery.com/.
23. 'About', Vagina Museum, 2018, https://www.vaginamuseum.co.uk/about.
24. Jamie McCartney, 'About', The Great Wall of Vagina, accessed 17 June 2018, http://www.greatwallofvagina.co.uk/about.
25. See https://mona.net.au/museum/general-collection/cunts-and-other-conversations-2008-11-greg-taylor-and-friends.
26. Brittany Spanos, 'Watch Janelle Monae Celebrate "Pussy Power" in "Pynk" Video', *Rolling Stone*, 10 April 2018, https://www.rollingstone.com/music/news/janelle-monae-celebrates-pussy-power-in-pynk-video-w518956.
27. Janelle Monáe, 'Janelle Monáe - PYNK [Official Video]', YouTube, 10 April 2018, https://www.youtube.com/watch?v=PaYvlVR_Bec.

Afterword

When I was in primary school, I was teased mercilessly for my ears. They were big and they stuck out. They were not small, neat, or tucked back, and they peeked through my fine and impossibly straight plain brown hair. I found hair in my face annoying, so I tucked it behind my ears like other girls, though it made my ears look even more conspicuous. Kids called me 'Dumbo', like the cartoon elephant. I remember that a girl suggested to me that perhaps the reason my ears stuck out was because I pushed my hair behind them. She must have felt sorry for me because she said I could get them 'pinned back'. This was a new idea to me. I had no idea what she meant and never asked anyone about it, but sometimes I would stand in front of the mirror with a forefinger on each ear and push them back to meet my scalp to see what I would look like as a normal person, as someone less ugly, and as someone unafflicted by what I was implicitly being told by others was a deformity. I didn't real-ise at the time that this girl was talking about cosmetic surgery.

'Cosmetic surgery' was a concept I had no access to as the white daughter of a white woman who had grown up on a farm in Richmond, in what was then a semi-rural town in New South Wales. Back in the 1980s, when I was at primary school, my family lived in a little suburb called Woodford, nestled at the edge of the Great Western Highway and backing onto the bushland of the Blue Mountains National Park, west of Sydney. For me, as for my mother, cosmetic surgery would have been something rich, fashionable, urban people did. Rural women were tough, pragmatic and self-reliant. There were no fashion magazines in our house, and as a teenager I never felt the need to read magazines like *Dolly* or *Cosmo* that other girls my age were reading because it simply wasn't part of how my mum and I defined ourselves, however much I might have wished to look 'normal'. Though I did enjoy flipping the pages of *Smash Hits* and I liked the way Madonna, Cyndi Lauper and Boy George looked with their colourful make-up and chunky jewellery. I realise now that I never really 'learned' how to do the femininity that came with the purchase price of female-oriented fashion and lifestyle magazines. And anyway, I preferred reading fantasy books. I now regard this comparative lack of exposure to media as a protective factor in the unusually impervious positive body-image that I have to this day, at the age of forty-one, with the passage of time and the creep of weight gain. I think that even if I hadn't consciously admitted it to myself, I knew that I treasured my brain and its capacity for gobbling up words on a page more than anything else.

Luckily for me, there was no 'body talk' or 'diet talk' in my lower-middle-class family home. My parents were both teachers, though my mum chose to stay at home to be the primary carer for me and my younger brother. I am grateful to her for protecting me from the every-day tribulations of female body management. At home, I could just be who I was and nothing was expected of me except that I do my home-work and find things to do in my leisure time—like ride my bike or climb a tree or visit the kids down the road—and go to bed on time. It was because I had a supportive and loving home environment that I came to accept my ears in spite of the bullying, which persisted into high school. Eventually, my head grew into my ears and I stopped worrying about them. At some point I must have decided that I couldn't do any-thing about people not liking me because my ears were too big—and I was too brainy in a public school where sportspeople were revered and 'nerds' who liked reading books were outcasts; but I didn't have to let them define me. So I went the opposite way instead, toward a defiant, and sometimes self-destructive, individualism—to express myself loudly and obstreperously, to swear and get drunk and smoke tobacco, to rage against the social world that tried to make me feel small, inadequate, iso-lated and most of all, ugly. There was never any way that I was going to stuff my gangly limbs and critical mind into that box labelled 'femininity'.

I relate this story to show that I have some understanding of what it's like to feel abnormal, and that I am not writing this book from a purely 'outsider' perspective peering into the alien world of cosmetic surgery, even though there is much of this world that *is* alien to me. As a girl, I experienced mental anguish over the ugliness of my ears; and later, as a liminal teen, I would come to understand what it was like to be sexually objectified, to be the object of sly sexual comments and unwanted touches, to be made aware of myself as a body that was not mine, though after puberty it was less about looking abnormal than about looking *female*. These social forces cornered me into regarding my body as an object of appraisal for the other's gaze in a way that was neither directed by me nor sexually empowering. I do not think my experience of being gendered female in these formative years is particularly unusual. And while I can only speak with authority on my own subjective white, lower-middle-class, heterosexual experience, the themes in this narrative go some way to explaining how central self-objectification is to many women's lives and why it is that women make up 90 per cent of cosmetic surgery patients in Australia and elsewhere.

Upon writing this book, I wonder what life might have been like if I had had access to cosmetic surgery as a jug-eared girl in primary school. Would I have had more friends? Would I be a different person now? Would I be more successful? Would I have the same belief in my own authority to judge my body and all its changes as perfectly normal and worthy of love? If I had grown up in the current digital-media-saturated era, would I be worried about my vagina too? These are questions that speak to the entwinement of the individual with the social, and the decisions we all face about the extent to which we empower others to define the conditions of our own happiness.

In the writing of this book, I have inspected my own body and found that my labia minora protrude to a degree that would be classified by cosmetic surgeons as 'hypertrophied', with characteristic wrinkling and darker colouration at the edges. If I view them through the lens of 'hypertrophy', they are a hideously ugly deformation: unfeminine, undesirable, unlovable. I do not need to put my faith in a description designed to make me feel bad about myself for *no reason* other than that I do not have something resembling a fictitious image of a 'normal' vulva. What this book shows is that the medical understanding of what a normal vulva ought to look like is a fantasy that has largely been concocted by men, who, notably, don't actually have vulvas. It is my hope that this book might empower ordinary girls and women from all walks of life to reject the body that history has made for them, and to craft stories that will be uniquely theirs in female-centred histories that are yet to be written.

INDEX